PENGUIN BOOKS

IN WITH THE EURO, OUT WITH THE POUND

Christopher Johnson was born in 1931 and educated at Winchester College and Magdalen College, Oxford, where he took a First Class honours degree in Philosophy, Politics and Economics. He was a journalist on *The Times Educational Supplement*, *The Times* and the *Financial Times* between 1954 and 1976. From 1977 to 1991 he was Chief Economic Adviser to Lloyds Bank, as well as a general manager of the bank (1985–91) and editor of *Lloyds Bank Review* and *Lloyds Bank Economic Bulletin*. He was Visiting Professor of Economics at Surrey University between 1986 and 1990, and still lectures to audiences in several countries. He is UK Adviser to the Association for the Monetary Union of Europe, Chairman of the British section of the Franco-British Council, and Specialist Adviser to the Treasury Committee of the House of Commons. In 1993 he was a visiting scholar at the International Monetary Fund.

His books include *The British Economy Under Mrs Thatcher 1979–1990* (Penguin, 1991), *New Players New Rules: Financing the 1990s* and, with Simon Briscoe, *Measuring the Economy* (Penguin; 2nd edition, 1995).

CHRISTOPHER JOHNSON

In With the Euro,
Out With the Pound

THE SINGLE CURRENCY FOR BRITAIN

PENGUIN BOOKS

PENGUIN BOOKS

Published by the Penguin Group
Penguin Books Ltd, 27 Wrights Lane, London w8 5TZ, England
Penguin Books USA Inc., 375 Hudson Street, New York, New York 10014, USA
Penguin Books Australia Ltd, Ringwood, Victoria, Australia
Penguin Books Canada Ltd, 10 Alcorn Avenue, Toronto, Ontario, Canada M4V 3B2
Penguin Books (NZ) Ltd, 182–190 Wairau Road, Auckland 10, New Zealand

Penguin Books Ltd, Registered Offices: Harmondsworth, Middlesex, England

First published 1996
10 9 8 7 6 5 4 3 2 1

Set in 10/12pt Monotype Bembo
Typeset by Datix International Limited, Bungay, Suffolk
Printed in England by Clays Ltd, St Ives plc

To Anne

Contents

Preface

Most of the economics literature on EMU is impenetrable even to the intelligent layman. I have tried to express the economic arguments in layman's language, although it is impossible to avoid using terms current in economic discourse. If my fellow-economists find some of the arguments over-simplified, they will be able to recognize from the notes the more complex versions on which they are founded.

I have tried to respond to the charge that the advocates of the single currency have not gone out into the arena and tried to explain what they are doing to ordinary men and women. People are often baffled, indifferent, or downright hostile to something they do not understand, not because they are incapable, but because the decision-makers have given up in advance trying to say something they think cannot be said 'in front of the children'.

First I set out here some of the main features of the present system of national currencies, so that readers have some kind of framework within which to place the discussion on monetary union and the single currency.

Money takes three main forms: coins, issued by the mint, normally controlled by the government; banknotes, issued by the central bank, which may or may not be controlled by the government; bank deposits, issued by commercial banks. Notes and coins are called fiduciary money, because their value depends not on their intrinsic content, but on people's faith in the government to maintain their value. Bank deposits are called scriptural money, because they are created by entries written down by banks. Most money is scriptural money nowadays. Money has three main functions: a means of payment, a store of value, and a unit of account.

The money issued in one country is called a currency. One currency is distinguished from another because the notes and coins look different, with different sizes and symbols. Domestic bank deposits of different countries are different because they have the names of different currencies. Two bank statements may have the same figures on them, but different amounts of money if they are in different currencies. (British banks do not put £ symbols on customers' statements, because it is taken for granted that they are in pounds.)

The price of money is called its rate of interest. The rate of interest paid on bank deposits and other forms of savings is expressed as an annual percentage of the sum deposited. It is the price banks pay depositors to borrow their money. Similarly, the rate of interest banks quote on loans is the price they charge for lending money. The currency of other countries is called foreign currency. The price paid for foreign currency in terms of domestic currency is called the rate of exchange. Rates of interest and rates of exchange vary according to financial and economic conditions.

Amounts of money in current pounds and interest rates in actual percentages are called 'nominal', to distinguish them from 'real' amounts and percentages which have been adjusted to take out the inflation element. For example, if inflation is 5 per cent, £100 of last year's money will be worth only £95 in real purchasing power this year, and an interest rate of 7.5 per cent will be only 2.5 per cent after inflation. (These are rough and ready calculations to illustrate a point; matters are a bit more complicated in reality.)

The normal practice is that a single currency circulates in a single country, and is legal tender in that country.[1] It is also quite common for the currency of a single country to circulate in other countries alongside its own as a foreign currency, although it is then not normally legal tender. What is not so usual is for a number of countries to have a single currency to the exclusion of domestic national currencies. There may be a currency common to all of them, but a common currency can coexist in parallel with national currencies, as do the US dollar and the ecu. It is therefore less confusing to refer to a single currency than to a common currency when discussing the replacement of European national currencies by one new European currency. I refer always to the European single currency, or the single currency for short, rather than to the single European currency. The former refers to a single currency for a still-to-be-decided number of countries in Europe, while the latter should be kept for the day when there is only one currency throughout Europe, and it is thus the single one in existence.

It was decided at the Madrid summit in December 1995 that the name of the new European single currency would be the Euro. Until it is better known, the name will lead to some confusion. Eurocurrencies, such as the eurodollar and eurosterling, have existed since the 1950s. The term originated when it was applied to US dollars used outside the national territory, at first in Europe, in order to avoid American restrictions. Gradually a eurocurrency came to mean any currency used outside its own national territory, not necessarily in Europe. The late Fritz Machlup suggested calling them xenocurrencies, after the Greek word *xenos*, meaning foreign, but it did not catch on. Some way will now have to be find of bypassing the ugly term 'euroEuro' for Euros used ouside European Union territory.

A single currency is the most advanced form of monetary union, or currency union. 'The adoption of a single currency, while not strictly necessary for the creation of a monetary union, might be seen . . . as a natural and further development of the monetary union.'[2] A currency union can consist of a number of national currencies linked by a system of fixed, possibly also adjustable, exchange rates. The exchange rate parities can be one-for-one, so that the different national currencies effectively become alternative names for the same units, or they can be whatever they were when the union was formed, either rounded, or with fractions and decimal places.

A monetary union is unlikely to last long unless there is a single monetary policy, either by agreement between countries or by a union central bank. Monetary policy covers the amount of money in circulation, the interest rates on various kinds of deposit and loan, and exchange rates. So a single monetary policy means a single decision about how much money to issue or let the banks issue, a single set of interest rates for similar kinds of loan and deposit, and a single view of what the exchange rate of the single currency should be against other currencies in the world. This requires a single central bank.

Different national monetary policies about how much money to issue, and at what interest rate, make it impossible to keep exchange rates fixed, if money can flow freely between members of the union. In that case, a difference between the demand of and supply for each national currency will affect its interest rate (its price). Different amounts of currency issued and different interest rates in each country must make exchange rates (the price of currencies against each other) vary up and down.

Acknowledgements

I thank the Association for the Monetary Union of Europe, in particular Bertrand de Maigret and Stefan Collignon, for helping my thoughts to take shape over the last four years thanks to a stimulating series of research projects, meetings and discussions. I would like to thank BAT Industries, in particular Richard Desmond, Heather Honour and Roger Lomax, for supporting me over this period in my role as UK Adviser to the Association. Other members of and visitors to AMUE too numerous to mention have played an important part in forming my thoughts. Some will find their names in the references. They know who they are.

Abbreviations

BIS	Bank for International Settlements
ECB	European Central Bank
ECOFIN	European Council of Finance Ministers
EEA	European Economic Area
EFTA	European Free Trade Area
EMI	European Monetary Institute
EMU	Economic and Monetary Union
ERM	Exchange Rate Mechanism
EU	European Union
IGC	Inter-Governmental Conference
IMF	International Monetary Fund
OECD	Organization for Economic Cooperation and Development

I

Introduction – The UK's Position

This book puts forward two main arguments. First, the European Union (EU) should create a single currency; second, the UK should join the European single currency.[1] The two are logically independent. The single currency might be a good idea for other EU members, but not for the UK. The single currency might not be such a good idea, but the UK ought still to join it if it is going to happen anyway. I maintain that the general arguments in favour of the single currency apply as much to the UK as to other EU members. It would be wrong to join the single currency just because it was there. It is right for the UK to join it, because the economic arguments are strongly in favour.

EUROPE'S OFFSHORE ISLAND

While the arguments both for and against the single currency will be dealt with in general terms, their application to the UK in particular will be set out. The book is addressed primarily to a British readership, although readers elsewhere should benefit from the general discussions, and cannot be disinterested as to whether the UK should or will join the single currency. The UK differs from other EU members by virtue of its history, its politics and its economy, and thus merits special treatment. It is crucial, in the sense that if it accepts the case for joining the single currency, other countries which have more in common with each other than with the UK should find similar arguments relatively easy to accept. Countries on the fringe of the EU which are even more different from the others than the UK will also be encouraged to join if the UK does, and discouraged if it does not.

The importance of Britain to the continent of Europe has often been recognized more clearly by the continentals than by the British. As Jean Monnet put it: 'The civilization of the West needs Britain; and Europe, to continue her unique contribution to that civilization, needs the qualities that reside in the British people.'[2] The British, far from being flattered that they are still welcome guests at a party they have tried to avoid attending, resent what looks to them like external interference in domestic decisions.

Britain's geographical position as an island (for about the last ten millennia, anyway) has given rise to an offshore mentality.[3] Yet throughout recorded history, the British have had ties of kinship, language, trade, politics and defence with the Continent, sometimes even closer than today. Britain alternates between defensive isolation and self-interested intervention. The Straits of Dover are wide enough for Britain to turn a blind eye to what is happening on the other side, but not wide enough for her to cut loose from the Continent. The Channel Tunnel may help to overcome the offshore mentality, as well as increasing the movement of goods and people between Britain and the Continent.

The post-war pattern of British involvement with Europe has been one of too little and too late. The European Economic Community was set up in 1958; the UK joined it fifteen years later in 1973. The European Monetary System (EMS) was set up in 1979; the UK joined its Exchange Rate Mechanism (ERM) eleven years later in 1990. As a latecomer, Britain had far less influence on the structure and staffing of the new institutions than if it had been a founder member. The UK is in danger of making the same mistake by delaying joining the single currency until the inevitably late entry deprives her of the influence she might still have had. Those who do not learn from history are condemned to repeat it.

DISASTROUS FLIRTATION WITH THE ERM

I have published a detailed account of Britain's turbulent relations with the EMS elsewhere.[4] The British Government persuaded itself, against the evidence, that it had done better by staying out of the ERM during the 1980s. Its decision to join in 1990 was taken at the wrong time, at the wrong interest rate, at the wrong exchange rate, for the wrong reasons, and in the wrong way. Having waited eleven years, the UK Chancellor of the Exchequer (John Major paused briefly on this rung to the Prime Ministership, but long enough to take the key decision) could have waited a few months longer.

The UK should have joined the ERM after and not before interest rates and exchange rates came down from their 1990 peaks. The decision should not have been taken because of the need to impress a Conservative Party conference with an interest rate cut. It should not have been taken unilaterally, but discussed with other EU countries, and underwritten by the German Bundesbank. Even so, the situation could have been saved had John Major, then Prime Minister, persisted with the option he considered in autumn 1991 of devaluing within the ERM rather than waiting to be forced out.

With hindsight, Mrs Thatcher can be praised for having a more flexible view of the ERM when she took Britain in than some of the other European governments, or her successors. 'For me, willingness to realign within the ERM – as other countries had done – if circumstances warranted it, was the essential condition for entry.'[5] John Major took this possibility seriously. 'In the autumn of 1991, the Prime Minister asked Sarah [Hogg, Head of the Prime Minister's Policy Unit] – very privately – to do him a paper on ways in which the pound might be allowed to settle at a lower rate without leaving the ERM . . . On reflection, the Prime Minister decided not to raise these options with the Chancellor' (Norman Lamont).[6]

The result was that British membership of the ERM lasted less than two years, and ended in the ignominious forced retreat of September 1992. The devaluation of the pound helped British exports just as the non-inflationary growth due to the fall in interest rates was promoting domestic economic recovery. The Government could hardly believe its luck. However, the short-term boost from leaving the ERM did little to tackle Britain's long-term economic problem of under-investment.

Whatever the economic advantages, the political pay-off from leaving the ERM was heavily negative. The abrupt change of policy (known in economic jargon as 'time-inconsistency') was seen as a major policy defeat. The Government was regarded as having broken its word both on the exchange rate and on the promise not to raise taxes, which helped Mr Major's surprise election victory in April 1992. The short-term policy success, if such it was, went with the deepest post-war period of political unpopularity of any government for at least the three years following the exit from the ERM.

British opinion has always been divided and vacillating on matters of European integration. There was no clear consensus in favour of entry into the European Communities in 1973, although it came to be accepted as a fact of life, especially after the 1975 referendum. The divisions have become particularly acute since 1992. The short-lived flirtation with the ERM can be interpreted in two ways. Either it shows that too close an involvement with the EU is harmful to British interests, and that the UK should continue to retreat, perhaps leaving the EU altogether. Or it shows that half measures do not work, and that the single European market, which has majority support in the UK, needs to be complemented by a full-blown single currency.

THE MIX OF ECONOMICS AND POLITICS

The technical nature of the issues has not made life any easier for the advocates of the single currency. The Eurosceptics have by general consent made the running in the debate. It is always easy to pick out particular faults in any institution, whether in Brussels, Whitehall or Westminster, and use them to denounce it in a general way. It is also easier to argue that the status quo, for all its imperfections, is more or less viable than to prove with certainty that a new policy departure will achieve all that is claimed for it. Barring constitutional change, we are lumbered with Whitehall and Westminster, but we can toy with the idea that somehow we can escape from Brussels by opting out and letting the rest of the world go by.

The case in favour of the single currency is primarily an economic one, based on what it is expected to do to improve economic growth, inflation, trade and investment. It is no more certain than any other proposition in economics, but, like other economic policies, it is more likely to succeed if those carrying it out, and the producers and consumers in the economy, are persuaded that it will succeed. The role of expectations is vital in economics. Persuasion, far from being an undesirable form of propaganda, is essential if people are to change their behaviour in such a way as to reap the benefits of policies such as the single currency.

There is also a political case for the single currency which is independent of the economic case. It forms part of Jean Monnet's functional approach to political integration, leading once warring nations to work together by integrating various functions of government one by one – coal and steel, atomic energy, trade, and now money. If the political case for EMU were overwhelming, it would be necessary only to prove that the single currency would be economically neutral, doing neither good nor harm to the economy.

Since many supporters of the single currency are against political integration, I do not base the economic arguments for it on a political foundation (although I happen to accept the political case as well). There are forms of political cooperation that may be required to make a success of the single currency, but they fall far short of political integration of the UK into a superstate. The economic case for the single currency can stand on its own. Its limited political consequences can be seen as a pragmatic and limited extension, already provided for in the Maastricht Treaty.

WHAT POLITICAL UNION MEANS

There has been a debate among successive British Chancellors of the Exchequer about whether the single currency also requires political union, although it has never been clear what they think political union means. Lord Lawson has on more than one occasion said that EMU and the single currency 'implies nothing less than a European government – albeit a federal union – and political union; the United States of Europe. This is simply not on the agenda now, nor will it be in the foreseeable future.'[7] Mr Kenneth Clarke has put the opposite view, which makes it easier to get support from MPs hostile to political union on grounds of national sovereignty.

It is quite possible to have monetary union without political union. It is a mistake to believe that monetary union need be a huge step on the path to a Federal Europe. The Austrian Schilling has been fixed against the Deutschemark for thirteen years and Dutch short-term interest rates have not diverged from German rates by more than 0.8 per cent in eight years. Yet nobody would deny that Austria and the Netherlands are sovereign states. Britain and Ireland enjoyed a *de facto* monetary union for some fifty years after Irish independence. And there are some examples of political union without monetary union. Scotland retained its own currency in some form for over 200 years after James VI of Scotland became James I of England.[8]

Germany has been the main advocate of political union, but it means different things to different Germans. To the Bundesbank, it means that there needs to be more pooling of sovereignty on fiscal policy, to keep budget deficits in check and prevent them undermining the stability of the single currency.[9] To some German politicians, it means that there needs to be more democratic control of EMU by means of the European Parliament.[10] To others, it means that the Inter-Governmental Conference starting in 1996 must add more flesh to the bones of the 'second pillar' of the Maastricht Treaty on the common foreign and security policy, to provide the political counterpart to the economic sacrifice Germany is making in giving up the D-mark under the 'first pillar' covering EMU.

The bargain between France and Germany was well summed up by M. Dominique Moisi, of the Institut Français des Relations Internationales (IFRI), in a talk at the Royal Institute of International Affairs in the summer of 1995: 'Countries always want what they haven't got. France wants a currency, and Germany wants a foreign policy.'[11]

The British are confused about the meaning of political union and federation. In the current European debate, political union does not mean the merger of existing EU nation-states into a single national entity like the USA. The crucial feature of the USA is that it is a single country in international relations. The nation-states of the European Union would continue to be separate countries, except in cases such as trade negotiations where they decided to pool their sovereignty for specific purposes.

Since decentralized federal systems of government can cover either a single state such as the US, or a group of states such as the EU, federation is in itself not a criterion of single statehood. Confederation would be a better word for a group of states with a federal system, were it not for the fact that Switzerland, a single-state federation, confusingly calls itself a confederation.

In this debate, political union, like economic and monetary union, means an institutional structure of cooperation between separately identifiable nation-states, and thus a supranational tier of government such as already exists in the shape of the Council, the Commission, the Court of Justice and so on. This structure is by its nature federal and not unitary, and the principle of subsidiarity is used to decide whether tasks are most efficiently allocated to the national or the supranational level:

In areas which do not fall within its exclusive competence, the Community shall take action, in accordance with the principle of subsidiarity, only if and so far as the objectives of the proposed action cannot be sufficiently achieved by the Member States and can therefore, by reason of the scale or effects of the proposed action, be better achieved by the Community.[12]

EMU is based on a bargain between France and Germany. France would get the advantages of monetary union by merging the strong franc into an even stronger D-mark to make up the single currency. Germany would get the advantages of political union, binding her into a European structure, and giving her more weight compared with France in foreign and defence policy. If the object of European integration is to prevent France and Germany ever going to war again, then it looks like a good bargain for the UK and other countries too. Chancellor Kohl has warned that the history of the Second World War could repeat itself if political and monetary union do not go ahead. The implication by Bernard Connolly (in his book *The Rotten Heart of Europe*) that EMU could actually cause another war between France and Germany is a far-fetched attempt to turn this argument on its head: 'The ERM and EMU are not only inefficient but also undemocratic: a danger not only to our wealth but to our freedoms and, ultimately, to our peace.'[13]

The political case for EMU is sometimes put by its advocates as if it tipped the scales between two finely balanced sets of economic arguments for and against. For those who accept the political case, this may be sufficient. However, I believe that the economic arguments in favour of the single currency offer advantages which far outweigh the economic arguments against.

BRITISH PUBLIC OPINION DIVIDED[14]

British opinion in general has been heavily against the single currency, in spite of more favourable views about the single European market. Even business opinion has been divided, with usually a small majority in favour. Not only have the Eurosceptics been more vocal and outspoken in debate; the Government itself has been deeply split, and thus unable to give a lead to public opinion.

A poll taken by the Association for the Monetary Union of Europe (AMUE) in 1988–9 showed 65 per cent of British senior managers in favour of EMU, compared with 24 per cent against. Of those in favour

75 per cent wanted a single currency, in other words 45 per cent of the total. This was when the ERM was riding high, and business was pushing for the Government to join it. The scores for the EU as a whole were even higher – 83 per cent for EMU and only 10 per cent against. In another study for AMUE, Ernst & Young found that British executives were much keener on the ecu as a single currency than just as a parallel currency. A CBI working group reporting in October 1989 recommended British entry into the ERM, and later into a common currency, if certain conditions were fulfilled.

The AMUE survey gave the main reasons for managers' support for EMU: 75 per cent wanted to reduce exchange rate fluctuations, 60 per cent wanted to lower the cost of administering foreign exchange risk, 44 per cent wanted to stabilize trade flows, and 33 per cent wanted savings on foreign exchange commissions. The rationale for these hopes is given in chapter 3.

Britain's departure from the ERM was a setback to such hopes. Yet by October 1993, a CBI survey showed that 51 per cent of members thought a single currency would be a help in the long run, though not a necessity, and another 28 per cent thought it was a necessary condition of the single market in the long run. There was thus a total of 79 per cent in favour, with only 8 per cent saying a single currency would be positively damaging. As many as 51 per cent expected the single currency to come about by 2000, but of these 35 per cent thought it would be for a minority of EU members, and only 5 per cent thought the UK would then be a member.

The September 1994 CBI survey, with different questions, showed a division of business opinion, but with a majority slightly in favour; a broader survey by MORI in September 1995 on behalf of the CBI and the Association of British Chambers of Commerce showed slightly lower scores (given in brackets), in view of the extension of its scope to smaller businesses. Asked what should happen if a group of countries went ahead with a single currency in 1999, 24(19) per cent thought the UK should be part of the leading group, 49(36) per cent wanted to keep open the option to be in the leading group, 17(22) per cent wanted to wait and see, and 10(12) per cent were against.

Polls show greater support among large businesses than among small. A British Chambers of Commerce survey in 1994 showed small firms evenly divided, with 46 per cent for and 46 per cent against the single currency. A *Management Today* survey in July 1995 showed 42 per cent for and 43 per cent against. An Andersen Consulting survey taken just before that showed 58 per cent of large companies for and 12 per cent against. Among the main arguments in favour by a majority vote, in descending order, were savings on foreign exchange transactions, higher economic growth combined with lower inflation, a more stable economic climate, the danger of protectionism by others if the UK stayed out, lower interest rates than outside, and more foreign direct investment in the UK. An overwhelming majority dismissed the argument that the single currency would put the UK at a disadvantage because its economic structure was too different from that of other members.

Opinion in the City is more divided than in industry. The EMU City Survey, carried out by the OMLX Securities and Derivatives Exchange, found that 89 per cent of City managers thought a two-speed EMU was the most likely, and 51 per cent that it was the most desirable outcome. Thirty-five per cent said the UK should be in the first tier, and 59 per cent that it should not. Thirty-eight per cent thought it would mean an increase in business for the City, 32 per cent that it would mean a decline, and 25 per cent that it would have no effect. Of those who thought business would decline, 95 per cent pointed to the foreign exchange market, 87 per cent to the interest rate derivatives market. Of those who thought it would increase, 88 per cent attributed this to the greater concentration of financial business in London.

British public opinion as a whole is more sceptical about the single currency than business opinion, although in favour of EU membership. The EU Commission's Eurobarometer survey showed a peak of 54 per cent of Britons in favour of the single currency in June 1991; this had slumped to 27 per cent by December 1993. The related Europinion survey showed that in the second quarter of 1995 there were still only 33 per cent of Britons in favour, and 62 per cent against, compared with a 47–46 split in the EU as a whole. Yet 52 per cent thought that they would be using the single currency by 2000, and 41 per cent that they would not.

A MORI poll showed 33 per cent of Britons in favour of the single currency in November 1994, and 56 per cent against. The support was even lower in Germany: 24 per cent for, 53 per cent against – a finding common to most such polls. An unusual poll was carried out for Granada Television by Social and Community Planning Research in April–May 1995. It showed only 16 per cent of 230 representatives of the general public in favour of the single currency. After a weekend of discussion with experts, this had risen to 28 per cent. The results, shown on television, showed higher scores, and similar changes of view, for a wide range of European policies.

It is no coincidence that the British feel themselves to be less European than other EU countries, and would thus not identify readily with the single currency as a symbol of European sovereignty. Eurobarometer found that 63 per cent of Britons thought the single currency would be important because of the loss of national identity – the highest proportion in any EU country. National currencies such as the pound are often seen as symbols of sovereignty, so that their abolition could symbolize an abandonment of it.

It is over a century since Mill denounced national currencies as barbarism, but barbarism lingers on:

So much of barbarism, however, still remains in the transactions of the most civilized nations, that almost all independent countries choose to assert their nationality by having, to their own inconvenience and that of their neighbours, a peculiar currency of their own.[15]

The survival of Scottish banknotes shows that the symbolism is devoid of real content, since Scotland has neither monetary nor political independence from the UK. The British are nonetheless more reluctant than other European nations to give up their national currency, in spite of its poor performance as a constant store of value over the years. The only exceptions are the Germans, who are equally reluctant to give up their national currency, but because of its good performance.

Currencies need not be regarded as national symbols, but as an international convenience. The US dollar is widely used as an international currency without detracting from the sovereignty of countries where it has become a parallel currency. If currencies with higher than average inflation are seen as national symbols, this can hardly further the national self-confidence of the countries concerned.

Inconsistent understanding of the issues among the British public is shown by poll evidence published by the Policy Studies Institute. Although only 33 per cent supported a single currency, 55 per cent were in favour of a European Central Bank. It must be assumed that 22 per cent would like to see a European monetary policy (otherwise what would be the point of a European Central Bank) but cannot or do not want to see that this would be far easier to achieve with one currency than with fifteen.

The poll evidence shows a clear picture. About two-thirds of big business is in favour of the single currency, about half small business, and about a third of the general population. Far higher numbers expect it to happen anyway, whatever they think of it. These figures reflect a background of hostility on the part of most newspapers, and agnosticism and division on the part of the Government. They show that sceptics can be converted by rational argument. If it was clear that the single currency was going ahead, and if a British Government decided to go in, a majority of the population might come round to it, some reluctantly, although there would always be a vocal minority against it. An NOP poll taken for the *Sunday Times* in December 1995 showed that, while 60 per cent of the population were opposed to the single currency, 50 per cent thought Britain should join if the other main countries went ahead, because it could not afford to be left behind. As the newspaper commented: 'People are suspicious of radical change, but even more fearful of missing out. They object to a further loss of national sovereignty but feel they cannot go it alone.'

POLITICAL PARTIES AT ODDS

The 1975 referendum set a precedent for a government party, whose ranks are divided, to campaign on a pro-European platform supported by a majority but not a totality of ministers. The political parties, in the 1990s as in the 1970s, are divided on the European issue. A majority of Labour and Liberal Democrat MPs appears to favour British entry into the single currency. A majority of Conservative MPs is against it. An *Observer* poll in April 1995 showed ministers equally divided 44–44 per cent on EMU, but Conservative bankbenchers against 61–30 per cent.[16]

In spite of tripartisan support, Mr Major's Government still had difficulty getting the Maastricht Treaty through the House of Commons in 1992 because of Labour and Liberal Democrat opposition to its opt-out from the Social Chapter. It is not the purpose of this book to examine the arguments for and against the Social Chapter, only to say that it should be possible to put this less important issue on one side so that it does not have the effect of enabling the views of a political minority to prevail on the more important issue of the single currency.

The single currency has become a political issue in Britain in a number of ways. It is a bone of contention not so much between the major parties as within them. It has become a symbol of sovereignty at a time when it is less clear than ever what the word means. Mrs Thatcher consciously carried out a surrender of sovereignty when she signed the Single European Act setting up the single European market in 1986. Her later claim that she did not know what she was doing lacks plausibility. 'The price which we would have to pay to achieve a Single Market . . . was more majority voting in the Community.'[17] A similar case can be made a decade later for surrendering a degree of monetary sovereignty for broader economic advantage, and to make the enlargement of EU to a host of small states in central and southern Europe workable.

British politicians claim to attach importance to the sovereignty of parliament, which has a longer history than its continental counterparts. They conveniently forget earlier complaints about the elective dictatorship of British Governments, which are accustomed to getting their legislation through the House of Commons by means of three-line whips. The back-benchers who have been the exception to this rule happen to be unrepresentative anti-Europeans whose activities undermine rather than support the doctrine of the sovereignty of parliament. In any case, there is every reason why national parliaments as well as the European Parliament should be more involved in monitoring the actions of the EU Council and Commission.

The opt-out from the single currency secured by Mr Major at Maastricht was presented as a policy triumph, but has created a policy vacuum. The illusion has been created that no British decision will be required until the moment when other countries decide to join the single currency. The hope lingers that the failure of other countries to go ahead may let Britain off the hook altogether, and end an embarrassing division among ministers. The most remarkable example of this attitude was the article by Mr John Major, the Prime Minister, in *The Economist* just after the second major ERM crisis of August 1993:

I hope my fellow heads of government will resist the temptation to recite the mantra of full economic and monetary union as if nothing had changed. If they do recite it, it will have all the quaintness of a rain dance and about the same potency . . . The plain fact is that economic and monetary union is not realisable in present circumstances and therefore not relevant to our economic difficulties.[18]

To take another example, *The Times* announced the 'Death of an EMU' in a first leader in October 1995, on the grounds that France could not meet the Maastricht criteria.[19] The disadvantage of the opt-out is that it has made it possible for the Government, if not others, to postpone a divisive debate until the last possible moment. Yet the issues are such as to require serious consideration over a period of time. If a government decision is taken to enter the single currency, it will take time to convert and educate public opinion.

The danger is that other countries will be ready to enter the single currency when Britain is only beginning a serious debate about whether to do so or not. The uncertainty about whether the UK will go in late or not at all will damage British economic prospects, and its absence from the inner circle of the single currency will allow others to take decisions that may be against British national interests.

In a much-quoted speech to the Royal Institute of International Affairs in October 1995, Mr Malcolm Rifkind, the Foreign Secretary, expressed the view that Britain might sometimes have to sacrifice influence in order to maintain national interests: 'Influence is a means not an end in itself. Occasionally it may be appropriate to accept a loss of influence if that is the only way we can protect our interests.'[20] This is surely a false antithesis. If Britain's influence is not exerted on the shaping of economic and monetary union, British interests will suffer.

This point was recognized by the Prime Minister when he told the Madrid summit in December 1995 that it would be folly for Britain to exclude itself from the decision-making process on the single currency, after having said that it would be folly for the countries of the EU to rush headlong into it. It may not be until nearer the day of decision in early 1998 that British policy-makers will finally decide which is the lesser of the two follies.

On the same occasion, Mr Major dispelled much of the fog that had settled around the vexed question of whether there should be a referendum on the single currency: 'If there were to be a referendum, the time for a referendum would be after the British Cabinet had decided that it wished to recommend going in, and it would then seek the endorsement of that in a referendum, were there to be one.'[21]

This statement implicitly makes a number of important points:

1. The Government in parliament is the main decision-making body. The role of referenda in the UK is not to take decisions, but to endorse or not some of the most important government decisions.

2. A referendum cannot be a substitute for government decision-making. It would be ludicrous for a divided Government to ask 'the people' to decide in a referendum what it should do. It is difficult to tell people what the arguments are, or even to formulate the questions put, in such circumstances.

3. A referendum is needed only if it is not clear whether a general election has given a Government support for a certain policy or not, and not clear from public opinion polls or other indications whether such support exists.

4. No Government would hold a referendum on a policy agreed by parliament if it thought it was going to lose. Either it would not hold the referendum, or it would deploy all the usual means of persuasion to win it, as the Labour Government – though not unanimous in its own ranks – successfully did in 1975.

5. A referendum campaign could be used to educate the public in the issues once the Government had made up its mind and done its homework – which was far from being the case at the end of 1995.

TEN DANGEROUS BRITISH ILLUSIONS ABOUT EMU

The British attitude can be summed up in a list of ten dangerous illusions about EMU and the single currency, which we try to dispel in chapter 10 after going through the arguments in the main part of the book.[22]

1. *It will never happen.* If France and Germany cannot get their act together, there will be no single currency to join. Britain will not have to make up its mind whether to opt in or out. The rifts in both major political parties will be healed. The French call this '*la politique de l'autruche*' – putting your head in the sand, like an ostrich.

2. *It is a mistake to have a timetable.* Many 'pragmatic' businessmen approve of the single currency in principle, but have short-term goals which will always appear to have a higher priority – such as increasing the price of their shares. The achievement of the convergence criteria before setting a date for the single currency is often put up as a smoke-screen to hide reluctance to think seriously about the Euro. If the convoy travels at the pace of the slowest ship, it stays together.

3. *It will do no harm to wait and see.* If a small group of countries is politically and economically ready to go ahead with the single currency, then Britain should perhaps not incur their odium by trying to prevent them. A narrow monetary union can be seen as a pilot experiment to settle whether Britain and other countries should join too. This would give a new British Government time to take stock. If the Euro was a flop the UK would be well out of it, and if it was a success it would not be too late to jump on the bandwagon.

4. *We can become more competitive before joining.* This is an argument often used by Labour Party spokesmen. If one believes, as they must profess to, that the British economy has been enfeebled by seventeen years of Conservative government, then it is logical to argue that it needs a few years of Labour government before it can be strong enough to compete with its rivals in continental Europe. Manufacturing industry in particular is thought to need more investment in machinery and skills before it will be competing on a level playing field.

5. *We will be better off outside.* Some British interests believe that the future lies in the Far East and not in Europe, and that Britain should model itself on low-public-spending economies like Hong Kong. The British economy, and the City in particular, is said to have prospered over the years by operating on a global and not just a European scale. The UK would be free to set its own rules and policies.

6. *The single market doesn't need a single currency.* There has been a big increase in UK trade with Europe even without the single currency, and exporters and importers are quite accustomed to dealing with foreign currency problems. There are single markets in other parts of the world that work quite well without a single currency, such as the North America Free Trade Agreement.

7. *Ordinary people wouldn't accept it.*　Currency is fundamental to national identity, and people would feel that it was the end of the monarchy and the British nation to lose the pound. The man in the pub has a gut instinct which politicians ignore at their peril. If the majority of the people are against it, that should settle the issue.

8. *It will divide Europe.*　If only a minority of countries are ready to go ahead in 1999, the others, including probably the UK, will be left on the sidelines with second-class status. This will jeopardize European unity, which has so far prevailed in the progress achieved in economic integration. The political fall-out could be even more damaging.

9. *It will make enlargement impossible.*　The political cohesion of post-Cold War Europe demands that the former Communist satellites should be included in the European Union framework as soon as possible. Enlargement is thus more urgent than the single currency, and should be given higher priority.

10. *It will mean the end of the nation-state.*　The single currency cannot be managed without much greater pooling of sovereignty than now envisaged, as the Germans keep insisting. The single currency, like the single market, is just a back-door route to political integration in a German-dominated European superstate.

2

The History of Monetary Unions

MONETARY UNIONS AND SINGLE CURRENCIES

In this chapter we look at gold and silver as single currencies, at examples of monetary union, notably the Latin Monetary Union and the two German monetary unions, the Bretton Woods system, the European currency snake, and the Exchange Rate Mechanism (ERM) of the European Monetary System (EMS). Valuable lessons for European Monetary Union can be drawn from all of them.

The history of single currencies of more than one country is linked with the history of monetary unions, which are more common because they do not often reach the stage of a single currency. Monetary unions also tend to go with other kinds of unions between states, such as customs unions and political unions. They require a degree of cooperation between states which is unlikely to be present if they are not linked by a more general desire to work together, which can apply to money, trade, defence, foreign policy, and other areas.

Currencies were in some ways more international before the rise of nation-states than they are today. In the Middle Ages many different currencies were used alongside each other in what could be regarded as either healthy competition or mind-boggling confusion. Gradually the power to issue currency came to be regarded as a badge of political authority and a valuable economic weapon.

The power of rulers to issue money as a way of financing wars became known by the medieval term 'seignorage', which originally referred to the duty charged by mints to turn base metal into coins bearing the ruler's head. The issue of paper money by governments has always been a way of borrowing without paying interest, because it can be used to finance public expenditure. It can also be regarded as a form of taxation. Even today, seignorage plays its part as a concealed form of taxation in countries with substantial rates of inflation. The higher the rate of inflation, the more interest the government avoids paying on the interest-bearing debt it would otherwise have had to issue. The rule 'one country, one currency' sounds sensible enough, but has turned out to be a recipe for malpractice by national governments.

GOLD AND SILVER AS SINGLE CURRENCIES

Many different commodities, ranging from cowrie shells to peppercorns, have been used as money in different times and places. The main requirement of commodity money is that it should be fairly scarce in the main area of use, that there should be enough in circulation to meet the needs of the economy, and that it should be reasonably expensive and difficult to obtain more of it.

The French historian Marc Bloch described the use of peppercorns as a a common, if not single, currency in many parts of medieval Europe, ranging from Normandy to Genoa:

Pepper fulfilled nearly all the conditions classical theory requires for a currency. It was sufficiently scarce and therefore had relatively high value with a relatively low bulk and weight. It was easy to store. It was more or less in the 'fungible' category, with differences in the quality of the different varieties probably barely perceptible. Finally, while being used as an instrument in an abstract way, it was a proper commodity, with a value in use independent of its monetary function.[1]

In some times and places gold and/or silver fulfilled these requirements better than anything else, and were thus used as money. However, it has never been common for the precious metals to be used simply by weight, so that, for example, the price of a loaf of bread might be an ounce of silver. It is highly inconvenient to have to weigh every coin when carrying out a transaction. So rulers who controlled mints stamped their image and a name and number on coins to guarantee their weight, and thus their value. In Britain in 1868 the weight of a gold sovereign was defined as being 113 1/623 grains (480 grains = one Troy ounce).[2]

Rulers often decreed a monopoly of coining, so that all gold or silver had to be sold to the mint at the official price. They also reduced the metal content of coins, so that they would buy more than they had cost to mint or mine. The ruler could get away with this, as long as he maintained confidence in the coinage, and did not issue so much that its value went down, and the price of other goods went up, causing inflation.

As economic activity expanded, it was necessary sometimes to supplement coins by other means, to avoid the danger of the price of gold or silver going up, and the price of other goods going down, causing deflation and slump. The gold coinage was often accompanied by silver at a fixed rate (ranging from 9 to 26 units of silver by weight for one of gold at different times in various places, but about 15.5 to one in the mid-nineteenth century). Coins were supplemented by banknotes and bank deposits. Notes and deposits, to maintain confidence, originally had to be convertible into coins, but as long as only a fraction of the population actually wanted to convert them, there was no need to have anything like the total equivalent amount of banknotes and bank deposits available in the form of coins sitting in bank vaults.

The shortage of gold and silver was thus prevented from putting a brake on economic development. What was more difficult for governments to control was the variable – usually falling – cost of mining new gold and silver, and the unpredictable discovery of new mines of the precious metals. Excessive supplies of gold and silver at different times in history have caused inflation, and the variation between the supply of the two metals has put strains on the fixed ratio between them. By Gresham's Law that bad money drives out good, excess supplies of silver caused gold to be hoarded, and excess supplies of gold caused silver to be hoarded. The validity of Gresham's Law depends on fixed exchange rates. If exchange rates are allowed to vary, an anti-Gresham's Law applies, where good money drives out bad: if the lira is falling, and the D-mark rising, people move out of the lira into the D-mark.

The simple way around Gresham's Law was monometallism, using either gold or silver as the main monetary standard and letting the ratio with the other metal vary with market conditions. However, many countries tried to hedge their bets by means of bimetallism, keeping a fixed ratio between gold and silver, and trying to manage supplies so that both stayed in circulation, rather as countries try to manage exchange rates today.

In the last quarter of the nineteenth century, most major countries moved on to the gold standard.[3] Gold thus became in a sense the major common currency of the world system. Yet it was far from being a single currency in the way now intended for EMU. Gold was supplemented by silver, copper, banknotes and bank deposits. It was the base of the monetary system, but not the most common means of payment. It was also minted by different countries in coins of different values and denominations, which could vary against each other by small percentages until the point was reached when it paid to ship gold to other countries where its value was higher.

THE INTERNATIONAL GOLD STANDARD

Gold was the single monetary base for different currencies, even if it was not a single currency. Each domestic currency was convertible into a gold reserve to which it was linked by a fixed rate. So these currencies were all linked with each other at fixed rates through gold – unless and until the gold value of the domestic currency was changed, as began to happen in the twentieth century. The gold standard was a system of fixed exchange rates, and thus had one important feature of a monetary union, even though gold was not the single currency.

Gold has an undeserved reputation for holding its value steady, an important virtue in any currency. British prices were as often rising (money falling in value) as they were falling (money rising in value) under the gold standard in the nineteenth century.[4] In either case, damage resulted to different sectors of the economy. It so happens that the price level was about the same in 1900 as it had been in 1800. For any level of prices in nineteenth-century Britain, there are a few widely spread years when prices were at that level. This is like saying that a clock which has stopped will show the right time twice a day.

Prices were not stable under the gold standard, but went down as well as up. Inflation was not zero, but either negative or positive in a particular year or series of years. Even in the heyday of the gold standard, world manufactured goods prices fell by 19 per cent between 1880 and 1896, and rose by 25 per cent between 1897 and 1913.[5] Prices depended on factors such as corn harvests, which fluctuated (with the weather), as well as on the supply of gold and silver.

The gold standard was supposed in theory at least to keep different countries' rates of inflation in line with each other, by means of the link between the domestic and the international functions of gold. This link, called the price–specie flow mechanism, was set out by David Hume in 1752.[6] If a country had higher inflation than its trading partners, it would get into a deficit on its external balance of payments, because imports would increase and exports decrease, as domestic goods became more expensive than foreign goods. The country would have to export some of its gold reserve to meet the deficit, and raise interest rates to attract money from abroad. This would cause domestic money to contract, and inflation to slow down again.

There is little evidence in fact for this theory during the main period of the gold standard. Countries' rates of inflation and economic growth showed little link with their balance of payments deficits, which did not disappear as they were supposed to. Balance of payments deficits and surpluses were large and persistent under the gold standard, and were financed by huge flows of capital. Payments imbalances today are smaller in relation to economic activity than they were then, even though there is no gold standard mechanism now.[7] The gold standard thus neither had much effect on inflation nor prevented imbalances in countries' external payments on current account. Gold is not now and never has been a good candidate for a single, stable currency, or the basis of one.

The gold standard is more often put forward by the opponents of the single currency as an example of what to avoid, than by its advocates as a model to imitate. Some countries that had left the gold standard during the First World War tried to return to it at the pre-war parities, even though prices had gone up in the meantime. Their currencies thus became over-valued, and there was pressure for price deflation. The UK's return to the gold standard in 1925 was at a rate only about 10 per cent above what was required to stabilize prices. This is less than the degree of misalignment of many currencies during the 1980s, but it was more difficult to lower the level of wages and prices in the economy when they were stable or falling than it would have been had they been rising. It meant absolute cuts, not just cuts in the rate of increase.

There was nothing about the gold standard which required countries that had gone off it to return at the same rate, except the misplaced pride of their governments. France and Germany returned to the gold standard after the First World War at a lower than pre-war rate, so that their currencies were undervalued in relation to the pound, with corresponding advantage to their trade.

More damaging than the gold standard itself were the exits and entrances of different countries at different dates, and the lack of any coordinated and collective approach to international monetary policy. It
is argued in favour of the gold standard that it was an automatic mechanism which obliged countries to behave in their own best interests
without any kind of overt agreement needing to be negotiated. The
mechanism did not in fact work in the way that it was meant to and it
was the lack of any negotiated agreement, particularly about exits and
entrances and currency rates against gold, which caused the downfall of
the system.

The EMS attempted to use the ecu as a unit of account to which to
peg exchange rates in the ERM, rather as gold had been used under
the gold standard. The ecu was never in practice used in this way. It had
the drawback that it was composed of a basket of the currencies for
which it was the numeraire, see Table 17. It was thus never an independent standard of value, and went down in value against the
stronger EMS currencies as the weaker ones in its basket were devalued or, like the pound, floated up and down.

The entrance of the pound into the ERM in 1990, and its exit in
1992, both decided unilaterally by the UK, recalled the country's
return to the gold standard in 1925 at too high a rate, and its panic-
stricken and unplanned departure in 1931.

THE UNITED STATES MONETARY UNION

Political union is not a necessary condition of monetary union in
Europe today, but it is not a sufficient condition either, as the history of
the United States shows. It took about 140 years for the United States
to achieve a well-functioning monetary union within its own borders.
The mistakes are glaring, and the lessons elementary.

The Federal Government adopted the dollar as the currency of the
United States from 1785, after one or two false starts, but failed to implement the policies to make it a viable and efficient currency. Two
Banks of the United States were set up to carry out more or less the
role of a central bank, but each lasted only twenty years and was then
wound up (1791–1811 and 1816–36). It was not until 1913 that the
Federal Reserve System of central banks was set up. It took another
twenty years to discover that each of the twelve Federal Reserve Banks

could not pursue an independent monetary policy, not even the powerful Federal Reserve Bank of New York.

For most of the nineteenth century, the US provides an illustration of the doctrines of free banking and competing currencies in operation. By 1905 the number of banks issuing currency had risen to 5,600. Even if they all issued dollars, they were paper dollars of varying degrees of value and reliability. Banks were chartered by individual states. There was no federal system of supervision, and in many cases not much at state level. The banking crisis of 1907–8 finally forced Congress to set up a proper Federal Reserve System to handle the issue of money, although the supervision of banks remains to this day divided and anomalous.

The monetary chaos of nineteenth-century America interrupted the otherwise rapid development of the economy, to an extent that is hard to measure with any precision, but the qualitative judgement of history is damning enough. 'Panic after panic – 1791, 1819, 1837, 1857, and so on down – has wrought havoc and destruction, like our Western tornadoes.'[8] The monetary order of the Federal Reserve System today is an aid to the growth of the economy and the control of inflation, even if the movement of funds by cheque around the country could be improved. Technically there are still twelve different dollars. Every dollar bill bears the name, letter, and number of the Federal Reserve Bank that issued it, although they all carry the seal of authority of the US Treasury in Washington DC. However, there is no question of the exchange rate between the twelve different dollars ever changing.

As Gertrude Stein might have put it, 'a dollar is a dollar is a dollar' (unless, of course, it happens to be Canadian). The US thus enjoys the economic advantages of monetary union throughout its vast territory: low transactions costs, free movement of funds, certainty of the value of investments, control of inflation, a common set of prices, and a global currency.

Short-term advantages could have been obtained at various moments in history if the dollar of one Federal Reserve Bank had been devalued against the others. For example, Texas might have found it easier to deal with the oil price fall of 1985 if the Dallas dollar had been devalued. This would have made it easier in the short run to cut incomes in the state, but this happened anyway without any change in the exchange rate. Adjustment was that much faster because it was known that there was no question of a cut in the exchange rate, and thus no alternative to a cut in prices and incomes in US dollar terms. In the long run Texas benefits by being part of the US monetary union.

The lessons of the US monetary union for Europe are clear, and most have been understood from the outset of EMU. Even Professor Martin Feldstein, who argues against EMU because the costs of not being able to devalue separate currencies in each region are high, admits that 'nobody seriously suggests that the dollar should be abandoned for a set of regional currencies'.[9] History shows that the costs to the US economy of not having a single currency would have been even higher. Free banking and competing currencies are a recipe for chaos, although the British Government retains a residual doctrinaire attachment to the idea.[10] A single currency needs a single central bank and a single monetary policy, even if its implementation can be devolved to a network of regional or national central banks, each putting its own name on part of the single currency. A single currency is a boon to trade and investment over a large and diverse area, see chapter 3. On the related questions of efficient money transfers and the supervision of banks, the US is more a lesson in what to avoid than in how to proceed.

A SCOTTISH NOTE

Scotland provides another example of a political union which did not for a long time lead to a complete monetary union. When the Act of Union between England and Scotland was passed in 1707 (a century after the union of the two monarchies in 1603), the rate of exchange was fixed at twelve to one; twelve Scottish to one English pound, and a Scottish shilling to an English penny. Attempts to fix the rate were not a complete success, and there were transactions costs. It was not until 1805 that the two currencies became exchangeable at par, and a full currency union came about. Even today, Scottish commercial banks still issue distinctive banknotes which are used instead of Bank of England notes in Scotland, but fully backed by Bank of England notes.

The Scottish example has been used by Sir Leon Brittan, a Vice-President of the European Commission, to justify a version of the single currency in which national currencies could be irrevocably fixed against each other at round number conversion rates other than one to one; in this example, it would be twelve to one.

Such concessions to national sensibilities are more trouble than they are worth. The example of Scotland has lessons more like those of Texas *vis-à-vis* the US monetary union. Scotland benefits by being part of the United Kingdom monetary union, even though the case could have been made for revaluing the Scottish pound upwards when the price of oil went up in the 1970s, and for devaluing it downwards when the price of oil went down in the 1980s. The Scottish pound has done better in the long run to remain at par with the English pound. An unforeseen consequence of the single European currency is that England and Scotland may for the first time have the same banknotes – perhaps with a distinctive thistle on the Scottish variety.

GERMAN MONETARY UNIONS

Since Germany is the key country for the success of the single currency, German monetary history is particularly relevant. Lawson has used the example of nineteenth-century Germany to show that political union is a necessary condition of monetary union. 'It is significant that whereas the *Zollverein* or customs union paved the way to the German Federation a century ago, it was only after Prussia and Bismarck had achieved a political union, with blood and iron, that a common German currency could be born.'[11]

The facts are more ambiguous. The German customs union (*Zollverein*) was set up in 1834. On the 'one market, one money' argument, the needs of trade and finance were thought to require fixed exchange rates, which is one form of monetary union. The chaotic diversity of currencies among the German states was gradually replaced by a fixed system. In 1853 one North German thaler was set equal to 1.5 Austrian florins and 1.75 South German guilders.

A form of monetary union thus preceded political union. The political unification of Germany by Bismarck in 1871 did not in itself guarantee a single currency. Austria–Hungary had dropped out after the Austro-German war of 1866. The German mark was introduced in 1875, after the new Reichsbank was set up to issue it. But there were still thirty-five commercial banks issuing currency, and it was not until 1909 that Reichsbank notes became the sole legal tender.

The great German inflation of the early 1920s shows that a central bank and a single currency cannot in themselves guarantee that the value of the currency remains stable. (The great Russian inflation of the early 1990s shows that even an *independent* central bank will not necessarily give top priority to stable prices.) The excellent record of the post-war Bundesbank in controlling inflation shows that Germany has learned lessons from its history. The reluctance of the Bundesbank to enter a single currency except under the strictest conditions is explained by the deep-seated fear of inflation that persists in Germany.

The monetary union between West and East Germany after unification in 1990 also provides lessons for the wider EMU.[12] The German Federal Government wanted to make unification irrevocable, before the Soviet leadership could change its mind. One obvious way of doing this was to merge the two currencies without delay, rather than allowing for a period of transition during which they could be gradually brought together. Even though the free market rate between the East and the West currencies was about four to one, monetary union was pushed through at one to one for current transactions and two to one for savings.

East Germany thus benefited from a windfall gain in purchasing power, but prices rose rapidly there. Eastern wages, which had been about one-third of Western at a one for one exchange rate, rose rapidly to about two-thirds, with trade unions demanding equality. With prophetic accuracy, the term German Economic, Monetary and Social Union (GEMSU) was used rather than just German Monetary Union. The wage catch-up went ahead in spite of productivity in the East being one-third of that in the West. The result was a sharp rise in unemployment, accompanied by a slower catch-up in productivity. The all-German inflation rate and budget deficit rose as the West poured consumer and capital goods into the East.

GEMSU has provided ammunition to the opponents of EMU, but most of it is wide of the mark. It does not show that monetary union is a bad idea, even between countries of the same nationality and the same language. After more teething troubles than the Federal Government expected or made provision for, GEMSU has worked. The monetary side was quickly carried out, and the economic and social side is becoming effective after a long period of adjustment. West and East Germany were further apart in living standards and economic structure than most of the countries in Western European EMU, and were thus poor candidates for a so-called optimum currency area (see chapter 5). If EMU can work between West and East Germany, it should be able to operate with less disorientation between, for example, Germany and the UK.

Nor does GEMSU show that EMU will be sabotaged by employees in lower-income countries claiming West German wages in spite of lower productivity, and thus causing a loss in competitiveness and a rise in unemployment. The East and West Germans were economically dissimilar, but they differed from other European countries in having a common language and a similar standard of education, as well as suddenly gaining freedom of movement and a common political system within Germany. So East German workers would have migrated West in even larger numbers had they not been paid to stay at home, enjoying increases in either pay or unemployment benefit.

The East German pay catch-up is unlikely to be repeated in EMU. Workers in different EMU countries are less mobile than the East Germans, because of differences of language, culture and housing. Mobility of labour is sometimes held to be a condition of monetary union, so that those who become unemployed can seek work elsewhere. It is equally plausible to argue that immobility is a condition of monetary union, to avoid cross-border equalization of wages where productivity levels are unequal.

Another supposed lesson from GEMSU is that EMU can be blown off course by unexpected shock events such as German unification. First there was an unexpected rise in demand due to West German spending in East Germany. This was a beneficial shock, in that the exports of Germany's trading partners, including the UK, benefited as Germany imported more, thus at the same time moderating her own inflation rate and dissolving the once intractable surplus in her balance of payments.

Not so beneficial was the rise in German interest rates to slow down the economic boom. Other countries in the ERM had to raise their interest rates too unless they were prepared to let their exchange rates fall against the D-mark. With hindsight, it is clear that there should have been a unilateral upwards revaluation of the D-mark. This would have moderated the German boom, without requiring such a big rise in interest rates, and allowed other ERM countries, notably the UK, to let their exchange rates fall and keep their interest rates down.

The mistake was to treat the ERM as a fixed exchange rate system before its time, rather than take advantage of its provisions for exchange rate adjustment in response to unexpected events. The pressure became such that Italy and the UK left the ERM in September 1992, when a D-mark revaluation at an earlier stage might have allowed them to remain on board.[13]

If a Europe-wide shock such as German unification had occurred within a single currency area, it could not have been dealt with by changing exchange rates. On the other hand, Germany would have been under pressure from the other countries in EMU to raise taxes earlier to finance unification, instead of letting the budget deficit soar and raising interest rates to offset it. The rest of Europe would have had a smaller shock to cope with than Germany itself, particularly East Germany.

It is hard to see what kind of unexpected event could occur to undermine EMU that would be on a scale comparable with German unification. A low probability of the unexpected is hardly a valid argument for not doing something. I do not call off a car journey because I know that there is a 10,000 to one chance that I may have an accident.

The other positive lesson from GEMSU is that the Bundesbank's view, which was hostile to the merger of the marks on the terms proposed, can be overriden by the German Government on broader political grounds. The Bundesbank has unquestioned authority over the domestic supply of D-marks, but not over external financial matters such as the exchange rate or monetary union. Here it may advise, but cannot dictate to the Federal Government. Whether Germany goes into the single currency is, like GEMSU, a political decision for the Government, not a monetary decision for the Bundesbank.

LATIN MONETARY UNION

Latin Monetary Union (LMU) is something of a misnomer. In French, the language of LMU, *monetaire* is the adjective of *monnaie*, which means a currency and a mint as well as money. LMU can thus equally well be called Latin Currency Union or Latin Coinage Union. Its scope was essentially limited to gold and silver coins, which were at the time a more important part of the money supply then they are today, rather than extending to bank deposit money.

The way had been prepared for LMU by a bilateral monetary union between Belgium and France, dating back to Belgian independence from the Netherlands in 1830, rather as the Anglo-Irish monetary union followed on Irish independence in 1921. Switzerland gave official status to French coins from 1848, to escape the chaos of cantonal currencies. Italy did the same in 1861, and in 1865 the LMU was agreed between the governments as a bimetallic system. The gold and silver franc coins of the four countries were declared equal to each other in weight and value (Italy kept the lira as equal to one franc). There were, however, transactions costs of up to 1.25 per cent for changing one kind of franc into another. Bulgaria and Greece joined in 1867.

The LMU was a convenience to travellers and traders and shows the advantage of a simple one-for one exchange rate between different currencies. However, it also shows the difficulty of controlling the supply of money, and thus the rate of exchange, throughout a union. There was no union central bank, only an inter-governmental agreement on how much coinage each member should issue. Then, as now, Italy was the suspect member of the union. Italian silver coins were minted at less than the agreed weight and thus tended to return to Italy. The Italian budget deficit also called into question Italy's ability to hold the lira exchange rate.

The exchange rate between silver and gold was a problem for the LMU, as it was for any bimetallic system. France managed only with difficulty to keep the exchange rate between the two at 15.5 to 1. The LMU could not stand out against the gold standard. The UK, as the leading economic power, had been on it since 1821, and Germany joined in 1873. In 1878, the members of the LMU also joined the gold standard, followed by the US next year.

The LMU was widely seen as an attempt by Napoleon III to extend French influence. After France's defeat by Prussia in 1870–1, Germany set out to establish her own influence by means of the new gold-backed mark. After 1878, the exchange rate stability of the LMU countries, such as it was, was due to their common membership of the gold standard, rather than to the LMU itself. Silver coins ceased to be cross-border legal tender in 1885. The LMU was not finally laid to rest officially until 1927.

Other more local monetary unions have taken place after the demise of the LMU. Denmark, Norway and Sweden formed the Scandinavian Monetary Union in 1872. It went further than the LMU in having an identical Scandinavian krona coinage in all three countries. Sweden left in 1905, because of its political separation from Norway, and the Union came to an end in 1914.

There are many examples of bilateral monetary unions. Both the Anglo-Irish and the Belgium–Luxembourg Unions were formed in 1921. The former ended when Ireland joined the ERM in 1979, while the latter survives, but nearly broke down in 1982 and again in 1993.[14] Such unions of one big and one small partner do not prove much about wider unions. They may show that monetary union does not require political union, but they also show that politically independent members of a monetary union are free to leave it.

THE WORLD MONETARY CONFERENCE

France tried to extend the LMU into a world currency. A major international conference was held in Paris in 1867 with this aim. The conference came down in favour of the gold standard, but the adherence of France and the other members of the LMU to bimetallism meant that no clear agreement was reached as to how the two should be reconciled. It also had to agree on a common monetary unit. A French gold 25-franc piece was chosen, to replace the existing 20-franc piece, because it would be roughly equal to the American 5-dollar half-eagle and to the British sovereign. It would have been necessary to devalue the sovereign by only 0.83 per cent, and the half-eagle by 3.5 per cent.

The British delegate was as unenthusiastic as his American colleague was enthusiastic. Some of the positions taken up then are scarcely altered today. The change in existing exchange rates in order to get round-number parities was resisted then as it has been today in response to proposals for a 2 D-mark ecu, or a 10-franc pound.[15]

Mr Rivers Wilson, the British delegate, refused to join. His decision was confirmed by a Royal Commission in 1868. He told the conference:

So long as public opinion has not decided in favour of a change in the present system, which offers no serious inconvenience . . . and until it shall be incontestably demonstrated that a new system offers advantages sufficiently commanding to justify the abandonment of that which is approved by experience and rooted in the habits of the people, the English government could not believe it to be its duty to take the initiative in assimilating its coinage with those of the countries of the continent.

The Royal Commission, while coming down against a change, published evidence in favour:

Smaller manufacturers and traders are deterred from engaging in foreign transactions by the complicated difficulties of foreign coins . . . by the difficulty of calculating the exchanges, and of remitting small sums from one country to another. Anything tending to simplify these matters would dispose them to extend the sphere of their operations.

Walter Bagehot wrote a series of articles in *The Economist* advocating that Britain join a world currency, but to no avail. He wrote:

If we do nothing, what then? Why, we shall . . . be left out in the cold . . . If things remain as now, [Germany] is sure to choose the French currency . . . Before long, all Europe, save England, will have one money, and England be left standing with another money.

As Morris Perlman comments: 'Belatedly his prediction may yet be fulfilled.'[16]

Once the opportunity had passed, it did not recur. The LMU did not generate the momentum needed to extend its idea to a world currency. The gold standard which succeeded it was only a partial realization of the dream. The 1944 Bretton Woods conference set up a system of fixed exchange rates within narrow bands, but adjustable by large margins. The US delegate, Harry Dexter White, was in favour of a more fixed system, but Lord Keynes, the British delegate, wanted the UK to keep its freedom to devalue.[17]

Bretton Woods gave long periods of stability, but they were interrupted by large and disruptive devaluations such as that of the pound in 1949 and again in 1967. Restrictions on capital movements made parities easier to maintain while favouring national monetary autonomy over world monetary union. Bretton Woods stood in for any separate

European exchange rate system, thus giving the European Economic Community the monetary stability it needed to develop the customs union from 1958 to 1971. It is no coincidence that the Werner Plan for EMU was introduced into the EC in 1972, a year before the Bretton Woods system was abandoned.[18]

THE EUROPEAN MONETARY SYSTEM[19]

The Werner Plan set up the European currency snake in 1972, see Table 1. This was a fixed exchange rate system, with narrower bands of variation than those agreed in the final two years of Bretton Woods; 2.25 per cent rather than 4.5 per cent. The UK left it in 1972 after only two months, with the forlorn hope of regaining control of its interest rate, exchange rate and inflation rate. Italy left after less than a year. France left twice and only rejoined once. Leaving once looked like a misfortune, but leaving twice looked like carelessness. By 1976 the snake was reduced to a D-mark bloc of Germany, Benelux and Denmark. Out of its ashes the EMS rose like a phoenix, after a political decision in 1978 by Valéry Giscard d'Estaing, the French President, and Helmut Schmidt, the German Chancellor, to take up a proposal put forward by Roy Jenkins, the President of the European Commission.

The core of the EMS was the ERM, a system of fixed but adjustable parities similar to that of Bretton Woods. The UK joined the EMS in 1979, but not the ERM, and was thus to all intents and purposes on the outside, until it finally joined in October 1990, see page 2. During the early years of the ERM, there were exchange rate realignments every year or two, with most other currencies going down against the D-mark. After 1983 there were only two general realignments, in 1986 and in 1987. After five years of unprecedented stability from 1987 onwards, the ERM almost broke down in 1992 and again in 1993, but survived in a more flexible form.

The ERM helped to bring inflation down from its early 1980s peak caused by the rise in the price of oil. Devaluations accommodated only about half of the differences in the inflation rate between countries, and governments used other policy measures to get inflation down and keep devaluations in check. By the end of the 1980s, the stability of ERM currencies against each other was seen as a 'dry run' for full

EMU, which was launched by the 1989 Delors Report and the 1991 Maastricht Treaty.

By the late 1980s the experience was regarded as so positive that the ERM was used as the launching pad for EMU. Stage one of the three stages of EMU laid down in the Delors Report began on 1 July 1990. The aim of stage one was that all EU members would join the ERM: Spain joined in June 1989, the UK in October 1990, and Portugal in April 1992. Those ERM members with wide 6 per cent bands around the fixed parities were to move to the narrow 2.25 per cent bands; Italy had done so in January 1990, leaving Portugal, Spain and the UK still with 6 per cent bands. All this was a prelude to stage two, beginning on 1 January 1994, after which the convergence tests had to be passed for entry into stage three – full EMU in 1997 or 1999.

The ERM, far from providing a smooth glide path into EMU, nearly wrecked the whole project. It became clear that exchange rates had been set in a mould that was going to be broken. Countries such as Italy and the UK succeeded in lowering inflation to annual rates not much higher than those of France and Germany. But their price levels were too high on account of inflation in previous years, which had not been offset by devaluation. When the financial markets realized how overvalued some currencies were, they tired of earning high interest rates on them under a quasi-guarantee of no devaluation. They began to sell them in the expectation that the ERM central banks would not have enough reserves to support their exchange rates.

The first major crisis of the ERM was in September 1992 when Italy and the UK left, and Ireland, Portugal and Spain devalued while staying in the ERM. The second major crisis was in August 1993, when the French franc and other currencies came under heavy pressure. The ERM countries then agreed to widen their bands around the central parities from 2.25 per cent (6 per cent for Spain and Portugal) to 15 per cent. This made it easier to keep within the bands, and removed any target for financial market speculation as long as a currency was nowhere near the edge of its bands. Even so, the peseta and the escudo had to be devalued when they had used up only about half their available wider bands.

Fixed exchange rates are, it can now be seen, neither a necessary nor a sufficient condition of full monetary union. Moderate exchange rate fluctuations, particularly around a constant average value, avoid the need for central bank intervention to prevent even minor deviations from parity during the run-up to monetary union. If other economic fundamentals, such as inflation rates, are in line with each other, then, once the monetary union begins, exchange rates can be first fixed then abolished in favour of a single currency without fear that they may be so far out of line as to make a single currency impossible to sustain.

The ability to fix any set of exchange rates for a trial period by massive central bank intervention or any other means does not prove that they are the right exchange rates at which to go into a monetary union. If fundamentals such as inflation rates are far apart, then the monetary union will not last, however much exchange rates may have been fixed during the run-up.

The ERM must be judged more successful than the snake which preceded it, see Table 1. The snake's original eight members were reduced to five during its first four years, and it was the three largest members apart from Germany who left. The ERM's original eight members are all still in it, apart from Italy, which left after thirteen years' successful membership. They were joined by three more members in 1989–92, of whom only one, the UK, left after nearly two years of membership, and by Austria in 1995. There are thus still ten ERM members, including France, Germany and Spain among the large countries. The main difference is that France behaved like Britain in the snake, but like Germany in the ERM. France did not stay the course in the snake, but remains a member of the ERM. The ERM also proved better able to handle exchange rate changes due to the oil price rise of the early 1980s than was the snake to handle the oil price rises of the early 1970s.

THE LESSONS OF HISTORY

The one-to-one link between currencies and nation-states is a fairly recent development in history. Rulers have long been aware of the power and prestige that a currency can give them, but they have not always made good use of it. Political union sometimes precedes monetary union, as in the United States, late twentieth-century Germany and the United Kingdom. Political union sometimes follows monetary union, as in the case of nineteenth-century Germany, but not always, as in the case of the Latin Monetary Union and the more limited Anglo-

Irish and Belgium–Luxembourg cases. Political union may or may not follow monetary union in Europe in the twenty-first century. If it does, it will be a much looser kind of political union than the formation of a unitary state.

None of these examples can be more than a rough guide, because the future environment for EMU will be so different from the past. Monetary technology has become faster and more efficient, and global money flows larger and less stable. It is harder therefore to fix the exchange rates of different currencies, but more feasible and perhaps more necessary to merge national currencies on a regional basis. The scope of trade, investment and financial markets is wider than the catchment area of most nation-states. Even if there is still a democratic political role for relatively small nation-states, they may be able to exist more prosperously and coexist more harmoniously if monetary policy is handled at a higher level.

The urge to merge among currencies is not new. While national currencies are sometimes abused as tools of political domination they are also sometimes put into the melting pot as a step towards more effective international cooperation. What technology makes more feasible, international economic development makes more desirable.

3
EMU Makes You Grow Faster

THE ECONOMIC GROWTH OBJECTIVE

Faster growth of the economy is the main economic aim of most governments. It opens the way to higher living standards and better public services. A major policy innovation such as opting in to the single currency could not be justified if there was not a good chance that it would raise the rate of economic growth.

The single currency should also help to keep the rate of price inflation down, another main objective of government policy. Low inflation is both an end in itself and one of the means to higher economic growth. The next chapter deals with EMU and inflation.

The other ways in which full EMU and the single currency can be expected to raise the growth rate are: lower cross-border transactions costs, an increase in trade within the single market, lower interest rates, more business investment, and greater competition on prices and products.

There is no economic growth convergence criterion in the Maastricht Treaty. It is sometimes argued that countries should demonstrate that they are capable of healthy economic growth before they enter into the competitive world of a single currency without recourse to devaluation. Growth rates among potential EMU members have nearly all clustered in the 1.5–2.5 per cent range for the last decade, so there has in fact been a convergence of growth rates, albeit in a range lower than governments and their electors would have liked.

A more sensible aim would be convergence of living standards, or GDP per head, as urged by the Delors Report: 'If sufficient consideration were not given to regional imbalances, the economic union would be faced with grave economic and political risks.'[1] This would mean that countries with lower living standards – the Mediterranean countries, for example – would need a faster rate of economic growth per head than their richer partners, so as to catch up with them. Such a convergence of living standards may be desirable on grounds of fairness across Europe, but it is not necessary to either the single market or the single currency. Countries with lower incomes per head have a chance to be more competitive in terms of unit labour costs, and thus to raise living standards by exporting more to their single-market partners.

Only Ireland has managed to have significantly faster growth than other EU countries, thanks partly to generous EU subsidies, which have not had such a marked effect in the Mediterranean countries. Table 2 shows that Ireland has grown by nearly 4 per cent a year since 1979; Spain and Portugal have grown at only 0.25–0.5 per cent a year faster than the EU average, and Greece 0.5 per cent a year slower. UK living standards measured by GNP per head are the same as the EU average, slightly lower than Italy's, and about a tenth lower than those in France and united Germany. Spain and Ireland have living standards about a quarter below that of the UK, Portugal and Greece about a third below. At this rate, it would take Spain half a century to catch up with the UK and the EU average.

The need for the catch-up countries to grow faster does not mean that the richer countries should grow more slowly than they wish to, or lock in to their recent disappointing growth rates. The British econ-omy has been growing at only 1.9 per cent a year since 1979, exactly the same as the French and Italian economies, and a fraction slower than the German and American economies. Not only has the UK not benefited by being outside the exchange rate mechanism (ERM) during the 1980s; its growth has been much more unstable than that of the three major continental countries or the US, see Figure 1. Nor have France and Italy benefited relative to the UK by being inside the ERM, because they have made sacrifices in order to get inflation down and qualify for full EMU by pegging to the D-mark exchange rate.

The single currency offers both the UK and the countries that have been in the ERM a chance to raise growth rates to a steady 2.75 to 3 per cent. It would be absurd, however, to insist that the UK should have a higher rate of economic growth as an extra convergence criterion before entering the single currency. The UK and its main continental partners have had exactly the same sub-standard rate of growth for the past fifteen years. None of them are likely to improve on it unless they all join the single currency. Nor can it be argued that the UK needs to catch up with the other richer countries before embarking on the single currency, when it is already so far ahead of the four countries that really need to catch up. The UK will do well not to fall further behind France and Germany in living standards.

Portugal and Spain, if not Greece, should be able to match Ireland's 4 per cent growth rate once they qualify for entry into full EMU. In this case, it would take Ireland and Spain no more than fifteen years to catch up with the UK. In the meantime, it would be pointless to insist that these countries reach Northern European living standards before they can join the single currency, when it may provide them with the best means of doing so. The EU budget measures taken so far have had only a marginal effect in helping the lower-income countries to catch up, see chapter 6.

The scope for improvement in the rate of economic growth is shown by the output gap – the shortfall of actual from potential economic performance if the economy was running at full capacity, see Table 2. The output gap is a rough measure of how far actual GDP is running below potential GDP. When the output gap is negative the rate of growth of actual GDP can exceed the rate of growth of potential GDP until the gap is closed. When it is positive, the opposite applies. All countries in the EU, except Ireland, have negative output gaps, while the US has a positive one. In the UK case, if the potential rate of GDP growth is 2.5 per cent, the actual rate of growth could go on at 3 per cent until 2000 before the gap is closed. If the gap is closed too quickly inflation may result; a good anti-inflation policy makes it easier to close output gaps, see chapter 4.

EMU may not be paradise, but it is better than the alternative that most European countries face. It is not a panacea. It will work only if a whole range of other policies go with it. One of its merits is that it creates a framework within which governments come under pressure to take sensible economic decisions outside the field of monetary policy.

Economic growth is made more difficult, because exchange rates and interest rates fluctuate unpredictably within the EU. Some countries maintain their central parities within the ERM while letting exchange rates fall below them; some devalue their central parities now and again; and some let their exchange rates float outside the ERM. EMU should be compared with the present wide-band ERM for those countries which are still members of it, and with floating for Britain and Italy, which have left the ERM. EMU should be compared with the present chaotic financial environment, not with some ideal world of freely floating currencies which has never existed. It should also be compared with a stage three of 'irrevocably' fixed exchange rates, which would be an improvement on the present chaos, but does not deliver all the advantages of the single currency.

TRANSACTIONS COST SAVINGS

When there is a single currency in the EU, there will by definition no longer be any exchange rate conversions when money moves across national boundaries. This will save time, trouble and expense. The banks and *bureaux de change* charge commissions, sell foreign currency more dearly than they buy it, and market derivative financial products such as forwards, futures and options so that their customers can hedge the risk that exchange rates will change. Hedging is like insurance. The greater the risk, the higher the premium.

The European Commission identified several different kinds of transactions cost saving arising out of the abolition of exchange rates within the EU.[2] About half the total saving will come from the elimination of bid–ask spreads and commissions in foreign exchange dealings between banks and their customers. The spread is the difference between the banks' buying and selling rates for foreign currency. Another 14 per cent will come from the ending of similar charges on banknotes, travellers' cheques and credit cards. Just over a quarter will be due to the reduction of companies' in-house costs managing foreign exchange risk, and the remaining 10 per cent to a reduction in the cost of cross-border payments once they are all in the same currency. The total saving was estimated at around 0.33 per cent of GDP. For the UK in current terms, this would be £2.5 billion, and for the EU as a whole $25 billion.

The UK has a special position, because London has the world's largest foreign exchange market, 30 per cent of the world total (see Table 23). There are therefore potential losses to the banks and other traders in the market, as well as savings to the companies and individuals who use it. The daily turnover of the London market has risen two-and-a-half times to $464 billion since the Commission made its estimates, see

Table 3. The increase in volume of business has caused a fall in spreads, but dealing profits and the transactions costs nevertheless went up sharply in 1995, as the increase in transactions volume was greater than the fall in spreads. We deal with London's position in the global foreign exchange market in chapter 8; here we are concerned with the effects of the single currency on the UK economy.

The share of intra-EMU currency trading in the London total is no more than 12 per cent of daily turnover. To this should be added something to cover the deals which now go 'through the dollar' to convert one minor EU currency into another, because it is cheaper. So up to a fifth of London's turnover could be lost, if all potential member countries joined the single currency at the same time, which is unlikely. The market would be likely to recoup some of the lost turnover by an increase in trading in major currencies, including the single currency itself, and in the currencies of the higher-income developing countries, such as Malaysia and Mexico. So 12 per cent might after all be a fair estimate of the loss of business.

According to the Association Cambiste Internationale (the foreign exchange dealers' association):

the ecu/dollar market and the ecu/yen market are expected to be larger than the present sum of the participating currencies against the dollar and the yen . . . These factors, however, are not expected to be enough to offset the loss of the intra-European foreign exchange markets . . . There will likely be a shake-out in the industry . . . We should ultimately expect to see fewer, larger players in the European foreign exchange markets.[3]

The 'big four' British clearing banks made foreign exchange dealing profits of just under £500 million in 1994, which was just under 9 per cent of their total pre-tax profits.[4] These dealing profits are before deduction of some staff costs, but they do not include profits from selling foreign currency through branch networks, so we can take them as a fair estimate of actual foreign exchange profits. If we assume that the big four had a 15 per cent share of the market between them, then total profits of all dealers would have been about £3 billion.

All British-owned institutions have 21 per cent of the market, North American 42 per cent, and Japanese 10 per cent.[5] These figures are consistent with those in the national income Blue Book, which began to show foreign exchange dealings as part of GDP for the first time in its

1994 edition.[6] They also fit in with the figures in Table 3, showing that the revenue from dealing spreads ranging between 0.02 per cent and 0.07 per cent comes to about $34 billion (£21 billion) a year. (It is assumed that there are effectively 200 active trading days in the year.) Brokers' commissions are payable on 35 per cent of this turnover, so we reduce it to $28 billion (£18 billion), assuming that revenues are equally shared between brokers and principals. Of this turnover, 23 per cent (£4 billion) must be taken off, because it is between banks in London. Another 52 per cent (£9 billion) is with banks in other financial centres, and the remaining 25 per cent (£5 billion) with British customers in industry and finance. The revenue from spreads may be higher than this, because the proportion of market turnover in spot deals has fallen to 41 per cent, with the other 59 per cent in forward deals, mainly swaps, where spreads may be wider. If profits are £3 billion, and net revenue £14 billion, costs are £11 billion.

Most of the potential loss in dealing profits due to the single currency would be incurred by foreign-owned banks in the London market. If the loss was 12 per cent, about £75 million would be incurred by British banks and other traders, and £285 million by foreign, making a total of £360 million. British non-bank customers' savings would be about £1.25 billion a year, assuming that they pay about twice the dealing spread that banks do. This fits in with our estimate of £2.5 billion total savings to British users.

BANK CHARGES TO CUSTOMERS

Transactions costs levied by banks are higher in percentage terms, the smaller the value of the transaction. If there is a fixed charge, it is obviously a higher percentage if the amount to be exchanged is smaller. It can cost £6.50 to buy £100 in foreign banknotes – which is 6.5 per cent – and more if you want to change some of them back again, see Table 4. For sums of £150 and over the percentage drops to 5.5 per cent, of which 4 per cent is the dealing spread charged, compared with 0.04 per cent paid by banks in the foreign exchange market.

Sending bank transfers across borders in the EU is even more expensive.[7] The EU Commission found in 1993 that the average cost of an ecu 100 cross-border transfer was ecu 25.4, and that 12 per cent of transfers took more than six working days. The Commission maintains that charges should not be levied on the sender and on the receiver of the money by the two banks at each end of the transaction, which happened in 36 per cent of all cases. Council agreed a directive in September 1995 to limit bank charges on low-value cross-border payments.[8]

The tale of the traveller who goes round the EU and loses half his money on the ten currency changes almost qualifies as an 'urban legend'.[9] One-third of the loss in value in the example given by the European Commission was due to the exorbitant cost of the lira–escudo and drachma–D-mark transactions, with the other eight exchanges resulting in a loss of one quarter. However, if the starting sum had been, say, £100 rather than the equivalent of £640, the loss would have been even greater. Our traveller would have done better to take US dollars around the EU with him.

Small and medium-sized enterprises using bank branches suffer more than large companies directly plugged into the wholesale forex market, because foreign currency charges are higher as a proportion of their foreign turnover, which may consist of many diverse small orders. It can be estimated that anything up to 30 per cent of a small firm's foreign currency earnings may be swallowed up by transactions costs, on the assumption that profits are 15 per cent of turnover and foreign exchange costs 4.5 per cent.[10] It is therefore surprising that the Institute of Directors, which represents small firms, should be hostile to the single currency. The Association of British Chambers of Commerce, which also represents small firms, with a higher proportion involved in foreign business, takes a more balanced view.[11]

Even if exchange rates were irrevocably fixed, transactions costs would not disappear. If banks were forced against their will to exchange different currencies at fixed parities, with no bid–ask spread, they would still have to levy charges to cover the costs of maintaining systems to handle all the different currencies with separate accounts. There would thus be a further saving to be made by moving from fixed exchange rates to a single currency, with money transmission charges no greater than those for domestic currency operations. Companies could also make savings on in-house costs of foreign exchange departments, although they would still need the capacity to deal with non-EU currencies such as the dollar.

Banks do, however, charge customers for the transmission of domestic money within national boundaries. The charges are not as high as they are for foreign currency. They are often cross-subsidized for customers getting 'free banking' with minimum credit balances thanks to charges on other products such as deposits and loans. British banks have been talking for years about extending money transmission charges to all customers, but have been held back because none of them wants to be the first to do it. Now that the banks are being pressed to bring down money transmission charges on foreign currency, they will find it more difficult to increase charges on domestic money transmission. Money transmission is costly for the banks, but it brings with it other, more profitable products, such as loans and deposits.

The cost of converting to the new single currency has been estimated by the banks at 8–10 billion ecu for the EU as a whole, and £914m for the UK (see page 151 and Table 18).[12] It must be assumed that the banks would plan their new systems for the single currency so as to yield the efficiency savings arising from the absence of transactions costs. At this stage we can do little more than guess that the total conversion costs for the whole economy including the corporate and the public sectors would amount to about £2.5 billion spread over about three years, in other words the same as the transactions cost savings, which would be permanent.

The full benefit of transactions cost savings is obtained only if all fifteen countries in the EU join the single currency. The advantages obviously depend on the size of the network covered by the new currency. Small economies get the best bargain, because each makes only a small contribution to enlarging the network, but gets access to a wide network by joining up with large countries.[13] The UK will still do well to join a monetary union consisting of Germany, France and Benelux, because these countries account for 50 per cent of the EU's economy, the UK 15 per cent. So the pound's currency area would be multiplied by over three, or by nearly seven if all fifteen join.

A single currency is like a telephone system; the more telephones there are, the more each user benefits. To mix metaphors, abolishing exchange rates is a bit like being able to send a fax down the telephone instead of sending a letter by post. It is both quicker and cheaper, but it is no good if you are the only person with a fax machine.

BENEFITS TO UK TRADE

Transactions cost savings are worth while in themselves. Their benefit will be particularly visible to personal shoppers, travellers and holiday-makers, who now suffer the higher percentage conversion charges. British tourists and business travellers spent £8 billion in the EU in 1994; if 3 per cent was lost on currency exchange, the saving from a single currency would be about £250 million, or a tenth of the total saving to the economy. Credit cards and charge cards are increasingly used to make transactions easier, but they have limitations. They cannot easily be used to shop from home at a distance, they have credit limits, they carry charges similar to those for other types of transaction, and they are open to loss and fraud.

Smart cards can be filled with foreign currency, but none has yet been invented which converts domestic currency into any one of a number of foreign currencies at the point of sale.[14] The cashless society, with electronic money for everyone, is still some way off.[15] Even if its use was widespread, it would not be a substitute for the single currency, but a way of lowering money transmission costs among single currency users. It is likely to take rather longer to introduce as a universal means of payment than the single currency itself.

The benefits to business and cross-border trade may be less in per-centage terms, but they will be more far-reaching. British exporters will be able to sell their goods on the Continent more cheaply, or make higher and steadier profits, so they will sell more of them. The same will apply to importers into the UK, which is good news for British dis-tributors and consumers.

International trade normally expands faster than domestic produc-tion, and the proportion of output traded thus rises steadily. Since the Second World War, trade has driven economic growth. What is true for the global economic system is even more so for the EU. British exports of goods to the EU rose from 9.3 per cent of GDP in 1980 to 10.6 per cent in 1994; the single currency should result in an even faster increase. We assume that UK earnings from the EU increase by 3 per cent – particularly invisible income earned by the City and the financial ser-vices sector – and outgoings to the EU by 1.5 per cent. This gives a once-for-all gain of £1.5 billion (based on the 1994 figures) in addition to the continuing trend.

The growth of trade may look like a zero-sum game, in which the growth of exports is cancelled out more or less by the growth in imports. The sum of the game is positive for several reasons: a wider variety of products comes on to the market, the most efficient producers drive the less efficient out of business, and international competition lowers prices to the benefit of all.

ONE MARKET, ONE MONEY

The single European market, agreed by the Single European Act of 1986, is a deepening of the original EC customs union, extending to many fields other than trade. Most of it came into being by the end of 1992 as planned. A number of measures were delayed in their implementation, and a few have not yet been agreed. Not only does the single market require the single currency to make it work better, but the single currency will improve one essential feature of the single market by stepping up competition by means of pricing in a single currency.

The common pricing of products throughout the EU in the single currency will be even more important than the savings in transactions costs. Businesses will save the 'menu costs' of a different set of prices for each market, and will be able for the first time to install price and product strategies for the whole of the EU. The single currency will be a better unit of account, as well as a cheaper means of payment, because it will for the first time be possible to make direct price comparisons of similar products being sold in different countries.

Price differentials will not disappear, any more than they have done within national boundaries where the same currency is used. Retailers will compete with each other by cutting prices. Large price differences for the same product in the same kind of outlet and on the same sales conditions will be competed away. It is hard to quantify this effect. It will be enhanced if the refusal by many manufacturers to supply foreign customers through 'parallel imports' bypassing the distribution trade is outlawed, and if consumers are legally protected against malpractice across borders as they are at home.

The motor industry would be more affected than most by the single currency. Before the 1992 ERM crisis the prices of many goods were higher in countries such as Italy and Spain, because they had higher inflation, but exchange rates fixed to the D-mark.[16] Subsequent devaluations reversed the position. The EU Commission has set guide-lines of 12 to 18 per cent for the maximum price variation of the same model of car across the EU, yet in May 1993 a Ford Fiesta cost 30 per cent more in Germany than in Italy (UK prices were somewhere in between). The manufacturers quite fairly blame exchange rate move-ments for the price differentials. Ford of Europe has said that it is 'an almost impossible task' to harmonize new car prices 'in a market which, itself, is neither stable nor harmonized'. Ford said it was 'not rea-sonable to expect manufacturers to make instant price changes, possibly as great as 30 per cent, purely because of exchange rate movements'.[17] The maximum difference had widened to 55 per cent by 1995, be-tween Austria at the top of the range and Italy at the bottom.[18]

Big exchange rate changes, by widening price differentials, invite the maintenance of barriers to trade, such as parallel import bans. German consumers can hardly be blamed for seeking out parallel imports from Italy, nor can the manufacturers be blamed for trying to limit them. This example goes to the heart of the 'one market, one money' argu-ment. Competition in one currency across borders would bring down the average price of cars, and consumers would get real increases in the value of their pay packets. The single currency is essential to the nar-rowing of differentials.

'One market, one money' is both the title of the European Commis-sion's book on the single currency and a proposition which still arouses controversy five years after the publication of the book. There are cus-toms unions and free trade areas which exist without a single currency, such as the North American Free Trade Agreement (NAFTA). But it is doubtful whether they can be called single markets as long as ex-change rates and other non-tariff regulatory barriers make it more dif-ficult and expensive to sell in one part of the area than in another. The member states of the EU are much smaller than those of NAFTA. The absurdity of trying to run a single market in Europe without a single currency is becoming increasingly apparent to businesses, if not to politicians.

It is illogical to support the single market and yet to oppose the single currency. It is more logical to advocate withdrawal from the single market, however misguided such a course would be, and then to jettison the single currency as redundant. The advantages of the single market and the single currency interact, so that their combined benefits are greater than the mere sum of each in isolation. The single market has reduced transactions costs by cutting down customs delays, but separate exchange rates continue to make exports more costly than home sales. The single currency will slash transactions costs by eliminating exchange rates, but customs delays will continue to make exports dearer if the single market is not completed or goes into reverse. Only the combination of no customs delays and no exchange rate barriers will put exports on a par with domestic goods.

COMPETITIVE DEVALUATION

Large exchange rate changes of the kind that have recently been seen are denounced by countries with high exchange rates as 'competitive devaluations' by the others. Not only do such changes distort the single market by unpredictable shifts of advantage between countries unrelated to fundamentals, but they carry the danger that the high exchange rate countries will refuse to dismantle the remaining non-tariff barriers to trade – such as manufacturers' bans on parallel imports – or even take action to protect their markets against what they see as unfair competition.

M. Philippe Maystadt, Finance Minister of Belgium, made the threat explicit in a widely quoted speech in May 1995: 'If it were impossible to establish proper and stable relationships and the currency union was threatened by countries which wanted to have all the advantages of the single market without accepting the disciplines of the single currency, then the use of a safeguard clause could not be ruled out.'[19] M. Maystadt's original French text said that 'to protect the single market against destructive monetary tensions' member countries seriously affected might have to use the protective measures allowed for in articles 109 and 115 of the Rome Treaty, covering balance of payments difficulties and commercial policy.

It is thus quite clear that the single market could be disrupted if the absence of a single currency leads to exchange rate misalignments big enough to distort trade flows. Few would give systems such as the ERM, which are intermediate between floating and a single currency, much chance of avoiding such misalignments except in the short run. The single market needs a single currency not just to push it forwards, but to stop it sliding backwards.

Table 5 shows that the evidence is ambiguous for the period following the major devaluations since the ERM crisis of September 1992. We have taken trade with the rest of the EU as a percentage of GDP as the appropriate figure on which to focus. Increases in exports of devaluing countries in national currency give an exaggerated picture. The bottom lines of the table are the balance of trade with the EU, taking exports and imports together. France maintained a balance of trade surplus with the EU of 0.2–0.4 per cent of GDP, in spite of the *franc fort* policy of keeping the franc almost up with the D-mark. Germany actually increased her balance of trade surplus with the EU from 0.4 to 1.3 per cent of GDP, in spite of the complaints from German industry about the adverse effects of the strong D-mark. In both cases, the slowdown in growth in 1993 helped the balance of trade.

Italy and Spain, the main countries in the dock on competitive devaluation charges, both improved their balance of trade with the EU by 1.5 per cent of GDP, after devaluations of 33 and 25 per cent against the D-mark. In Italy's case, there was a swing from a deficit of 0.6 per cent of GDP to a surplus of 0.9 per cent of GDP, larger than Germany's. In Spain's case, the deficit with the rest of the EU was cut from 2.6 per cent to 1.1 per cent of GDP. The UK, with a devaluation of 21 per cent against the D-mark, was able only to cut its EU trade deficit from 0.9 to 0.6 per cent of GDP (about £4 billion). The main beneficiary has been Italy; once it left the ERM, the devaluation of the lira was greater than that required to correct the previous overvaluation. Spain has done no better than correct what was an excessive deficit by moving to a reasonably competitive exchange rate. By keeping Spain in the ERM, the EU has been able to control the devaluation of the peseta.

The European Council meeting at Cannes in June 1995 asked the European Commission for a report on the effect of currency fluctuations on the internal market, which was published at the end of October 1995.[20] The Commission concluded that the effect had been a slowdown in economic growth in the EU of 0.25–0.5 per cent in 1995, because of the uncertainty caused among businessmen. (This is the converse of the argument that the single currency, by ending currency fluctuations, will increase economic growth, see above.) The effect had been more on exporters' profit margins than on trade balances. It had

been particularly pronounced in the car, clothing, shipbuilding and textile industries, and in frontier regions.

The Commission findings for intra-EU export volume growth in
1992–4 are consistent with our own. French exports fell by 2.5 per cent
a year, and German by 6.3 per cent. British exports rose by 3.6 per cent
a year, Italian by 2.2 per cent, Spanish by 8.7 per cent. Structural and
cyclical factors, as well as exchange rate changes, played a part.

The Commission concluded that the exchange rate uncertainty
might lead to a misallocation of resources and create difficulties in
terms of the location of production activities, thus curbing investment
and slowing growth. Inflation and interest rates were rising in the de-
preciating currency countries, notably Italy. However, new measures
designed to correct the effects of the currency fluctuations might ag-
gravate the problems:

re-fragmentation of the single market, curbs on trade, and a further slowdown
in growth at the expense of employment ... The introduction of anti-
competitive practices in the form of limits on parallel imports or state aid linked
to exchange-rate movements would clearly contravene Community rules on
competition. Such measures risk setting off a process of re-fragmentation of the
internal market, a reduction in intra-Community trade and a slackening of
growth in Europe.

The Commission argued that the causes not the symptoms should
be tackled, and called for greater convergence, leading to the single
currency.

LOWER INTEREST RATES

The single currency can be expected to lower interest rates throughout its area. This is an even bigger potential benefit than the transactions cost savings. It will lower interest rates in countries other than
Germany, because they will no longer need to raise them above
German levels in order to stop their currencies falling against the D-
mark. Separate exchange rates have required a risk premium against
the D-mark, particularly for countries in the ERM. The risk premium
compensates D-mark investors for any fall in the value of investments
in other currencies due to a drop in their exchange rates against the

D-mark. The size of the risk premium is debatable, but it rises in a disruptive manner at times of exchange rate crisis.

Even German interest rates may be lower than before, because the Maastricht Treaty rules on keeping budget deficits down will mean that interest rates do not need to be so high in order to finance excessive government spending and keep inflation down. German interest rates were exceptionally high in the wake of unification in the early 1990s, because Germany did not have to cut her budget deficit at the time and put interest rates up without taking other countries' needs into account.

Real long-term interest rates averaged 4.5 per cent in six major countries in 1980–94, see Table 6, compared with 2.9 per cent in the 1960s and 0.8 per cent in the 1970s. This is attributed by Group of Ten and IMF studies to the rise in government debt and deficits.[21] According to classical economic theory, a shortage of supply of savings relative to investment demand pushes interest rates up and reduces investment. It is governments which are mainly responsible for reducing the supply of savings by letting their spending rise faster than tax revenue, and increasing both annual deficits and the outstanding stock of debt. In a world of free-flowing capital, no one government can buck the trend by saving more, although some governments can become 'free riders' by running bigger deficits. The general level of real long-term interest rates is set in a global capital market, after allowing for differences in inflation and exchange rate risk.

This analysis is a powerful additional justification for the Maastricht fiscal criteria designed to limit EMU governments' deficits and reduce their debt, and for a degree of fiscal policy coordination in an area where national policy can have only a limited effect. The justification extends to fiscal policy coordination between the EU and the US and Japan, both major participants in the world government debt market. For detailed analysis of the Maastricht fiscal criteria, see chapter 6.

Unless EMU can reduce real long-term interest rates down to the 1960s level of 3 per cent, the economic growth objective will not be achieved. High nominal rates also need to be reduced, see chapter 4 on the effect of interest rate inflation on borrowers. (The low real interest rates of the 1970s did not help economic growth, because they were due to abnormally high inflation, which nominal interest rates barely kept up with.) If the interest rate consistently exceeds the rate of national income growth (whether in real or nominal terms), the economy is saddled with a permanent interest burden which diverts resources from more productive outlets, see page 120.

Full EMU and the single currency should provide a complete contrast to the ERM. According to Christopher Taylor, the former Chief European Adviser of the Bank of England, 'the direct effect could be equivalent to a reduction in average real interest rates of 1–1.5 per cent for the EU as a whole'.[22] To err on the side of caution, this would mean a cut from 4 per cent to 3 per cent. The evidence of the Group of Ten study is that a one percentage point change in the debt–GDP ratio for OECD countries moves the global long-term interest rate by 0.25 per cent. The debt–GDP ratio for the EU countries could be reduced from 75 per cent at present to 65 per cent, close to the 60 per cent Maastricht guideline. This could reduce global and thus European long-term interest rates by 1 per cent, given that the EU has nearly 40 per cent of total OECD GDP. The reduction could be greater if the US and Japan maintain the fall in their real interest rates to about 2.5 per cent which took place in 1995.

The ERM years may have helped to reduce inflation in member countries, but the achievement was at the cost of keeping interest rates high. German real long-term interest rates were as high as American in 1980–94, see Table 6, and in both cases over 2 per cent more than the real rate of economic growth. France paid the penalty, with an average risk premium of 0.6 per cent against Germany. Both Italy and the UK had slightly lower real rates than Germany, but any advantage was offset by higher nominal rates, which impose a different kind of burden. Dividend yields in equity markets also showed that risk premiums of 1–2 per cent were needed in the case of France and the UK to attract investment to the shares of companies in countries with currencies weaker than the D-mark.

THE SINGLE BANKING MARKET

The European Single Market in financial services will also bring down interest rates by promoting greater cross-border competition between banks on lending rates. The single currency is even more necessary to the single market in financial services than to that in goods. It is intuitively obvious that the existence of separate currencies must divide the market in money even more than those in other goods and services.

Financial and business services are the UK's largest industry, accounting for a quarter of the national income. They had faster than average growth during the 1980s because of financial deregulation, but that has now run its course. If the UK is to continue exploiting its comparative advantage in this field, it must enter the single European market in a full-blooded way that has up to now not been possible. The obstacles consist partly of regulations in other countries which are gradually being dismantled, and partly of the multiplicity of national currencies and payment systems. In this chapter we look at the domestic banking industry within the single market; we survey the international prospects for the City of London in chapter 8.

Cross-border differences in interest rates for similar kinds of loan are due much more to divergent expectations about exchange rates than they are to variations in banks' pricing strategies. The single market in wholesale financial services predates the 1986 Single European Act and still uses the dollar as its main currency. The single market in retail banking and insurance has not developed as expected, in spite of the completion of free capital movements in 1990. Differences of regulation, tax and culture have been more difficult to bridge than was anticipated. The single market in retail financial services was not open for business on 1 January 1993 as planned, and has not made much progress since then.[23] Above all, borrowers and depositors are understandably averse to taking exchange rate risks. The single currency will for the first time make it possible to compare the price of money across frontiers in the same currency in terms of interest rates.

The more efficient banks are likely to profit at the expense of their sleepier rivals. To quote Professor John Kay of the London Business School, it will be a case of 'more competition, more consolidation'.[24] The banks that win the competition will not necessarily be the existing market leaders. The shake-up in banking will be good news for borrowers. Small firms and personal mortgage and consumer borrowers will do particularly well, because they will have an alternative to the domestic banking/building society networks. Both the general level of interest rates and the spread above it, reflecting the riskiness of the type of loan, should come down.

British mortgage borrowers could expect, for example, to pay a spread of only 1 per cent over a money market rate of 4.5 per cent, making 5.5 per cent, and to be able to fix the rate indefinitely. At the time of writing, variable mortgage rates are 7 per cent, 1 percentage point above money market rates of 6 per cent. The mortgage market suffers from both uncertainty of borrowers about their incomes and unpredictability of mortgage rates. The single currency might cushion the effects of the withdrawal of mortgage tax relief and float the British housing market out of the negative equity trap.

The UK's variable mortgage rates, and their tendency to rise in times of crisis, are sometimes given as a reason for not joining the single currency, on the grounds that monetary tightening by the European Central Bank would have a severer effect than in other countries, where more mortgages are on fixed rates.[25] The move to fixed mortgage rates in the UK has not refuted this argument because most fixed rates are for a limited period and apply only to new loan contracts. Fixed rates became popular when they fell below variable rates, and borrowers decided that variable rates were more likely to rise than fixed. Their popularity peaked in the second quarter of 1994, when 65 per cent of all new first mortgages were granted at fixed rates, but this fell rapidly to 28 per cent in the first quarter of 1995, as fixed rates rose. In mid-1994, no more than 21 per cent of all mortgages outstanding by value were at fixed rates. This could fall as new fixed rate mortgages tail off, and existing short-term contracts switch to variable rates.

The move to a single currency will change the position radically. As nominal and real rates fall, fixed rates could become low and stable compared with short-term variable rates. The UK could fairly rapidly switch to a continental – or indeed American – pattern of fixed-rate housing finance, reducing the uncertainty for owner-occupiers trying to cope with variable incomes as well as variable interest payments. Fixed-rate loans account for about nine-tenths of French and two-thirds of German mortgages; only in other high-inflation countries such as Italy and Spain does the proportion of variable rate mortgages approach that in the UK.[26] What this means for monetary policy in EMU is discussed in chapter 4.

A cut in household interest rates will bring down the cost of living. The traditional way of measuring the Retail Price Index (RPI) in Britain includes mortgage interest. The single currency should therefore reduce it, and thus help to get inflation down. Depositors will not necessarily lose to the extent that borrowers gain. The banks' spreads between lending and depositing rates will be squeezed by competition, just as their spread between buying and selling rates for European currencies will be eliminated by the single currency. Lower mortgage rates will stimulate consumer spending, and bring back the 'feel-good' factor which was absent from the 1992–5 recovery partly because of the morose condition of the housing market.

The deep-rooted nature of Britain's inflationary psychology was shown by the general reaction to the news in December 1995 that mortgage rates had fallen to 7.5 per cent. This is still about 4.5 per cent in real terms, and far higher than it should be, or could be if the UK joined the single currency. Hamish McCrae made the point:

If anyone, five years ago, had said that home loan rates would be back to the level of the 1960s, they would have been greeted with a mixture of disbelief and jubilation . . . Our interest rates, far from being low, are actually quite high. A mortgage rate of 7.5 per cent may sound wonderful compared with the double-digit rates of yesteryear. But it is a killer if house prices in 25 years are going to be no higher in money terms than they are today.[27]

See page 147 on the transition from sterling to Euro mortgages.

We assume that there would be major interest savings to personal and corporate borrowers, with lending rates coming down by 2 per cent – 1 per cent off the real rate and 1 per cent off the inflation rate. Because there would be an increase in the efficiency of the financial system due to greater competition and lower risk provisions in the more stable economic environment, deposit rates might come down by only 1 per cent, leading to a 1 per cent squeeze on the margins of banks, building societies, and other financial firms. The result would be a total saving of about £11 billion in borrowing costs, offset by a total reduction of £4 billion in deposit income – a net saving of £7 billion or 1 per cent of GDP, £5 billion to households and £2 billion to companies. This is logged in UK statistics as a transfer payment, but is better seen as a reduction in costs, and thus an increase in value added, or GDP. Financial institutions might lose 25 per cent, or £1.75 billion of the £7 billion, from their profits. Some would increase their profits, and others would disappear or be taken over, as competition led to consolidation.

Our view is confirmed by Dr Hilmar Kopper, Chairman of Deutsche Bank. He said that monetary union would trigger a wave of cross-border banking mergers. It would force European banks to compete more efficiently on an international scale. 'Only the big boys will survive in the global banking markets,' he said.[28] The expected shake-up in banking was described by the foreign exchange dealers' association: 'A single currency, by eliminating foreign exchange risk and converging interest rates . . . will result in a greater willingness on the part of customers to look outside national borders for financial services. Banks will attempt to defend their domestic markets while at the same time expanding outside their borders.'[29]

INVESTMENT AND GROWTH

The other main effect of a cut in interest rates and share yields will be to stimulate business investment on capital expenditure. Investment projects will become economic which were not so when they had to earn higher returns to repay expensive borrowed money, compensate for exchange rate uncertainty, and hand out high dividends to shareholders. The rate of interest is also the discount rate used to measure the present value of future earnings. A 12.5 per cent cut in the nominal interest rate from 8 to 7 per cent raises the present value of a future earnings stream by 14 per cent, and makes it that much more likely that it will go ahead. The fall in inflation that may be expected over and above the cut in real interest rates will also make investment more attractive by reducing the financing burden in the early years of the project, see page 64.

If nominal interest rates fall by one percentage point from 8 per cent, and real interest rates fall by the same amount, capital spending by British industry, which has been running at about 10 per cent of GDP, could go up by 10 per cent to 11 per cent of GDP, and the output of the economy might rise by 5 per cent over a period of, say 10 years, a cumulative £42 billion (see Table 24). This would add 0.5 per cent to the UK's long-term growth rate of 2.5 per cent.[30] In November 1995 the UK Treasury raised its estimate of the trend rate of growth from 2.25 to 2.5 per cent a year, because of supply-side reforms.[31] The interest rate effects of the single currency could raise this another 0.5 per cent to 3 per cent.

A permanent increase of even 0.25 per cent in the UK growth rate, from 2.5 to 2.75 per cent, would be of immense value. Our estimate of the net present value of such a rise in the growth rate is that it is worth about seven years of current GDP, or £5,000 billion.[32] Such an increase would be 'endogenous', to use Mr Gordon Brown's terminology, if it could be brought about by increasing capital investment and enhancing labour skills. An 'exogenous' increase in the growth rate of the same kind could also occur if, for example, there was a stimulus to the 'animal spirits' in the economy due to optimism about the effects of the single currency.

Part of the 0.25 per cent increase in the trend rate of economic growth already claimed by the Treasury is due to the single market and the increase in efficiency from cross-border competition. This will be hard to disentangle from the stimulus to growth to be expected from the single currency and lower interest rates. In the case of the single market, the rise in the productivity of capital gives a once-for-all rise in investment. In the case of the single currency, the fall in the rate of interest will leave productivity unaffected, but raise investment by making capital cheaper. Some of the single market effect may already have occurred by anticipation in the boom of the late 1980s. The remaining effects may depend on the single currency now coming to the rescue of the single market project.

Even if the rise in the stock of business capital due to lower interest rates comes to an end after ten years, and the rise in the growth rate does not last, there will be a permanent rise in the *level* of national output and living standards. In the case of the UK, for capital spending by business to increase by 1 per cent of national income (£7 billion), something else has to fall: personal consumption, government expenditure, or net exports (exports have to fall, or imports have to rise). Since GDP itself will be rising by an extra 0.5 per cent a year, it will take only two years for the additional investment to be paid for by the extra growth of output. After that, other sectors of the economy begin to benefit, as well as the capital goods industries. Personal consumption need not suffer if the budget deficit can be reduced, or the balance of payments goes into deficit for a time to finance imports of capital equipment.

An additional attraction of the single currency is that balance of payments deficits become easier to finance. They ultimately become as easy to finance as balance of payments deficits between regions of one country. British banks transfer surplus deposits from rich widows in

Bournemouth as loans to creditworthy manufacturers in Birmingham, without any trace in the statistics.

Lord Lawson recalls shocking the Germans by saying at the IMF meeting in Berlin in 1988, 'I chose as my heretical theme the thesis that the balance of payments on current account did not have the central importance as an indicator of success or failure that popular comment supposed.'[33] Unfortunately, in a world of separate national currencies, an excess of such flows can disrupt exchange rates and interest rates, and governments cannot then sit on the fence. The single currency would remove the exchange rate risk from such flows within the EU, and interest rates would not need to rise in deficit areas unless their borrowers became less creditworthy than others.

The lifting of the balance of payments constraint which has bedevilled British economic policy since the war would be a major advantage to the UK if the country joined the single currency. It would be the end of sterling crises, and rises in bank rate which can defend the pound only by attacking the real economy. Deficits on current account would be offset by surpluses on capital account, as foreign investors found the UK an attractive base for operations in the EMU. The trend could be reversed, as British companies invested more on the Continent, with a surplus on current account offset by a deficit on capital account.

Table 7 shows that business investment levels in France, Italy and the UK have fallen well below those in Japan, the US and Germany. Although the UK had an investment boom in the late 1980s, it could not be sustained because inflation, the balance of payments deficit, and then interest rates all rose. The UK recovery of the mid-1990s did not produce the forecast surge in business investment, because interest rates were raised at an early stage in the cycle to forestall the danger of inflation. The single currency should lower interest rates, and stimulate investment in the non-German countries towards German levels, with corresponding benefits to economic growth and living standards.

It is possible that the single currency will bring about a permanent increase in the rate of economic growth as well as an extended medium-term once-for-all increase. The way in which this could happen depends on the so-called 'new economics', which maintains that returns to investment increase with its amount, rather than diminishing or remaining constant.[34]

It cannot be shown that the single currency will in itself create more jobs, but the interest rate, investment and growth effects should do so. It would be counter-productive to follow the Governor of the Bank of England in arguing that unemployment will make EMU more difficult to achieve, when the single currency itself will have a major effect in reducing the general level of unemployment, even if it redistributes work between industries and regions.[35]

Unemployment rates differ widely across the countries of the EU for reasons of economic and social structure and statistical convention. The countries with the highest unemployment rates – France, Ireland and Spain – are those keenest on the single currency. Germany and the UK, with relatively low unemployment rates, are the least keen. If countries themselves regard high unemployment as a reason for joining EMU rather than staying out of it, others should not seek to prevent them. As long as the existing convergence criteria in the Maastricht Treaty are met, there is no need to add unemployment to them – as the Governor of the Bank of England conceded.

FOREIGN INVESTMENT AND EXCHANGE RATES

The UK is one of the leading countries to have made successful foreign investments around the world, and one of the most popular destinations for foreign investment from other countries. Such investments consist of direct investment by businesses in foreign subsidiaries, portfolio investment by pension and insurance funds in foreign shares, and loans by banks. The UK has a surplus of foreign investments abroad over and above foreigners' investments in Britain, and the income from the former is usually about £3–4 billion more than the outflow from the latter.

Exchange rates are an important barrier to foreign investment. If a British business invests in a high exchange rate country such as Germany, the returns will be good in terms of pounds sterling, but the D-mark cost of making the investment will also be high. If it invests in a low exchange rate country, the assets may be cheap, but their value, and that of the earnings from them, will fall as the exchange rate falls. So companies generally require higher returns on foreign direct investment in order to cover the foreign exchange risk.

Companies' ability to deal with exchange rate changes is limited by the fact that foreign exchange derivatives – forwards, futures and options – normally run for periods of months rather than years. A long-term investment in selling or production facilities in another European market will therefore produce uncertain returns in terms of domestic currency. A higher yield or a quicker pay-off will be needed to compensate for the uncertainty, so investments that would have been attractive at home will not be made abroad.

Accumulated direct investment abroad by British companies is 38 per cent as much as the value of their capital equipment in Britain. The UK's direct investment abroad is about $250 billion, or 15 per cent of the OECD total. This is nearly half the US share, about the same as the Japanese share, and nearly double the share of France or Germany. This helps to make the UK the third biggest earner of foreign investment income in the world after the US and Japan, and the fourth biggest earner of all kinds of 'invisible' income after France if services exports such as tourism are included.

The UK is the second most popular destination in the OECD for incoming foreign direct investment, with $200 billion or 17 per cent of the total accumulation – about half that in the US, nearly double France's 9 per cent share, and over three times Germany's 5 per cent share. Much of the recent inflow into the UK has been from multinationals seeking a base from which to export to the whole of the single market, and choosing the UK because of its relatively low labour costs and internationally minded business ethos. If the UK does not join the single currency, fears that it might lose some of the advantages of the single market could lead some multinationals to relocate or set up new operations in the heartland of the single currency rather than in the UK. Continental companies now investing in the UK as a centre from which to supply the whole single market would also think twice.

Not all potential investors think in this way; a minority would take their chances on the less regulated and more competitive environment of the UK. But the UK's freedom to devalue is a double-edged weapon for foreign investors; while making it easier to export from the UK to the continent of Europe, it reduces the asset value of their stake.

It is well known that the UK gets over half her merchandise export revenue from the other EU countries, but for all kinds of foreign income this falls to only 44 per cent, see Table 8. Only 36 per cent of

UK foreign investment income comes from the EU, and only 30 per cent of income from exports of services such as finance, and tourism. British direct investment in the EU has risen rapidly in the last decade, by 12 per cent a year in cash terms, compared with 7.5 per cent for all direct investment abroad, and 6 per cent for domestic investment. It has risen from 27 to 38 per cent of all UK outflows of direct investment. In terms of total value, UK direct investment was at end-1992 42 per cent in North America, 27 per cent in the EU, and 31 per cent in the rest of the world, mainly developing countries.

In spite of the UK's high past accumulation of foreign direct investment, there has been a notable decline in foreign direct investment in the UK by both the EU countries and the rest of the world since 1989, see Figure 2. The recession of the early 1990s affected foreign direct investment both out of and into the UK. From 1992, UK outward investment picked up but inward investment continued to decline. By 1994, EU direct investment in the UK had fallen to a fifth of its 1990 peak, and world investment to two-fifths of its 1989 peak. Some of the fall can be accounted for by the change from boom to recession, but some may well be due to uncertainty about the UK's future role in Europe. In 1995, there was a sharp recovery in foreign direct investment in the UK, to the 1989 peak level, but it remains to be seen whether it will be maintained.

In spite of ministerial boasts that the UK is an attractive destination for foreign investment because it has not signed the Social Chapter of the Maastricht Treaty, the British Government's lukewarm attitude to the single currency and to the EU generally appears to have had a far bigger negative effect. If the UK does not join the single currency, British and other foreign companies are likely to increase their direct investment on the Continent. Continental and other foreign companies are unlikely to reverse the decline in their direct investment in the UK. Growth and employment in the UK will suffer.

4
The Virtues of Stable Prices

INFLATION AND ECONOMIC GROWTH

One of the three main functions of money is as a store of value. If the single currency is to fulfil this function better than the existing European currencies, it will have to bring about stable prices. This means that the annual rate of price inflation will have to be between 0 and 2 per cent. The attractions of price stability are not quite as obvious as those of economic growth. Zero or very low inflation is a policy objective of most industrial country governments, but sometimes it can be achieved only at a high cost in lost output and higher unemployment. Governments need to remember why they are pursuing it, if they are not to jettison it for electoral reasons when the going gets rough.

The link between inflation and economic growth has been examined at some length by economists.[1] In the first quarter of a century after the Second World War, higher growth was often associated with higher inflation, for example in Japan. It is still the case for rapidly developing countries such as China. If economic growth runs ahead of capacity, the laws of supply and demand push up prices for a time, and the inflation rate has to be lowered by a temporary tightening of policy. Lower inflation then goes with a slowdown in growth rather than stimulating growth.

Lower inflation helps to raise the growth rate if it can be sustained for long periods. A typical estimate is that 10 per cent on the inflation rate reduces economic growth by around 0.25 per cent and vice versa.[2] Thus if the UK could reduce its current 3.5 per cent inflation rate to zero, or if it had had Germany's 2.9 per cent inflation instead of its own 6.4 per cent since 1979 (see Table 9), then the growth rate might have been nearly 0.1 per cent higher. This is only £700 million in one year, but it would accumulate to over £40 billion a year after thirty years.

The link between inflation and economic growth is weak, but there is more of a link with national income per head. The most advanced economies are those which have achieved the lowest inflation rates.[3] Switzerland is a good example, because it has low inflation, low economic growth, but high national income per head. Countries with high living standards and substantial personal savings have an even greater interest than others in preserving them by preventing the fall in the value of money which inflation causes.

The higher the inflation rate, the more variable it is. This makes it particularly hard to predict or provide against future inflation on the basis of past and present inflation. It is no coincidence that the rate of economic growth is also more variable as inflation rises. If governments cannot forecast inflation correctly, they are likely to make their policies either too tight or too loose, causing unwanted recessions and unsustainable booms. Low or zero inflation makes it possible to stabilize the management of the whole economy, like that of each business and household in it. British inflation since 1979 has been more unstable as well as higher than that in other major countries, see Figure 3.[4]

SAVERS GAIN FROM LOWER INFLATION

The advantage to savers of lower inflation is obvious. Their money keeps its purchasing power for longer. It was Keynes who wrote:

If we are to continue to draw the voluntary savings of the community into 'investments', we must make it a prime object of State policy that the standard of value, in terms of which they are expressed, should be kept stable.[5]

If prices rise, they are seldom adequately compensated for by higher interest rates. Even if interest rates are high in real terms over and above the inflation rate, the UK and most other countries tax the inflation part as well as the real part of the interest.

Say the interest on a £10,000 deposit is 8 per cent, or £800 a year, and inflation is 5 per cent, so that the real rate of interest is 3 per cent. A 20 per cent taxpayer pays £160 tax on the interest, leaving £640 net of tax. She needs 5 per cent, or £500, to maintain the purchasing power of the deposit. So she is left with £140, a 1.4 per cent real after-tax return. Protection against inflation would require a tax-free inflation allowance of £500. The 20 per cent tax on the remaining £300 would be £60, leaving a real after-tax return of £240, or 2.4 per cent. The loss due to inflation is £100, or 1 per cent.

This example refutes the point sometimes made, that inflation can be made harmless by indexation, so that all values are raised each year by the inflation percentage. Indexation loads the economy with huge accounting costs, can never cover every transaction, and perpetuates inflation instead of abolishing it. In economies with single-figure inflation, there is not such an incentive to index as there has been in some Latin American countries, and the damage due to inflation is unchecked. Some gilt-edged government bonds are indexed in the UK, but few other kinds of saving enjoy this benefit. Some tax allowances are indexed, but others are not.

As more people become self-employed, the proportion of the population able to beat inflation goes down. Many self-employed people work at fixed rates, which cannot be increased annually as full-time pay awards can. There is a fixed money income component in many pension incomes, for example many annuity incomes bought with personal pension plans, which makes them vulnerable to inflation. It is difficult to plan decades ahead for retirement if you do not know whether prices will remain stable, double, or treble over your working life. Price stability would mean that pension funds would need fewer assets to meet their unknown future pension liabilities, and that individuals would be encouraged to save more themselves because of the reduction of inflation risk. According to a Goldman Sachs estimate:

A drop of 1 per cent per annum in the measured rate of retail price inflation, with everything else staying the same, would mean that a typical pension fund could be 10 per cent smaller and still achieve solvency. If wages were to rise less rapidly in response to the decline in measured price inflation, the average pension fund could decline by 20 per cent.[6]

Inflation redistributes income haphazardly and unfairly, makes it harder to draw up long-term business or personal plans, and undermines the moral foundation of contracts. It adds to short-term transactions costs rather as fluctuating exchange rates do. Cash and current account deposits paying no interest are eroded by inflation, so the utility of this most basic kind of money is reduced. People spend time and effort switching their holdings around so as to minimize the amount of wasting cash in their possession. They put money into savings accounts simply in order to earn enough interest to offset the losses due to inflation, and may be led to overcompensate, and thus keep money idle that they could be using to good purpose.

The kind of saving generated by inflation is as much a case of money illusion as are inflationary pay awards. Far from switching from money into goods to beat inflation, people often react by spending less. According to an OECD study: 'The majority of evidence appears to support the hypothesis that the relation between the rate of inflation and the rate of saving is positive.'[7]

THE COSTS OF INFLATION TO BUSINESS

If savers benefit from zero inflation, do borrowers suffer? In one sense they do, because the principal of their loan is not devalued by inflation, and it is therefore a bigger financial burden when it has to be repaid. Yet they are also better off, because they have to repay less interest in real terms in the early years.

This is shown in Table 10. We compare the discounted servicing profile on a loan of £10,000, first for a 10 per cent nominal rate of interest and 5 per cent inflation, then for a 5 per cent nominal rate of interest and zero inflation. Although the real inflation-adjusted rate of interest is 5 per cent in both cases, the real servicing burden is more up-front with 5 per cent inflation. Under 5 per cent inflation, 9.1 per cent of the total payments fall in year 1, compared with 4.8 per cent under zero inflation; the extra 4.3 per cent is the burden imposed by inflation. To look at it another way, inflation adds 90 per cent to the first-year interest, rather than the 5 per cent inflation rate. It is not much consolation that at the end of ten years 5 per cent inflation reduces the discounted principal to 39 per cent of its original value, compared with 61 per cent under zero inflation. The Bank of England pointed out in a recent analysis that matters become even worse if there is a sudden jump in inflation and nominal interest rates where loans are at variable rates of interest.[8]

The effect on British business borrowers has been to encourage them to look for high real returns and short payback periods from investment projects, and to discourage ventures with lower rates of return and longer paybacks. Financial obligations are distorted by being loaded into the early years, long-run investment in major industries and infrastructure is reduced, and resources are misallocated. According to the Bank of England, the recent fall in inflation has not reversed this attitude:

Many companies remained to be convinced that inflation and interest rates would remain low and stable over the long term. Many firms continued to seek rates of return which partly reflected past higher and more variable inflation and interest rates . . . If excessively high target rates of return continue to be used as the recovery progresses and as the financial constraints on investment are further relaxed, there is a risk that they will limit the level and type of investment undertaken by UK firms.[9]

Low inflation should therefore increase the extra investment already expected because of lower interest rates due to the single currency, see page 55. British industry may not, however, be convinced that low inflation is permanent unless and until the UK joins the single currency. Real interest rates should fall if exchange rates are abolished, and nominal interest rates should fall by even more if inflation comes down. With a 2.5 per cent rate of inflation, a 6.5 per nominal and 4 per cent real interest rate could fall by 1 per cent in nominal and real terms to 5.5 per cent nominal and 3 per cent real, because of a lower exchange rate risk premium. It could fall another 1 per cent in nominal terms if inflation fell from 2.5 to 1.5 per cent, to 4.5 per cent nominal and still 3 per cent real, see Table 11.

Businesses incur 'menu costs' because of inflation. They have to decide afresh each year what each employee and manager should be paid even if there has been no material change. They have to assimilate a new set of prices for their inputs once a year or more, and publish a new price list for their outputs. Any substantial rate of inflation makes it harder to spot which items are changing in price relative to each other. In a zero inflation world, some prices stay the same, some go up, and some go down. The market system of free prices can perform with full efficiency only if it can be seen at a glance what is getting scarcer and what more plentiful, by looking directly at price changes, rather than having to strip out the general rate of inflation.

British employees have not suffered from inflation, as long as they have remained in work, because pay awards have more than made up for it, and employers have been able to recoup the cost from productivity rises, price increases, and devaluation of the pound. Employees suffer from 'money illusion', thinking that they have done well with an in-crease that looks big on paper, and makes modest real pay rises look even better in money terms.

The unholy alliance between the two sides of industry has to change if EMU is to benefit the economy. There is some evidence that em-ployees and their unions bargain for a 'risk premium' in pay awards to forestall the danger of inflation being higher than expected. When, as has been happening in the mid-1990s, inflation turns out lower than predicted, pay rises are higher than expected and the inflation predic-tion is eventually validated by employers having to put up prices to pay for the excessive pay rises.

ADVANTAGES OF INFLATION

Inflation is sometimes held to have advantages, especially if it is low and well controlled. It is claimed that real pay cuts, which may be justified by poor performance, are easier to carry out by leaving nominal pay unchanged, and letting inflation make the cut. An inflation rate of a few per cent may thus oil the wheels of business.

If employees are fooled by such tactics, then the signal that the real pay cut is supposed to give is blurred. If they are not fooled, then the exercise is pointless, since it would have been easier to make a pay cut in nominal terms which would also have been a real terms cut if inflation was zero. Similarly, the effect of real price cuts in shops is dimmed if they can announce only that they have held the price of their goods steady while everything else has gone up. Shoppers are more likely to respond to price cuts, and shops to make them, if the general level of prices is stable.

Governments benefit from the so-called 'inflation tax'. They can fi-nance their debt partly by issuing notes and coins on which no interest is paid. The higher the inflation rate, the greater the advantage of this seignorage from money issuing powers (see page 17). With inflation al-ready quite low, the inflation tax brings in only about 0.5 per cent of GDP in most EU countries; if tax revenue is one third of GDP, then it brings in 1.5 per cent of tax revenue.[10] In the higher inflation Mediter-ranean countries, the inflation tax has had a higher yield, ranging up to 3 per cent of GDP in Greece.

Governments benefit from inflation as borrowers because they can repay in devalued money. They also get the same disadvantage as private borrowers, that the interest they have to pay is higher in real terms in the early years of a loan because of inflation. Government bond rates also carry two kinds of risk premium. There is the domestic premium, with investors wanting an interest rate which may turn out to have a higher inflation component than the actual inflation rate, because their inflation expectations err on the side of pessimism. There is the international premium, which has to be paid in the global market for funds. Investors want compensation for a possible fall in the exchange rate of the issuing country compared with their own, which may again turn out to be too high because of pessimistic expectations.

Another supposed advantage of inflation is that in so far as it is unanticipated, it can give the real economy a boost, and reduce unemployment. Governments can get away with inflationary cuts in taxes or interest rates only for a short time. Then the new and higher rate of inflation will be anticipated, and the next boost will drive inflation even higher. Soon unemployment stops falling, while inflation goes on rising. The cost of getting inflation back down again by tightening policy is that much higher because the government has lost any credibility its inflation forecasts ever had. So in the long run, higher inflation countries have higher, not lower, unemployment.[11]

The UK has long suffered from relatively high inflation (see Table 9). In the years since the ERM was formed in 1979, the UK has had an average inflation rate of 6.4 per cent a year, and the value of the pound has sunk to 39p. Italy has had a worse record, France 0.7 per cent better, Germany 3.5 per cent better. The value of the pound has sunk to 2p since 1914.

Britain's poor performance can be measured in terms of the German D-mark (see Table 12). The pound's exchange rate fell by four-fifths in the thirty years 1965–95, from DM11.20 to DM2.31. The Italian lira fared worse, losing 86 per cent of its value. The French franc, in line with the US dollar, lost only two-thirds of its value, falling from 82 to 43 pfennig. The D-mark went down only against the yen, which rose from DM1.11 per 100 yen to DM1.75. In the first fifteen years of the ERM, the pound lost two-fifths of its value against the D-mark, compared with one-third for the French franc and nearly three-fifths for the lira.

In spite of the damage done by inflation to the economy, British

governments have persisted in the delusion that by retaining 'sovereignty' over monetary policy they can improve on their abysmal past
record. Inflation was unusually low in the mid-1990s. The Government
may or may not achieve its 2.5 per cent target, but there is no guarantee
inflation will remain low. As long as governments retain the power to
buy votes with inflationary budgets in the run-up to general elections,
Britain's inflation record will remain poor and patchy. We examine
how it might be improved by EMU, compared with the curious new
cat-and-dog ménage of the Treasury and the Bank of England introduced after departure from the ERM in 1992.

INFLATION UNDER EMU

The ERM helped its members to reduce their inflation rates, but at a
high cost in terms of interest rates and unemployment, see page 51. By
pegging their exchange rates to the D-mark, and limiting the size and
frequency of devaluations, other countries were able to use the system
as an anti-inflation discipline. They acquired an incentive to take measures that non-members such as the UK were able to take independently, with similar costs, but less permanent benefits. They also ended
up in most cases with overvalued exchange rates, which plunged the
ERM into crisis in 1992 and 1993.

Full EMU and the single currency offer a cheaper way than the
ERM of reducing inflation or keeping it down where it has already
fallen to a low level. Only the Netherlands, which did not devalue
against Germany after 1983, established full credibility for its anti-
inflation policy under the ERM, and even that took time. EMU will
have a European Central Bank (ECB) to run the single currency. This
should make low inflation credible, as the Bundesbank has done in
Germany, at a lower cost than the traditional policies of freeze and
squeeze which the ERM perpetuated under a different brand name.

Zero or low inflation is a good aim in its own right for any domestic
economic policy. It is also helpful to the establishment of a single currency, although the convergence of inflation rates is neither a necessary
nor a sufficient condition of the single currency. Countries with different inflation rates, such as the UK and Ireland, can form successful
monetary unions. For example, between 1962 and 1979, when Ireland
left the monetary union with the UK to join the ERM, consumer

price inflation averaged 8.8 per cent in the UK and 10 per cent in
Ireland, making the Irish price level nearly 20 per cent higher over
the period.[12]

Different regions of monetary unions such as the UK and the
USA have different inflation rates. Nor do similar inflation rates guarantee that countries can have the kind of exchange rate stability between them on which a monetary union might be founded. The
swings between the dollar and the yen are far greater than the inflation difference between the US and Japan could justify. Between 1979
and 1995, the inflation differential of 2.8 per cent a year would have
justified a 33 per cent fall of the dollar against the yen; in fact it fell by
60 per cent.

If inflation rates diverge too much for fundamental reasons, such as
widely different increases in unit labour costs in similar business sectors,
countries will be able to abandon exchange rates and form a monetary
union only at the risk of some becoming less able to compete with
others, and getting into unemployment and recession of a kind that
could undermine the union. The Maastricht Treaty therefore stipulates
that inflation rates should converge at the time when the decision to go
ahead into the final stage of EMU is taken:

A price performance that is sustainable and an average rate of inflation, ob-
served over a period of one year before the examination, that does not exceed
by more than 1.5 percentage points that of, at most, the three best performing
Member States in terms of price stability. Inflation shall be measured by means
of the consumer price index on a comparable basis, taking into account differences in national definitions.[13]

It is not clear whether this means 1.5 percentage points above the
average of the three best performers, or above the best performer. It
could make quite a difference if, say, the three best performers had rates
of 0, 2 and 3 per cent.

The inflation criterion is oddly drafted, because it sets only a relative
and not an absolute standard. It could be satisfied by convergence on
inflation rates averaging 5 per cent or more. The assumption was that
Germany and one or two other countries at least would be the low inflation benchmark; a hope that seemed to have been dashed when
German inflation approached 5 per cent as a result of the unification
boom in 1992, but revived when Germany reduced inflation close to

2 per cent in 1995. If 2 per cent is the standard, then 3.5 per cent becomes the limit.

Inflation convergence is the easiest of the criteria for EMU, partly because inflation has fallen worldwide under the twin impact of stronger international competition and weaker commodity prices. Even countries such as Britain, Italy and Spain, with traditionally high inflation rates, may be able to bring them close to or within the limit. Inflation convergence, unlike the convergence of budget deficits, does not have to continue once the single currency is set up, because it is assumed that the ECB will act to keep inflation down.

Some divergences in national inflation rates are bound to continue. Even if inflation is zero for the EU as a whole, relative prices will continue to change. Countries which happen to sell more goods and services whose relative price is rising will have higher inflation rates than those selling more goods and services whose relative price is falling.

The UK, with a relatively small manufacturing sector and a relatively large services sector, may have a permanently higher inflation rate than Germany, if the price of services, with a high pay component, continues to rise faster than the price of manufactured goods. This will not matter if the difference in national inflation rates is only a percentage point or two.

The EU Commission is devising a common standard to measure consumer prices throughout the area.[14] There are numerous differences among national statistical methods that have to be ironed out. The UK uses at least three consumer prices indexes, and many other ways of measuring inflation besides. There is the old Retail Prices Index (RPI) including mortgage interest; there is RPIX, excluding mortgage interest, the government's target; and there is RPIY, excluding changes in indirect taxes such as VAT.[15] The treatment of housing – consumption or investment? – and of sales taxes are among the most difficult points to agree.

The ECB will have to target a consumer price index covering the whole area of the single currency as the objective of its monetary policy, and allow for the fact that different countries have different rates of inflation because of the variety of their economic structures. Putting together national inflation figures can be only a stopgap, because they will not reveal how much of the differences are due to economic structure and how much to general inflationary pressures in a particular country.

One of the most elusive difficulties in measuring inflation is to allow for improvements in the quality of products over the years. If prices rise, this may be because the product is better, not because the same product is more expensive. It is also difficult to allow for new products, because by definition their price this year cannot be compared with their price last year, when they did not exist.[16] Computers and everything associated with them have both fallen in price and improved in quality, while accounting for an ever-larger share of spending.

On the other side of the ledger, some top-of-the-market branded goods have become more expensive because of the prestige of their name, with no perceptible improvement in quality.[17] This may not have much effect on consumer price indexes, because such goods are generally excluded from their terms of reference; the British RPI does not seek to measure the prices paid by the top 5 per cent of income earners. Some estimates suggest that many inflation increases in advanced countries should be reduced by a percentage point or two because of quality changes. So 2 per cent measured inflation could mean to all intents and purposes none at all.[18]

THE INDEPENDENT EUROPEAN CENTRAL BANK[19]

The Maastricht Treaty, following the Delors Report, sets up a European System of Central Banks (ESCB), incorporating the national central banks, such as the Bank of England, but controlled by the European Central Bank (ECB). The main aim of the ECB is price stability, which could in practice mean 0–2 per cent inflation, see above. Monetary policy will be taken out of the hands of national institutions and given to one central institution, with national central banks helping both to decide it and to carry it out. There will be a single European monetary policy, otherwise there could not be a European single currency. Its aim will be to control inflation, although national economic policies affecting taxation, expenditure and employment will continue to have important consequences for inflation.

The ECB is closely modelled on the German Bundesbank. The seat of its forerunner, the European Monetary Institute, was placed in Frankfurt when it was set up in January 1994. It must be assumed that the ECB will also be in Frankfurt. Its physical presence in Germany will help to give it some of the Bundesbank's credibility in financial markets and may reconcile hostile German public opinion to the loss of the D-mark as a tried and trusted currency.

The control of inflation by monetary methods was discredited in the UK under the name of 'monetarism'. Between 1976 and 1985, governments tried to control inflation by limiting the increase in the supply of money. The policy was based on too simple a theory, and carrying it out in practice was too complicated. At first sight it looks as if the ECB concept is a return to monetarist methods. The Bundesbank claims to control inflation by aiming at the intermediate target of money supply. In practice, German money supply targets are as often missed as hit,[20] and the Bundesbank is effectively using interest rates, not money supply, to control inflation. It is monetary, not monetarist policy.

The ECB, like the Bundesbank, is based on the assumption that central banks which are independent are more successful in controlling inflation than those that are not. The evidence is persuasive, but not conclusive.[21] If the central bank's objective is price stability, can it achieve this more effectively if it is independent of the government, or if it is closely integrated with the finance or economics ministry? An independent central bank is supposed to be less subject than its government to short-term political pressures, yet if it is independent and unelected, it may pursue unpopular policies but not be able to carry them through, particularly if the government is opposed.

Where price stability has been achieved, central bank independence, and monetary policy in general, have been only two of a number of contributory factors. The Bundesbank's success as an independent central bank in keeping inflation low has been helped in Germany by responsible trade union behaviour. Lack of central bank independence, however, did not prevent Japan from achieving even greater price stability than Germany after the 1970s.

The case against central bank independence is that the separation of key policies such as monetary and fiscal (tax and public expenditure) policy and their allocation to different and possibly conflicting agencies can lead to higher costs than otherwise in lowering inflation. Professor James Meade was a leading exponent of these doubts:

Close co-ordination between monetary and fiscal policies is greatly to be desired. We should attempt to bring them closer together rather than to separate them. It is not only useful to have two rather than one club to play a round of golf; it is also useful, indeed necessary, to know whether one is on the tee or in a bunker before one decides whether to make use of the driver or the niblick.[22]

For example, Germany may have had higher budget deficits, higher interest rates and lower economic growth in the aftermath of unification because the Federal Government's responsibility for fiscal policy was separated from the Bundesbank's responsibility for monetary policy. If the German Government had had to take the blame for high interest rates, it might have raised taxes sooner to reduce the Federal deficit quicker. We return to the links between monetary and fiscal policy in chapter 6.

This argument can be met by showing that where the government and the central bank agree on policy objectives, welfare losses can be reduced, because inflation expectations are lower than otherwise, and the unemployment cost of lowering actual inflation is therefore less.[23] In such a case it may not matter too much whether the central bank is independent of the finance ministry or subordinate to it, if the policy outcome is the same. Conversely, if the central bank and the finance ministry are at loggerheads, independence may not help the credibility of the central bank's inflation performance if the welfare sacrifice its policy demands goes beyond the bounds of what is acceptable to the population of a democracy.

One possible compromise, adopted in New Zealand, is for the government to subcontract monetary policy to the central bank, and make it responsible for achieving precise inflation objectives, albeit with some escape clauses. This has worked well in New Zealand, but it does not ensure long-term credibility, because the government can change the central bank's objectives from one period to the next. In the absence of a European Union federal government, this solution is not open to the EMU in any case. Nor has it been adopted in the UK, in spite of the recommendations of the Treasury Select Committee.[24]

FAILINGS OF UK ANTI-INFLATION POLICY

The UK has failed to control inflation adequately by means of monetary policy over the years. The Bank of England has never been independent since it was nationalized in 1946. It has advised on and carried out monetary policy but the Treasury has taken the decisions. The government has always been free to control interest rates to further its own political ends. Interest rates have tended to rise early in the life of a parliament and to be cut in the run-up to general elections. Democratic sovereignty over monetary policy has furthered the electoral ends of politicians, not the public interest in keeping inflation down.

The new policy regime installed after the UK's departure from the ERM in 1992 was an improvement, but it did not make the Bank of England independent, nor did it prevent the political manipulation of interest rates. The Chancellor of the Exchequer still decides interest rates, even if the Bank of England's advice is more influential because it publishes a quarterly inflation report and the minutes of meetings between Governor and Chancellor (with a six-week delay).

The new system had its first real test in the summer of 1995. The Governor of the Bank, Mr Eddie George, had already persuaded the Chancellor to raise interest rates three times in the five months to the beginning of February. At the fourth time of asking, when base rates had risen to 6.75 per cent, the Chancellor refused, and there was an open rift between Bank and Treasury. By the autumn, the Governor climbed down and withdrew his advice because the danger of inflation had lessened, although he still believed that the 2.5 per cent inflation target might be missed.

As long as the final decision is the Chancellor's, the Governor has little to lose by taking the hawkish side in the argument, and recommending precautions to avoid inflation by raising interest rates. If the Chancellor takes his advice, and it turns out right, the Governor's reputation is enhanced; if it turns out wrong, the Governor can still claim the credit for taking no risks with inflation. If the Chancellor rejects the Governor's advice and is proved right, the Governor can still claim the credit for taking no risks; if the Chancellor is proved wrong, the Governor can say 'I told you so', and next time round he will be unassailable (at least for his five-year term of office).

This is quite different from a system where the central bank is independent. It then has to take into account the possible effects of its interest rate decisions on the real economy to a much greater extent, instead of leaving that side of things to the finance ministry. The US Federal Reserve Board was given the dual objectives of full employment and price stability by the Humphrey-Hawkins Act in 1978.[25] The German Bundesbank also has to take account of the government's economic policy, as the ECB will have to: 'The primary objective of the ESCB shall be to maintain price stability. Without prejudice to the objective of price stability, the ESCB shall support the general economic policies in the Community.'[26]

National central banks are to be given independence before stage three of EMU begins, according to the Treaty.[27] This may appear paradoxical, since they will immediately lose their independence to the ECB when they become part of the ESCB at the outset of stage three, although their governors will sit on the Governing Council of the ECB. The aim is to make them independent of their governments, so that governments accept that monetary policy has been taken out of their hands. Many people in the UK, who do not necessarily support the single currency, are in favour of making the Bank of England independent to improve monetary policy and keep inflation low. They range from Thatcherite monetarists, through the Liberal Democrat front bench, to the Confederation of British Industry.

Once it is accepted that monetary policy is taken out of the political arena and run by unelected guardians of the public interest, there can still be an argument about whether they should be in a national institution such as the Bank of England, or a European federal institution such as the ECB. The ECB should turn out to have greater credibility than the Bank of England because it will inherit the credibility of the Bundesbank, just as the IMF turned out to have greater credibility than the British Government in the 1976 financial crisis.

MAKING THE ECB CREDIBLE

Credibility will depend on a number of detailed ways in which the ECB's independence is established:

Neither the ECB, nor a national central bank, nor any member of their decision-making bodies shall seek or take instructions from Community institutions or bodies, from any government of a Member State or from any other body.[28]

The President, Vice-President and four other members of the Executive Board will serve eight-year non-renewable terms, which gives them no motive to please politicians. They will be appointed by the EU governments, but they are not to take any instructions from governments or other EU institutions. Their powers are entrenched by the Maastricht Treaty, while those of the Bundesbank and the Federal Reserve depend only on federal law, and not on the constitution.

The six members of the Executive Board will be outnumbered by the national central bank governors, who join them to make up the Governing Council. Originally there were to have been twelve, now there will be fifteen because of the enlargement of the EU in 1995, and the number could rise with future enlargements. The Executive Board will thus be in a minority which is shrinking as time goes on, but it can be expected to 'divide and rule' the national governors, who are unlikely all to take the same line on anything. Eventually, the number of national governors may have to be limited by a system of merger or rotation: the first was adopted in Germany after unification; the second applies in the US, where only five of the twelve chairmen of Federal Reserve Banks sit with the seven Federal Reserve Board members on the Open Market Committee which decides monetary policy.

It is clear that one national central bank governor, be he British, French or German, will have little power in isolation in the ECB, but he will be able to join coalitions. The ECB will be independent of any one country's central bank, including Germany's, which could explain why the Bundesbank drags its feet about EMU from time to time. Its performance will depend on the quality of the Executive Board and the national governors, who will need to be chosen more for their political skills in monetary policy than for their expertise in sorting out bank failures or managing issues of government debt.

Independence is usually taken in the institutional sense, but other kinds of independence can be defined: the personal independence of the President and the Executive, operational independence and financial independence.[29] There is a good measure of all these set out in the Treaty. There will be a separation of powers between the ECB and other national and European bodies, as there is in the American system of government.

The ECB will be independent, but it will be accountable.[30] Like the Bank of England, it will have to publish a quarterly report. The President will also have to report at least once a year to the European Parliament, the EU Commission, and the European Council of Finance

Ministers (ECOFIN) and the European Council (of heads of government). The ECB will be sensitive to criticism and to pressure to take the needs of the real economy into account when deciding monetary policy. While the ECB is not accountable by the Maastricht Treaty to national parliaments, there is no reason why national governors, and perhaps also members of the Executive Board, should not make periodic reports to them, as the Governor of the Bank of England does to the Treasury Select Committee of the House of Commons.

National governments are in many cases reluctant to surrender sovereignty to independent national central banks, and may be even more reluctant to surrender it to the ECB. However, the absence of a European government in charge of economic policy will make the proposed ECB the only federal policy-making organ at European level. There will be no European government with which the ECB can have a relationship of dependence or independence. (The Presidents of the Commission and the Council will be able to attend the ECB Governing Council as observers, without voting powers.) In time, however, ECOFIN may develop into a virtual European finance ministry.

HOW WILL THE SINGLE MONETARY POLICY WORK?

There will be limited scope for variations of monetary policy between countries. A single monetary policy means the same interest rate for similar loans and deposits in every country, subject only to pricing differences between different banks based on varying views about creditworthiness (see page 52). Even in the ERM, other countries have to accept German interest rates as setting a floor below which they cannot move. In EMU, the Bundesbank will no longer be free to set its own interest rates and challenge other countries to adjust. There will have to be collective decisions in the interests of Europe as a whole.

The ECB will have to agree on its policy instruments. The European Monetary Institute (EMI) has already gone some way to narrowing the differences.[31] There are several issues on which the Bundesbank, the Bank of England, and other central banks disagree. This is hardly surprising, in view of the wide differences in functions and powers among the national central banks of the EU.[32]

a) *Monetary targets*   A common definition of EC money supply rather than the widely varying national definitions is needed if targets are to be used. Will the ECB target a broad monetary aggregate ('M3' or 'M4'), like the Bundesbank, or monitor a narrow one ('M0') and target inflation directly, like the Bank of England?[33] There is some evidence that a money supply target would make more sense for Europe as a whole than for individual countries.[34] The Bank of England's short experience of targeting inflation since 1992 shows that it is difficult either to forecast inflation or to influence it through monetary policy over a period of up to two years ahead.

One alternative would be a credit target, such as domestic credit expansion (DCE), which could be applied to each country as well as to the EU as a whole. DCE allows for the fact that the amount of money in each country, though not the amount of bank credit, varies as external payments move in and out of surplus and deficit. It seems unlikely that the exchange rate (of the single currency against the dollar and/or the yen) would be a monetary policy target. It might form part of a 'monetary conditions' target, including both interest and exchange rates. We deal more fully with EMU external exchange rate policy in chapter 8.

Will the M0 monetary base or short-term interest rates be the main policy instrument? Here the Bank of England's view that monetary base targets cause very volatile short-term interest rates may prevail.[35] Most central banks do in fact use short-term interest rates to achieve their monetary policy objectives. There is still scope for argument about which particular rates to use, and how to go about achieving them.

b) *Minimum reserve requirements*   Will commercial banks have to have quite large non-interest bearing reserves, as in Germany and most other countries, or minimal working balances at the central bank, as in the UK? Reserves are a kind of tax on banking and need to be uniform if the playing field is to be level. It is doubtful whether they give a central bank more control over monetary targets than interest rates alone, and if there are no monetary targets the question is academic. One compromise is to have reserves paying market rates of interest; another is to have zero reserve requirements – not as daft as it sounds, because it prevents banks borrowing from the central bank.

c) *Market intervention*   This is also known as open market operations (OMO), with the central bank buying and selling financial assets to control the monetary system. The Bank of England prefers OMO to operating on the level of bank reserves as a monetary control technique. Should intervention be partly in commercial bills, as in the UK, or entirely in government paper, as in other countries? The Maastricht Treaty bans the purchase of government debt by the ECB at the time of first issue, because it would be a form of inflationary monetary finance,[36] but there is no ban on ECB dealings in the secondary market for existing government debt. Sale and repurchase agreements ('repos'), such as are used by the Bundesbank, are likely to be widely used.

Should intervention be continuous during the day, as in the UK, or carried out once or twice a week, as in Germany? Should it be done through intermediaries such as discount houses, or by direct dealings between central banks and commercial banks? The wide variety of central bank techniques in different countries can be overcome only to the extent that financial assets converge and become closer substitutes. Some degree of decentralization in the execution of monetary policy is provided for, with the ECB using national central banks such as the Bank of England 'to the extent deemed possible and appropriate'.[37] Both the ECB and national central banks might at different times intervene.

d) *Banking supervision*   The Maastricht Treaty leaves this fairly open.[38] Should the central bank be responsible for banking supervision, as in the UK, or should there be a separate supervisory organ, as in Germany? The two policy objectives of supplying liquidity to the banking system, and deciding whether a bank is well enough managed to be worth rescuing, are connected, but it does not follow that they must be carried out under the same roof. There is a case for a European banking supervision organization, to ensure that banks from poorly supervised member countries do not abuse the 'single passport' that they will enjoy in the single European banking market. This is parallel to the case for a UK bank supervisory authority separate from the Bank of England, which has gained support since the Barings affair in February 1995.

HARMONIZATION OF FINANCIAL CULTURES

The German Bundesbank wants to go further than the harmonization of central bank operating procedures and harmonize what it calls 'financial cultures':

An effort should be made to achieve the maximum harmonization of the underlying conditions in the financial sector – with the aim of promoting a convergence of the 'financial culture' in Europe. From the point of view of monetary policy, it would be useful to gradually eliminate existing differences in the financial structures of EMS members in the wake of the progressive integration of the European financial markets. One outstanding example of such persisting differences is the prevalence in the UK of floating-rate loans as opposed to the preference in Germany for longer-term locked-in interest rates. For this reason changes in short-term interest rates that are subject to central bank influence have a comparatively large impact on disposable incomes in the UK where households moreover have a relatively high level of indebtedness; this may well have implications for the deployment of the central bank's set of instruments, as was demonstrated by the events of the EMS crisis in 1992. Clearly, this could give rise to problems for monetary policy cooperation in the EMS and for the later single monetary policy.[39]

The point has been acknowledged by the Bank of England and private sector UK commentators. A former Bank of England analyst, writing in a broker's circular, put it as follows: 'The way in which a given change in European interest rates will affect various countries is likely to differ greatly. So even if inflationary pressures were the same throughout the currency area before a change in monetary policy they could not be after.'[40]

The Bank of England's evidence is that the UK differs from other countries less in its corporate financial culture than in its household financial habits, notably mortgages.[41] Although most bank loans to British companies are at variable rates of interest, 35 per cent of their outstanding debt is in fixed-rate bonds, so perhaps a total of 40 per cent is at fixed rates, including some bank loans. The comparable figure for France is also about 40 per cent, and for Germany about 50 per cent. Small and medium enterprises, which cannot issue bonds but have to rely on banks, suffer from having most of their debt in variable-rate form.

By contrast, about 80 per cent of UK mortgages, and most consumer credit, is at variable rates of interest (see page 53). In 1990, British households were paying out 10.9 per cent of their income in interest, about three times the European average. By 1994, this had fallen to 6.5 per cent, with the fall in interest rates and the slowdown in the mortgage market.[42] It was the prospect of sky-high mortgage rates following 15 per cent bank base rates which tipped the political balance towards the UK's departure from the ERM in 1992.

Differences in financial culture are deep-rooted and bound to persist after the single currency has been set up. The Bank of England might be justified in pointing out to the Bundesbank that Britain's cult of the equity – the use of share issues as an important source of company finance – might have some advantages for the German corporate sector, which is financed to a relatively great extent by bank loans and bonds rather than shares. The high proportion of equity finance gives the UK one of the lowest interest-to-corporate-income ratios in the EU, in contrast to the position of the UK household sector with its relatively high interest burden.

The principle of subsidiarity must leave a good deal of independence to national financial systems, after the requirements of the single monetary policy at European level have been met. The operation of the single market in financial services will bring about some convergence, but it should not be for the ECB to dictate its pace and nature.

While continental corporations may find advantages in the diverse and flexible financial culture offered by the City of London, British mortgage borrowers will be attracted by the continental fixed-rate system, provided that the level of rates is fixed at a low enough level, see page 53. The differences in financial culture, far from being a reason for the UK not to enter the single currency, offer opportunities for improvement in financial packages for both corporations and households thanks to cross-border competition on product and price.

The Bundesbank's point, that the transmission mechanism of monetary policy differs between countries, remains valid, if something of a truism. The implication is that national central banks will need to use some of the discretion allowed to them by the Treaty in the application of the single monetary policy to local conditions. It will no longer be the function of monetary policy to prop up exchange rates under full EMU, because there will not be any other than external rates against the dollar and the yen. So the 1992 ERM crisis is irrelevant to the future. If the ECB is to use monetary policy to damp down the growth of demand so as to avoid inflation, then the high British proportion of variable rate finance could be an advantage, because a fairly small rise in interest rates would have a big real effect, and it would not be necessary to raise rates to punitive levels.

The different impact of monetary policy in different countries will make it necessary to use fiscal policy as well to get the right balance between growth and inflation, see chapter 6. The tighter fiscal policy can be, the lower interest rates can be set by the ECB. A bias towards tight fiscal and loose monetary policy will keep a rein on public expenditure and favour private investment and economic growth. If fiscal policies are not tight enough, the ECB will have to raise interest rates to keep inflation under control, thus jeopardizing the boost to economic growth expected from the single currency through lower interest rates. If the ECB can use short-term variable interest rates to achieve its targets, and companies and households can shift more to long-term fixed rates, damage to the real economy could be kept to a minimum.

5

Costs and Benefits of Giving Up National Currencies

THE END OF MONETARY INDEPENDENCE

If a country enters a single currency, it gives up its national currency. That might seem to mean the end of its monetary independence, and the surrender of a national monetary policy for a transnational monetary policy. Some further proof is needed. Sharing in a single currency is neither a necessary nor a sufficient condition of having a single monetary policy.

Different countries can try to fix their exchange rates irrevocably, and a system of their central banks can operate a single monetary policy without a single currency yet existing, as is planned in the early part of stage three of EMU.[1] Such a system is very much a second best, because it means giving up monetary independence without reaping all the advantages of a single currency. Unless it is a short and unavoidable transition phase, it may break down, because financial markets may not believe that exchange rates are fixed irrevocably, and credibility will be lost.

Different countries can try to use the same currency, but issue different amounts of it with different interest rates, thus pursuing different monetary policies. This was the case in the former Soviet Union after 1991, as the rouble area broke up into separate sovereign countries. It was an unstable and unsustainable state of affairs, because there was no agreement among the various central banks on a single monetary policy, and the Soviet rouble split into several currencies, with different exchange rates against each other.[2] The Russian central bank was unable to control the monetary policy of the other central banks, which made inflationary issues of roubles, so it kept the rouble and told them to issue their own currencies.

A single currency must quickly lead to a single monetary policy, carried out by a single central bank, or a system of national central banks,

as outlined in chapter 4. Otherwise it will not survive the tensions arising out of divergent national monetary policies. Monetary policy operates through the quantity of money issued, the short-term interest rates
set by the monetary authorities, and the exchange rate. The three are related. The monetary authorities can try to use all three instruments, but
in deregulated domestic and international financial markets they
cannot succeed. They cannot fix both the interest rate and the money
supply. They cannot fix both the interest rate and the exchange rate.
They cannot fix both the exchange rate and the money supply. They
often end up switching attention among the three and failing to control
any of them.

The difficulties were summed up in a classic quotation by Tommaso
Padoa-Schioppa, Deputy Director General of the Banca d'Italia: 'The
Community will be seeking to achieve the impossible task of reconcil-
ing (1) free trade, (2) full capital mobility, (3) fixed . . . exchange rates
and (4) national autonomy in the conduct of monetary policy. These
four elements form what I call an "inconsistent quartet" . . . At least
one has to give way.'[3]

In EMU, with a single currency taking over from fixed exchange
rates, it is national monetary autonomy that has to give way. Under the
Bretton Woods system national monetary autonomy could coexist
with fixed exchange rates (for most of the time) because there were restrictions on free trade and, when they were reduced, curbs on capital
mobility. Central banks were able to use official foreign exchange reserves to prevent markets moving exchange rates.

The single European market brought about freedom of trade and
capital movements by 1990, within the 1992 deadline set by the Single
European Act. The ERM tried to fix exchange rates from 1987 to
1992. Three instruments in the inconsistent quartet were then in play:
free trade, full capital mobility, and fixed exchange rates. The countries
which managed to stay in the ERM after the 1992 crisis in effect gave
up the fourth instrument in the quartet, their national monetary
autonomy, in favour of German monetary leadership. Those which left,
notably the UK, were not prepared to do so, and reverted to national
monetary autonomy at the cost of giving up fixed exchange rates.
Some have suggested giving up freedom of capital movements in order
to preserve the other three elements of the quartet.[4] This could not be
done without abandoning the free market in financial services to

which the EU is committed, nor is there any guarantee that capital controls or transaction taxes would be effective.

The ERM allows for a less than total surrender of monetary autonomy by members. Interest rates can and do vary in line with countries' divergent needs to control inflation, and financial market pressure on their exchange rates. Exchange rates can vary within bands originally set at 2.25 per cent (in a few cases 6 per cent) each side of the central parity, then widened to 15 per cent in August 1993. The two uses of interest rates – domestic and external – sometimes conflict, and in such cases monetary autonomy is of limited use.

This happens according to the 'Walters critique', named after a former economic adviser of Mrs Thatcher.[5] If exchange rates are expected to be fixed for, say, a year ahead, then ERM members wanting to keep their exchange rates fixed must all have the same interest rate. If this interest rate is some kind of compromise between national rates, it is too low for high-inflation countries which need high interest rates to get inflation down, and too high for low-inflation countries, where it causes deflation and unemployment.

In a more extreme version of the Walters scenario, the high-inflation country raises interest rates for domestic reasons, then finds its exchange rate rising, which may help to damp down inflation, but makes it even more uncompetitive in foreign trade than the existing inflation is already doing. The opposite happens in the low-inflation country, which cuts interest rates and finds its exchange rate falling and pushing inflation back up again.

The Walters critique ceases to apply once financial markets expect exchange rates to change. Then the high-inflation country can and must raise interest rates, not only to deal with inflation, but to protect its exchange rate. Even then, there is no conceivable annual interest rate high enough to compensate holders of the currency for an exchange rate loss of several percentage points overnight. The low-inflation country is under the opposite pressure to cut interest rates, but will still attract money from abroad in the expectation of a rise in its exchange rate, and face the danger of inflation from an increase in its money supply rather than a fall in its exchange rate.

These examples illustrate the point that even when countries are free in theory to change their interest rates and exchange rates, their ability to do so is limited in practice, and they may fail to achieve their ultimate policy aims. A country may have sovereignty over its own interest rate, but the financial markets have sovereignty over its exchange rate. Intervention by its central bank, and other central banks, to fix its exchange rate by buying or selling its currency cannot be counted on to work. The central banks do not have as much money as the big banks and corporations in the financial markets, to put it mildly. Official foreign exchange reserves amount to about $1,000 billion; this is less than world foreign exchange market turnover of $1,572 billion in one day (see Table 22). A rise in the interest rate on a currency, which normally follows official buying to support it, may also be intended to raise or stabilize the exchange rate, but it may lower it if the financial markets infer that there is a danger of devaluation.

The British Government regained autonomy over its interest rate after leaving the ERM in August 1992. It was able to cut bank base rates below German levels to a low of 5.25 per cent, instead of raising them to 15 per cent, as it announced that it would on 'Black Wednesday' in September 1992 – without ever doing so. It lost control of the exchange rate, which fell at one point to 25 per cent below its central ERM parity against the D-mark. By a stroke of luck, this exercise of monetary sovereignty gave the UK a moderate dose of export-led growth with few inflationary consequences in the short term. It would be unwise to count on miracles being repeated to order.

There are two ways in which monetary autonomy can go wrong. First, it can fail to achieve the intended aim, even if the aim is above reproach. Second, it can be used by politicians for short-term electoral advantage, for example by cutting interest rates before an election, even if higher interest rates are likely to be needed to reduce inflation after the election. The first failing is one to which the European Central Bank may not be immune, although the scale of its operations should give it an advantage over any national central bank. The second failing is one which can be avoided by making the central bank independent. This can be the national central bank, as monetarists want, or the ECB, as supporters of EMU want.

Even when a currency is floating, it is a mistake to think that it has monetary autonomy because it is free to choose its interest rate. Monetary conditions depend on the exchange rate as well as the interest rate. If the exchange rate rises, it is like a rise in the interest rate: import prices, then home prices, fall, and exports fall because they are dearer. If the exchange rate falls, it is like a cut in the interest rate: import prices, then home prices rise, and exports rise because they are cheaper. The exchange rate normally moves up and down with the interest rate, but it is impossible to predict how much, and it may move in a perverse direction. In the UK, a one percentage point rise in the interest rate is sometimes said to have the same effect as a four percentage point rise in the exchange rate.

Because the monetary authorities cannot tell what the effect of an interest rate change is going to be on the exchange rate, they cannot ever be in full control of monetary conditions. There is no such thing as full monetary autonomy in a world of floating exchange rates and free capital movements.

ADVANTAGES CLAIMED FOR MONETARY AUTONOMY

Advocates of monetary and exchange rate autonomy argue that it may not be perfect, but it is preferable to the alternative. The dishonour of a national currency may seem better than its death. Monetary sovereignty is sometimes felt to be part of national sovereignty, so that giving it up involves a loss of political independence, and ultimately political union (see page 5). It is almost a case of 'my country, right or wrong'.

The role of the House of Commons in national finance is also given as a reason for keeping monetary sovereignty, even though MPs have little say in practice on interest rate decisions which the Treasury and the Bank of England announce first and argue about afterwards. As Lord Lawson told the Treasury Select Committee in late 1987 about interest rates: 'When I think they ought to go up they go up, and when I think they should come down they come down.'[6] If monetary policy is too dangerous a weapon to be left in the hands of politicians, it could be even more dangerous in the hands of fickle backbench MPs than in those of the Chancellor of the Exchequer and the Prime Minister. As it is, the Chancellor's obligation to deal with parliamentary questions at times of financial crisis can be acutely embarrassing.

Sir Robin Butler, the Cabinet Secretary, told the Scott Inquiry in 1995 that ministers sometimes had to withhold information from the House of Commons. For example, Mr James Callaghan did so when he was Chancellor of the Exchequer at the time of devaluation in 1967. Mr Callaghan denied that what he had said to the House was a lie, but the point was that even twenty-five years ago it was not possible to have frank discussions on the floor of the House of Commons about interest rates and exchange rates, because of financial market reactions.[7]

One reason given for keeping control of interest rates is that different countries have differently phased economic cycles, and that they therefore need to put domestic interest rates up and down at different times. It can happen that countries think that they are in different phases of the cycle, and are making divergent forecasts about future inflation because they are using different models to predict the behaviour of the economy. We assume none the less that such cyclical differences can and do occur.

Figure 4 shows how much monetary autonomy countries had in the shape of different short-term interest rates in the first half of the 1990s. Germany kept rates high, raising them to nearly 10 per cent to offset the inflationary budget deficit due to unification spending. From mid-1992 the Bundesbank gradually reduced rates to under 5 per cent over three years. France followed German rates and managed to bring hers down to only half a percentage point above Germany in the heyday of the ERM in 1991 and early 1992. The ERM crisis in August 1992 forced France to raise rates to 12 per cent so as to hold the franc within its 2.25 per cent band against the D-mark. By early 1993, France was able again to come down to within half a point of Germany, but the gap widened in 1995 with doubts about the *franc fort* policy both before and after the election of President Chirac in May.

Lira interest rates managed to come down as low as franc rates in early 1991, but then had to climb to 14 per cent in 1992. Even so, the lira had to leave the ERM. After that, Italian rates were able to fall to 7 per cent over the following year, but could not go below German rates, or the lira would have fallen even faster than it did. The political and economic uncertainty surrounding the Italian Government meant that rates had to rise again after that.

Britain was able to lower interest rates to French levels by the spring of 1992 while holding the exchange rate within its 6 per cent band, thanks to ERM membership. Departure from the ERM, unlike in the case of Italy, allowed the UK to lower interest rates below French and

German levels for a time, but in 1994 they were raised again for domestic reasons, above German then above French levels.

US rates behaved quite differently. They were falling to 3 per cent while European rates were rising, remained there when European rates started falling, then doubled to 6 per cent in 1994 and 1995 as German rates continued to fall.

Europe clearly has monetary autonomy *vis-à-vis* the US – and divergent exchange rates to match. Within Europe, France's monetary policy is governed by Germany's. The granting of independence to the Banque de France in 1993 did not change this. Italy regained monetary autonomy after 1992, but was not able to use it to much advantage because of the uncontrollable fall in the lira's exchange rate. Britain made the most of monetary autonomy to cut interest rates after a sharper than expected depreciation of the pound by the markets, then used it to raise interest rates again, but without the rise in the pound's exchange rate that might have been expected.

There is a trade-off. Lower average interest rates should arise out of the single currency in future (see page 51), but with the same level everywhere, and changes in interest rates by the ECB happening at the same time for everyone. Average interest rates are higher at present than they will be under full EMU, but they can be changed in different countries at different times. In the long run, the first alternative offers better prospects for faster and steadier economic growth, but the second still tempts politicians with an eye on the short term.

In theory different regions of the same country might benefit from having different interest rates, and even different currencies. In a monetary union such as the UK, regional interest rate differences can exist only if the mix of different kinds of borrowers varies, as it must do to some extent. The housing market in the south-east might have benefited from having lower interest rates than the rest of the country in the early 1990s, but this was not possible.

Regional differences within one country therefore have to be dealt with by changes in government spending and taxation. The same would be true over a wider monetary union including Britain and the continental countries. Fiscal policy has to take over some of the present functions of monetary policy, see chapter 6.

Economic cycles in the different countries of Europe are in any case likely to converge more closely as a result of further economic integration in the single market. The recession followed a very similar pattern in Germany, France and Italy in 1992–4, with all showing negative growth in 1993, but occurred two years earlier in the UK, see Figure 1. This can be seen as a hangover from Britain's disastrous independent monetary and fiscal policy before joining the ERM in 1990.

Economic cycles in Europe should become less pronounced under EMU, because the present ups and downs of inflation will no longer result in volatile stop-go growth as governments struggle to bring them under control. There should be less variable inflation and growth for the whole single currency area. At the same time, variations between different countries should diminish, because their industrial structures tend to be diverse in similar ways, even if each branch of industry is integrated across frontiers in terms of trade and investment. Each country has some kind of oil, chemical, motor, textile, retail and financial sector, whether or not they are in national ownership. As countries become more open to trade with each other, economic impulses both positive and negative will move across borders more rapidly throughout the area, and business cycles will diverge between industries rather than between countries. Fiscal policy will have to be more closely coordinated through the ECOFIN Council of Ministers, because changes in tax and spending in one country will have more effect on others.

DEVALUATION – THE ULTIMATE WEAPON

The ultimate economic weapon is devaluation of the exchange rate, and it is this that countries are most reluctant to give up. (Giving up revaluation is also a sacrifice, but would affect fewer countries; it is one which Germany might be ready to make in view of the damaging effects revaluation has had on industrial competitiveness there.) Freedom to devalue may be no more than freedom to choose one's own rate of inflation, as the British Government discovered after leaving the European currency snake in 1992. It may also be the most painless way, in the short-term at least, of escaping mounting economic and financial pressures.

Devaluation can be more disease than cure. If foreign exchange markets decide, rightly or wrongly, that a country's policies are not sufficient to keep inflation under control, they sell the currency, and that makes it worse. For the sake of the argument, we assume that a country

wants to devalue and is able to do so. It is easier to carry out a devaluation in a fixed but adjustable system such as Bretton Woods or the
ERM than in a floating system. Even then, the country's partners in
the system may not allow it to devalue by the full margin that it wants.
On the other side, one intended devaluation may lead to another un-
intended one forced by the financial markets. Under a floating system, a
country cannot choose its rate of devaluation, but its currency depreci-
ates in the market by a margin which is itself floating.

If a country decides on and is able to carry out a devaluation of, say,
10 per cent, will it be a real devaluation, with no effect on the country's
prices? See Table 13, showing a £–DM nominal devaluation of 10 per
cent; this means that the cost of the DM in £ terms is revalued upwards
by 11 per cent. In case 1, a nominal and fully real devaluation, the price
of a typical item stays at £100 in the import market, the home market
and the export market. German exporters to the UK get only DM180
instead of DM200 for their sales, so they sell less because profits are cut;
British exporters to Germany can charge DM180 instead of DM200,
so they sell more because goods are cheaper. There is a real impact on
quantities sold and an improvement in the UK balance of payments in
sterling terms. (There is also a boost to demand in the UK, from both
exports and import substitutes, which will have to be offset by action to
prevent it becoming excessive, unless there is spare capacity to be used
up.)

In case 2, a nominal but not a real devaluation, UK exporters to
Germany keep prices at DM200, and their sterling prices rise from
£100 to £111. German exporters to the UK also keep prices at
DM200, and raise their sterling prices from £100 to £111. Home
prices and wages also end up rising by 11 per cent as imported components and the influence of both higher import and export prices
push them up, and employees demand full compensation in terms of
pay. At first German exporters sell less because their goods are dearer
and British exporters sell more because their goods are more profitable;
after a short time the rise in home costs and prices cancels out both
effects. There is only a temporary benefit to the balance of payments,
but a permanent rise in the British price level.

Case 3, a nominal but only partly real devaluation, is a typical compromise, halfway between the extremes of cases 1 and 2. UK import
and export prices rise by 5.5 per cent in sterling (i.e. German export

and import prices fall by 5 per cent in DM), and British home prices rise by 5.5 per cent in sterling. There is a lasting effect on both quantities sold and prices.

Case 4 shows what would have to happen within a single currency area to produce a similar real devaluation without a nominal one. If the DM price of UK exports to Germany and German exports to Britain is to fall by 5 per cent from DM200 to DM190, then home prices and wages have to be cut by 5 per cent in sterling terms as well, with export and import prices coming down by the same amount; if they do not, exports will be too expensive, whether they are British exports in Germany or German exports in Britain. These cuts should be interpreted as being relative to German wages and prices over a period of a few years; they could, for example, mean increases of 3.5 per cent in the UK and 9 per cent in Germany. The example is not far-fetched. In 1993 and 1994, consumer prices rose 7.9 per cent in Germany and 3.8 per cent in France, so French prices fell by 3.8 per cent relative to German.

Thus the typical extent of relative pay and price cuts needed to avoid a devaluation may be only half the extent of the devaluation. Compared with relative pay and price cuts, a devaluation may be twice as effective if it is all real, but effective only in putting inflation up if it is all nominal.

PROS AND CONS OF DEVALUATION

The larger the share of foreign trade in a country's economy, the more likely it is that a devaluation will be nominal than real, and affect prices more than consumption and exports. As members of the single market do more trade with each other, devaluation becomes less effective as a way of boosting the economy, and more harmful to the single currency aim of lower inflation. In large countries such as the US and Japan, which trade a lower percentage of their national income, the dollar and the yen have big real devaluations and revaluations, because the exchange rate has less effect on home prices.

Devaluations will not be needed for balance of payments reasons in full EMU as they are now, because surpluses and deficits will be financed in the single currency without any risk of exchange rate changes making it more expensive for a devaluing deficit country to repay its foreign currency debts. Countries might still wish they could devalue, however, to boost activity and reduce unemployment in areas lagging behind. Devaluations might also seem attractive, as in 1992 for Italy and the UK, to offset increases in inflation which had made a country's exports uncompetitive. This would be less likely in full EMU, because members would already have had to demonstrate that their inflation rates had converged downwards.

Countries try to avoid deliberate devaluation, and regard it as a last resort when other methods have failed. It is generally seen as a failure, and as a breach of faith with foreign investors in the currency who had not bargained for it. Such was the case with the British devaluations in 1931, 1967 and 1992. All three led to satisfactory recoveries in economic activity, but were they the best way of achieving the aim, or were they used only because other policies had been tried and failed?

Devaluation is more effective when it is unexpected. Then it is not factored into inflation expectations by employees when bargaining for pay increases, and it is not followed so quickly by increases in wages and prices. This means that a devaluation can be more real than nominal, and have more beneficial effects on exports and economic growth. The reason why the British devaluation of August 1992 was so successful in real terms was that the government had persuaded everyone in advance that it would never happen. So pay and prices hardly rose by more than they would have done in the absence of a devaluation. Dishonesty may be the best policy once in a decade, but it brings diminishing returns because it destroys credibility.

The alternative to devaluation, once it is thought to be necessary, is to seek a fall in pay and prices in the industry or area affected, relative to pay and prices elsewhere; this could mean a standstill, while there are increases in other industries and areas. Incomes are then cut directly instead of by means of devaluation, and export prices fall because home prices fall. The effect on incomes and output is more sudden, but equally sure, but the impact on prices is to lower them, not to raise them as devaluation usually does.

Real wage rigidity makes it difficult to carry out price and real wage cuts; but if it is a problem, then it is equally so if devaluation is used, because devaluation is effective only if it results in real wage cuts. So there is then no case for preferring devaluation to direct operation on pay and prices. Real wage rigidity could make it difficult for a country to

pass the Maastricht inflation convergence criteria, or to survive the increased competition of EMU under a single currency. In this case, devaluation would be a second best forced on it by failure to enter EMU,
rather than the preferred solution.

Real wage rigidity has two elements. One is the extent to which
money wages keep ahead of inflation by a constant real margin. The
other is the extent to which money wages slow down with a rise in unemployment. If money wages do not respond much to a rise in inflation, and/or if the rise in inflation can be reversed with only a modest
increase in unemployment, then real wages are flexible.[8]

Not only would this make devaluation more effective in real terms; it
would also make it easier for a country such as the UK to adjust to a
single currency by wage and price movements alone, even without devaluation. National differences in labour markets and unemployment
rates could make it more difficult for some countries in EMU to adjust
to shocks without devaluation, but the UK does not appear to be one
of them. A change of regime such as entry into the ERM or, better
still, full EMU, is designed to change labour market behaviour.

The Governor of the Bank of England warned of problems of adjusting to different rates of unemployment without exchange rate
changes:

The longer-term problem of unemployment reflects, at least in part, structural
features of the European labour market, which also differ from one country to
another . . . it could, in fact, become more difficult to resolve within monetary
union as a result of on-going differences between member countries . . . It
cannot be ruled out that there will be a continuing need for exchange rate
adjustments.[9]

The warning applies less to the UK than to some other countries,
because British unemployment fell in the mid-1990s, and the labour
market became more flexible in terms not only of pay, but also working
hours, hiring and firing, and mobility between occupations.[10] UK real
wages, after being the most rigid in the industrial world, became more
flexible in the 1990s, since nominal wages appeared in 1995 to be rising
by slightly less than the 3.5 per cent rate of inflation. Other countries
can be left to decide for themselves how to tackle unemployment,
which is not a criterion for EMU entry, as long as they meet the existing ones.

Devaluation is most effective where a whole country is affected differently from other countries by what economists call a shock, which could take the form of a domestic wage explosion, or a rise in the world price of oil. It is not effective if, as often happens, one region of a country is hit in a way which leaves the rest of the country unaffected. Then it would be using a sledgehammer to crack a nut. The US dollar was not devalued because Texas was hit by the oil price fall in 1985 (see page 23). The traditional remedy for depressed regions within one country is an outwards movement of labour and an inwards movement of finance.

If one country is suffering from a shock in a similar way to other countries, devaluation in that country is also ineffective, because it will improve its position, if at all, only at the expense of its neighbours in adversity. This leads to accusations of 'competitive devaluation', see page 47. The case for devaluation is that it can deal with an asymmetric shock, confined to one country; it is not the right policy to deal with a symmetric shock, affecting all countries more or less equally. If the shock is symmetric only for all EMU countries, and does not affect the US or Japan, devaluation for the single currency against the US dollar and the yen could be the right policy. This would leave the single currency intact, and be a matter for its external exchange rate policy, see page 172.

It is quite difficult to think of asymmetric shocks of a kind that would justify devaluation for one whole country in EMU rather than for one region of one country. The reason is that industrial structure is fairly diversified, as a result of each national economy's independent development in the post-war period. North Sea oil and gas is now only 1.5 per cent of Britain's GDP. A shock which hits one industry is thus more likely to affect all major countries in EMU rather than one only.

It has been argued by a former Bundesbank economist that the EU is less at risk from asymmetric real shocks than from asymmetric monetary shocks. While devaluation may sometimes be the appropriate way of dealing with the former, the single currency is the obvious way of dealing with the latter. In other words, any advantage of a national currency can be nullified by financial market shocks of the kind which monetary autonomy is ill-equipped to deal with.[11]

It is sometimes argued that exchange rate changes, while not appropriate to EMU in the long run, would be needed in the early years to correct the misalignments resulting from the merger of currencies at whatever their exchange rates were on the starting date. John Williamson has proposed a 'proto-EMU' in which there would be stable real exchange rates rather than nominal exchange rates.[12] This means that countries with higher inflation rates would devalue to prevent their currencies becoming uncompetitive. While this has been in effect the solution adopted for exchange rate misalignments in the ERM, it should no longer be needed once full EMU has begun. The convergence criteria, see page 132, are designed to ensure that countries enter the single currency on a level playing field.

Convergence of real rather than nominal exchange rates could mean divergence of inflation rates. Countries would perpetually adjust to higher than average inflation rates by devaluation, which would prevent inflation being brought down. This would be a step back from the inflation rate convergence that has already been achieved. The danger is that divergent nominal exchange rates would cause inflation rates to diverge again.

Once there is a single currency, there can still be changes in real exchange rates even without changes in nominal rates. Pay and prices can rise at different rates in different countries and industries to allow for divergences in productivity and competitiveness. Annual differences of at least 1.5 per cent are permitted under the Maastricht inflation convergence criteria. Differences of this kind should be allowed to persist once full EMU is reached, as a necessary adjustment mechanism. If prices go up faster in one country than in others, a real upwards revaluation takes place even within one currency area. It is just as if the country had a separate currency which had been revalued, making its imports cheaper and its exports more expensive; in both cases there is an incentive for prices to come down again, giving a real devaluation, or the country will not be able to compete. With separate currencies, the real revaluation due to inflation could be reversed by a real devaluation due to a nominal devaluation rather than only to relative price changes.

Countries in EMU will still be able to carry out real devaluations by having lower price increases than their neighbours, even when the nominal type of exchange rate devaluation is ruled out. This kind of competition, encouraged by the single market, will help the single currency's objective of keeping inflation low. Real exchange rate changes can obviously be measured by relative movements in consumer prices.

They can also be measured by means of relative wholesale prices, export prices, or unit labour costs, which are all, in different ways, more relevant to international trade than are consumer prices, and are thus better measures of competitiveness.

What applies to countries applies even more obviously to industries. Industries that are being priced out of the single market will be under pressure to increase productivity, get unit labour costs down, lower prices, and let surplus workers go to other sectors. For an industry in one country, or for its manufacturing sector as a whole, nominal devaluation of the currency removes the incentive to control costs and prices, because both employers and employees know in advance that it is available as an escape from excessive wage rises. Currency devaluation, like patriotism, may be the last refuge of a scoundrel rather than a glorious manifestation of national independence.

SURPLUS COUNTRIES WITH HIGH EXCHANGE RATES

Changes in industrial structure have made devaluation even less relevant to the needs of industrial economies than before. Countries with the most sophisticated exports and the highest balance of payments surpluses tend to have the most overvalued currencies, see Figure 5. Those with the highest deficits tend to have the most undervalued currencies and the least sophisticated exports. So the conventional wisdom that devaluation helps exports and improves the balance of payments is true only in some cases. A currency is devalued because its country has a weak balance of payments; the balance of payments does not become strong just because the currency is devalued.

Countries such as Germany and Japan have advanced and competitive industrial export sectors, so their currencies rise. Consumer goods and services become expensive by foreign standards, but the price of exports rises less, on account of productivity gains in manufacturing. Many of these exports are in any case new and exclusive goods whose prices cannot easily be related to prices at other times or in different places. The problem of allowing for quality increases and new goods is well known for consumer price indexes, see page 71. It is even more acute for exports of new capital goods.

Figure 5 suggests that there is a slight positive relationship between the real exchange rate and the balance of payments on current account, as shown by the upwards sloping line, rather than the negative one postulated by conventional economics.[13] France, Denmark, Belgium and Switzerland all have current account surpluses which are larger, the higher the country's real exchange rate; Japan is an extreme example of this trend, partly because of the recession in the home economy. The US, Spain, Canada and Australia all have deficits which are bigger, the lower the country's real exchange rate. The UK is in the middle, with a zero current account balance in 1994 and a 6 per cent fall in the real exchange rate since 1991.

The exceptions to the rule are Germany, Austria and Portugal, which have small deficits and overvalued exchange rates; in Germany's case, surpluses are more normal, and the deficit is due to the unification boom. Other exceptions are Italy, Finland and Sweden, with small surpluses and undervalued exchange rates.

The moral is not that devaluation cannot improve the balance of payments, but that there are many factors other than the exchange rate determining a country's external position, notably its domestic business cycle, the quality of its export trade, and its balance of capital imports and exports, which must come to the same as its balance on current account, with a capital surplus financing a current deficit, and vice versa. The balance of payments causes the exchange rate even more than the exchange rate causes the balance of payments, because foreign exchange markets buy the currencies of strong countries and sell the currencies of weak ones.

IS EMU AN OPTIMUM CURRENCY AREA?[14]

One of the tests applied by economists to EMU is to ask whether it is an optimum currency area. The concept of an optimum currency area was first defined by Robert Mundell in 1961.[15] It has been reworked in many different ways since then. The original inspiration was to ask whether a shock to an area, a fall, or even a rise in the demand for its products, say, could be best dealt with by a change in the value of its currency against the rest of the world, or by movements of capital and labour.

For example, when Scotland was hit by the decline in shipbuilding, should the Scottish pound have been devalued against the English? Or was the actual solution adopted preferable: movement of labour out of shipbuilding and into other sectors, and foreign investment of new capital in oil and electronics in Scotland?

We could conclude that nation-states are optimum currency areas, because labour and capital can move more freely within them than between them. All this proves is that there are generally fewer restrictions on the movement of people and money between regions of one country than there are between countries. This is not always the case, anyway. There is about as much movement of labour between Ireland and England as between Scotland and England, even though Ireland is a separate state and Scotland is not. An example in favour is Italy, where labour has moved from south to north and capital has moved from north to south; however, the south might have been better served by devaluation, since its people would in many cases rather have stayed at home, and much of the capital invested there has been unprofitable. Italy satisfies the normal conditions for an optimum currency area, but shows that they do not always give the optimum result.

The argument about optimum currency areas becomes interesting only if we ask whether they are narrower or wider than existing national currency areas. Mundell suggested that the eastern parts of Canada and the US might form one optimum currency area, and the western parts another; the currency dividing line would thus run north–south, at right angles to the political frontier of the 49th parallel. The reason would be that eastern North America is stronger in manufacturing, and western North America stronger in natural resources. This idea was taken further by Joel Garreau in *Nine Nations of North America*. The nine nations, spanning the existing boundaries of Canada, the US, Mexico and the Caribbean, are: the Breadbasket, Dixie, Ecotopia, the Empty Quarter, the Foundry, the Islands, Mexamerica, New England and Quebec.[16]

The lifting of restrictions on movements of labour and capital in the last thirty years suggests that potential optimum currency areas should have become larger rather than smaller than existing national currency areas. Language, culture and immigration laws have put a brake on labour movements, but the technology of financial markets has been an accelerator for capital movements.

The case for EMU is that the EU will become an optimum currency area, and would be better served by having one currency than several, with exchange rates changing against each other. The single market set

out, in effect, to make the EU into an optimum currency area by establishing the free movement of capital and labour while improving that of
goods and services. The first was enacted for the most part by July 1990;
the second is still in the making. People are free to move between EU
countries in search of jobs, but differences of language and difficulties
of housing have kept such movements fewer than those between states
of the US.[17]

It is lucky that free movement of the factors of production has
turned out to be lopsided. It is better in human terms that when workers are unemployed capital investment should come and create jobs for
them in their own homes, than that they should have to uproot themselves and look for work in a strange country. Too much labour mobility is even undesirable in an area where wage and productivity levels
vary widely, as between East and West Germany, see page 26. If employees can move too easily to areas where pay is higher, wages will be
bid up to keep them where they are, even if productivity levels do not
justify such an increase. Low mobility of labour also makes it easier for
countries to have different tax systems, and allows them to preserve
some degree of fiscal independence, see chapter 6.

Free movement of labour in the single market should allow individuals to match skills to opportunities at the appropriate rate of pay,
rather than being the solution to unemployment in whole regions. Regional unemployment is more easily dealt with at national level by
migration within countries. It is in any case less of a problem in the
UK than it used to be; the variance of regional unemployment rates
has fallen sharply, as the south-east gets a taste of the woes that used
to be the preserve of the north.[18]

To ask whether the EU is an optimum currency area or not is short-
sighted. The whole point of the integration agreed in the single market
is to make it an optimum currency area, both creating the conditions
for a single currency and using its advantages to feed back into the
better working of the single market. If it can be shown that the single
market or parts of it are not yet an optimum currency area, that is an
argument for removing the remaining barriers to free movement of
labour and capital, not for retaining separate exchange rates.

The desire for exchange rate changes, and thus a separate currency, is
an argument against joining an optimum currency area. The more
trade countries do with each other, the less real advantage a devaluation

or revaluation can give, because the effects will more quickly be wiped out by price changes. So free movement of goods is in effect a third criterion for an optimum currency area. Again, the EU is in a dynamic situation, where the lifting of non-tariff barriers, following that of tariffs at an earlier stage, is increasing trade between its members.

Countries such as the UK, whose trade with the rest of the EU is increasing less rapidly than that of other members, appear to have a better case for keeping the power to devalue. But the continuation of a separate exchange rate will continue to hold back the growth of UK trade with the rest of the EU, so the argument is circular. Entering the single currency would justify itself by increasing UK trade with the rest of the area to the point where devaluation against it made less sense than before.

Another criterion for an optimum currency area is industrial diversity, which has been shown to make devaluation less useful. If each country in an optimum currency area has a similar range of industries, they are affected symmetrically by a shock to demand in any of them. If each country specializes in a different industry, a shock to that sector has an asymmetric effect on that country, such that it might wish to have freedom to devalue or revalue. The EU is more industrially diverse than other monetary unions, such as the US or, formerly, the Soviet Union, because it consists of separate national states which have inherited a range of industries from the days of autonomous economic policies.

The EU's distinguishing mark of separate nation-states paradoxically makes it a better candidate for a single currency than even the US, because of its industrial diversity. There is less diversity in the different regions of the US where, for example, the motor industry is more concentrated in the Midwest than it is in any country in Europe. Two-thirds of US auto production is concentrated in the Midwest, only 38 per cent of Europe's in Germany.[19] There was an even greater degree of concentration in the rouble monetary area in the former Soviet Union. There, each major industry was concentrated in only one or two republics; now that the republics have become independent, there is a case for separate currencies and exchange rates to deal with asymmetrical shocks, as, for example, an oil price fall in Azerbaijan.

One possible result of the single market and the single currency might be, paradoxically, greater industrial specialization among countries. This would create the possibility of asymmetric shocks, and the case in theory for separate exchange rates. Since the new structure of industry would have been brought about in part by the single currency and the freedom from exchange rate risk, it would be ludicrous then to break up the single currency because of a different kind of risk that could be dealt with by other means in a more integrated economic area.

The eventual result of the single market and the single currency may be that the EU industrial structure becomes more concentrated: cars in Germany, finance in the UK, and so on. For that to happen national, sometimes nationalized, monopolies in sectors such as airlines, telephones, gas and electricity will have to be more free than they are now to merge and concentrate across borders. The single currency is likely to be up and running long before such long-run changes can occur. It is no more likely that the single currency will split up again in future because of industrial concentration than that the dollar will split up today because of similar developments in the US.

COSTS AND BENEFITS

A simple economic model can be used to show the balance of costs and benefits in a monetary union, see Figure 6. The benefits due to the abolition of exchange rates, the lowering of interest rates, and the elimination of inflation (see chapters 3 and 4) increase with the degree of economic integration (see the line sloping upwards to the right). The costs of giving up a separate national monetary policy, interest rate and exchange rate fall with the degree of economic integration (see the line sloping downwards to the right). For each country, there comes a crossover point in the integration process at which the advantage of a separate national monetary policy falls to where it is no greater than the gains from a single currency. After that point, as economic integration continues, the benefits of a single currency rise, and those of a separate national monetary policy fall.

It is difficult to measure exactly the benefits due to closer integration, or the costs of giving up a separate currency. The graph has been drawn with purely illustrative numbers. It is based on the assumption that a country which is 50 per cent integrated with other countries in the monetary union gains 5 per cent of GDP from integration, and loses nothing from not being able to devalue. A country which is not integrated at all gains a maximum of 2 per cent of GDP from being able to devalue, and obviously gains nothing from integration. The crossover point comes at 14 per cent integration, where a country gains 1.4 per cent of GDP from integration, and loses 1.4 per cent of GDP from not being able to devalue.

We can, however, measure the degree of integration, see Table 14 and Figure 7. It is taken as the product of two factors: the importance of trade as a proportion of GDP, and the percentage of trade done with other EU members. We have been able to include services as well as goods in the former, and in the latter case we take the percentage of goods trade done with the EU as a proxy for the percentage of goods and services trade. Trade is the average of exports and imports.

The proportion of GDP traded is a function of the size of the country. Small European countries trade between one-third and two-thirds of GDP, large ones 22–28 per cent. It is thus not surprising that the small countries are generally those keenest to join the single currency. The percentage of trade done with the rest of the EU depends not on size, but on history and geography. It is just over half for Denmark, Italy and the UK, and between three-fifths and three-quarters for Benelux, the Iberian countries and Ireland.

There are wide differences in the resulting figure for the degree of integration in terms of the amount of GDP traded with the EU, shown in Figure 7. Belgium–Luxembourg was in 1994 about 50 per cent integrated, Ireland about 40 per cent (mainly with the UK), the Netherlands about 33 per cent, and Portugal about 25 per cent. Denmark is only about as integrated as Germany, in the middle 15–16 per cent range. The four other major countries are the least integrated, at about 12–13 per cent. It is impossible to say that, by this criterion, France is more integrated than the UK, for example. France does more of its trade with the EU, but the UK trades more of its GDP, so the result is about the same.

If Figure 6 and Figure 7 are taken together, it is clear that, on the highly artificial assumptions of the former, all the smaller countries benefit to a greater or lesser degree from EMU, with Belgium at the head of the list. Denmark and Germany get a moderate benefit. France, Italy, Spain and the UK were just below the crossover point in 1994, but as integration continues in the single market, they will all move above it by the time the single currency becomes a reality at about the turn of the century. Different ways of drawing the graph would give different results. Our way of drawing it reflects the main arguments of this book.

In the end, the criterion for membership of a single currency is how like each other countries' economies have become. Do they do more trade with each other? Do they invest more in each other? Do their inhabitants travel around a lot? Do they react in the same way to good or bad news? Do their unions bargain in similar ways? Do their firms increase or cut prices for similar reasons? As economic and monetary integration goes on, countries will study each other more closely to find out who has the best way of doing things. That in itself will make them converge towards optimal solutions. An optimum currency area is simply a monetary union which has decided to do whatever is needed to make a single currency work to its economic advantage. You do not look around for optimum currency areas and create single currencies in them; you look around for areas suited to monetary union and make sure that they become optimum currency areas.

An important contribution to the analysis of optimum currency areas is that of Tamim Bayoumi, of the IMF Research Department. He points out the penalties to a country of being left out of a monetary union that is going ahead whether or not it joins. Since his analysis is particularly relevant to the UK, I quote it at length:

The incentives for a region to join a currency union are different from the incentives to admit a region into a union. The entrant gains from lower transmission costs on trade with the entire existing union, while the incumbent regions gain only on their trade with the potential entrant. As a result, a small region will always have a greater incentive to join a union than the union will have an incentive to admit the new member. A corollary of this is that, even if a country would prefer a free float across all regions, it may still have an incentive to join a currency union with other regions if it is going to be formed. This is because most of the welfare losses from the nascent union will occur whether or not the region decides to join. This set of incentives may explain why some countries in the EU who are not particularly convinced of the merits of EMU are also worried about being relegated to the second division of a two-speed EMU.[20]

The advantages of separate currencies, such as they are, will be less than those of a single currency if European integration goes on becoming a reality. The whole world is gradually becoming more integrated in terms of trade flows and capital flows. If large countries such as the US and Japan could see the merits of giving up autonomous monetary policies, the world might turn out to be an optimum currency area. For the time being, a single world currency remains a distant dream, but there have always been visionaries who have not been afraid to dream it.

6

How Governments Will Still Tax and Spend Under EMU

THE MIX OF MONETARY AND FISCAL POLICY

A single currency can be run either in such a way as to give member governments as much freedom of economic decision-making as possible, or as little as possible. If the principle of subsidiarity[1] is interpreted in the first rather than in the second way, then EMU should be designed to leave governments free to make their own economic decisions as far as possible, without interfering with the success of the single currency. In this chapter we look first at the way in which fiscal policies can still be independent, and then at the ways in which they will be constrained.

It makes good sense to pool sovereignty on monetary policy rather than on other aspects of economic policy. Monetary policy, even in one country, cannot easily be the subject of public and parliamentary debate. It is generally decided by finance ministries or central banks, but is often blown off course by the vagaries of international financial markets. It would be more difficult to centralize taxing and spending – fiscal policy – with the same types and rates of tax and the same tax burdens and levels of public expenditure throughout a wide community of nations.

Even self-confessed federations forming single nations with a federal government leave differing degrees of fiscal autonomy to their member states: Australia, Canada, Germany, Switzerland, the United States, for example. Federal expenditures as a proportion of total government spending range from 70 per cent in the US to 30 per cent in Switzerland.[2] Even unitary systems such as the United Kingdom leave some fiscal autonomy to local governments, although in this case it has been sharply reduced in recent years.

The paradox of EMU is that member states will have to use fiscal policy more actively to offset their loss of control over monetary policy, yet that very same monetary policy requires some limits on fiscal policy. It is Germany, the guardian of monetary orthodoxy, which is most anxious to tighten the central oversight over national fiscal policies, even beyond the Maastricht Treaty, see page 5.

Each country's macro-economic policy has two main elements: monetary policy, or interest rates; and fiscal policy, or the budget, which is in surplus or deficit according to whether taxes and other receipts add up to more or less than public expenditure. The combination of the monetary and the fiscal elements is the policy mix which then influences economic growth and inflation. If a policy mix is to be made looser, either interest rates are cut, or the budget deficit is increased, or both. If a policy mix is to be made tighter, either interest rates are increased or the budget deficit is reduced, or both. If a policy is to remain the same in its broad economic impact, the mix can be changed within it. If interest rates are cut, the budget deficit has to be reduced (the UK case in 1992–3). If interest rates are raised, the budget deficit has to be increased.

In full EMU, the monetary part of the policy mix will be handed out to national central banks from the ECB. They will have only the degree of control over it conferred by the presence of their national central bank governor on the governing council of the ECB, and their responsibility for executing it in their own national territory (see page 79). Governments will have no control even over their own independent national central banks, let alone the ECB. So to achieve a given policy result for the management of their economies, governments will need to complement ECB monetary policy with a suitable dose of fiscal policy, which may need to be tightened in some countries and loosened in others. They will not be able to use monetary policy by having different national interest rates because they are at different points on their economic cycle, see page 88, but they can and must use fiscal policy. As the European Commission put it:

The need for fiscal autonomy and flexibility arises from the loss of the monetary and exchange rate instrument for individual countries. Indeed, EMU will place new demands on fiscal policy at the national level for short-term stabilization and medium-term adjustment purposes in the case of country-specific disturbances.[3]

Countries worried about unemployment and deflation will be able to increase public spending or cut taxes, or both. Countries worried about overheating and inflation will be able to cut public spending or increase taxes, or both. Such fiscal action will have to be within the Maastricht Treaty limits, see below. Nevertheless, the need for greater national use of fiscal policy should reassure those who fear that governments will be surrendering all their economic decision-making powers.[4]

Fiscal activism is sometimes derided by policy-makers of the 1980s, such as Lord Lawson when he was Chancellor of the Exchequer:

Tax policy needs to be seen in a medium-term, not to say long-term, supply-side context. In other words, taxes should be changed (reduced or reformed or both) in order to improve economic performance. Unnecessary fluctuations in tax levels are inimical to economic performance.[5]

Their view was that the government's main job was to control inflation by means of monetary policy (which ended in a massive failure), and that economic growth was a matter for the private sector. The task of fiscal policy was to lower the tax burden as far as possible to give the private sector incentives to grow. The budget deficit had to be reduced by means of public expenditure curbs, so as to provide the private sector with cheaper and more plentiful finance. (Again, the failure was such that by the early 1990s taxes, public expenditure and the budget deficit all rose sharply.)

The structure of a country's tax system is not to be tampered with lightly, because it is built into personal and business planning and expectations. Short-term fiscal management is more concerned with tax rates and allowances than with the kind of tax to which they apply. It is dangerous to proceed on the assumption that tax rates should move in only one direction – downwards. If that is the general expectation, the shock and horror resulting when they have to move upwards, as UK VAT had to in 1993 and 1994, makes it harder to use fiscal policy in a neutral manner according to the needs of the economic cycle. Indeed, political pressure was such that the second half of the imposition of VAT on domestic fuel had to be withdrawn.

The use of fiscal policy is sometimes dismissed as 'fine tuning', not so much because it is undesirable, but because it is thought to be impossible. It is true that it takes a few weeks or months to implement tax and spending changes, but not true that they can be announced only once a year at the time of the Budget (now at the end of November in the UK). As soon as fiscal changes are made, it is quite easy to measure their exact size in terms of money given or taken away from different kinds of household or company. It is more difficult to assess their impact on economic behaviour, which may take longer to have effect.

Monetary policy is in no way superior to fiscal policy on most of these points. A change in bank base rates by the authorities results in an immediate announcement of a new figure. The effect on other interest rates, notably long-term rates, takes more time and is uncertain. The effect on exchange rates, a vital part of the monetary policy mix, cannot be predicted. The total impact of interest rate changes on the economy may take up to two years to work through, hence Milton Friedman's famous phrase about 'long and variable lags'.[6]

National fiscal systems need to be overhauled to make them more efficient as a tool of economic management. It is a quarter of a century since Professor James Meade proposed using the rates of national insurance contributions and VAT as economic regulators.[7] At that time, the creaking antiquity of the tax collection system was among the many excuses for not taking up the idea. It is hard to believe that after quarter of a century the Inland Revenue and Customs and Excise will not be able to handle this type of change by the end of the century.

It does not follow that governments should always be using the accelerator and the brake by changing tax rates at the slightest indication of a change in economic trends, which may later be revised by the statisticians or reversed by the real world. There is something to be said for putting the economy on cruise control, and letting it travel at a selected speed until there are compelling reasons to change it. The main short-term influence on fiscal policy will be the level of interest rates set by the ECB, and its decisions whether to raise or lower them. Fiscal policy-makers in finance ministries should probably wait and see how monetary policy goes rather than trying to second-guess or override it by over-active fiscal policy.

POLICY COORDINATION IN EMU

The way EMU is set up implies a one-to-one assignment of policy instruments to policy objectives, with each main instrument in different hands. The ECB uses monetary policy to control inflation, and governments use fiscal policy to regulate growth. This is an over-simple framework. Monetary policy affects output as well as prices, and fiscal policy affects prices as well as output. So each of the two partners – governments and ECB – are bound to consider the effects of their policy actions on both objectives; there are limits on the optimal degree of central bank independence, see page 73.[8] The institutional arrangements should ensure that they will work together rather than separately.

There is scope for the union-wide policy mix to be influenced by constant interplay between the European Council of Finance Ministers (ECOFIN) and its key committee of officials on the one hand and the ECB on the other, by attendance at each other's meetings and other forms of communication. The stage two Monetary Committee will be succeeded by an Economic and Financial Committee at the beginning of stage three, including two members from the ECB. The President of the ECB may be invited to take part in ECOFIN meetings, and the President of ECOFIN may attend meetings of the ECB Governing Council.[9] If the general fiscal stance is too loose, the ECB can be relied upon to raise interest rates. If the general fiscal stance is then tightened, the ECB should logically lower interest rates. This is what happened between the Bundesbank and the German Government in 1991–5.

If EMU is to achieve its aim of lower interest rates, governments will need to put their heads together to get lower budget deficits than otherwise. Even the threat of monetary tightening by the ECB could be enough to force fiscal tightening on governments. It would be more credible than similar threats such as national finance ministers or central bank governors make to their government colleagues who want to cut taxes and spend money to buy votes in advance of an election.

There is a case for fiscal policy coordination among governments, as well as coordination of fiscal and monetary policy between the governments in the ECOFIN Council and the ECB. This case was set out by Alexandre Lamfalussy, now President of the European Monetary Institute, in the Delors Report; it was accepted by member governments and written into the Maastricht Treaty: 'Member States shall regard their economic policies as a matter of common concern and shall coordinate them within the Council.'[10] In October 1995, M. Delors returned to the question by calling for a 'fiscal roof', in the form of a 'European economic government', which would decide policy at the level of the Heads of Government Council rather than leaving it to the ECOFIN Council.

The EU as a whole will have to have a policy mix. The ECB's monetary policy will have to have as its counterpart an appropriate union-wide fiscal policy. If this is left to chance, the fiscal policies of separate countries may not add up to a fiscal policy that is right for the EU as a whole. The risks are generally on the side of too loose an EU fiscal policy, which would make the ECB have a tighter monetary policy than it wished. However, the Maastricht criteria could also result in too tight an EU fiscal policy. If most countries implement them according to the timetable, or even go below them, the result could be a highly deflationary fiscal policy requiring a cut in ECB interest rates to offset it.

Another argument for coordination is that fiscal changes in one country may have effects that spill over into other countries. Such 'spillovers' are difficult to measure, but are more likely to be important the more open to trade with each other countries are. If the effect of a tax cut in the UK is to boost demand, then some of it will spill over into imports from other countries. The main effect is still likely to be on the home economy, as intended.[11]

The effects of a fiscal change, whether at home or abroad, depend on exactly what it is, and what the different effect is likely to be on consumption, investment and imports. An increase in the number of nursery teachers, for example, will have quite a different effect from a cut in the rate of corporation tax. If the EU governments collectively take spillovers into account, each can carry out a more moderate fiscal expansion when all act together, compared with what it would have had to do on its own, in order to achieve a desired effect on demand. Uncoordinated fiscal expansion could result in an excessive fiscal deficit for the EU as a whole.

Not only will excessive budget deficits result in a looser fiscal stance than the ideal for EMU. They will also absorb savings that might have gone into more productive private investment, and raise long-term interest rates – the so-called 'crowding-out' effect. In a monetary union with free flows of capital and no exchange rate risk, countries with large budget deficits may absorb more than their fair share of total EMU savings.

However, if bigger than average public sector deficits are incurred to finance worthwhile and remunerative investment in infrastructure, then the logic of the single market dictates that they should be free to attract funds from anywhere in EMU, or indeed the rest of the world, particularly from countries with a surplus in the balance of payments on current account. Freedom to allocate savings to the most profitable opportunities could thus be at variance with controls on deficits. If savers are risk-averse, they may be even more likely to invest in government bonds across the EMU than in corporate equities and loans. The risk on public bonds, if a country has passed the criteria for entry into EMU, may be seen as lower than that on corporate securities, even if the return is also less. Budget deficits are not all bad. They create a form of low-risk saving tailored particularly to the demands of growing pension and insurance funds as well as individuals' long-term needs for security.

There are other arguments for limiting budget deficits. One is that countries can be tempted to compete in fiscal laxity in order to win the votes of their electors, or the siting of new business ventures. Votes can be bought either by cutting taxes, or by increasing spending on desirable public services such as health, education and social security. Industries can be attracted by infrastructure facilities, by investment allowances or by tax holidays. There is evidence that such incentives are not the strongest factors determining location, but they may tip the scales where a decision is finely balanced. Competition to cut tax rates can be healthy in reducing excessive tax burdens, but it can also result in undesirable cuts in essential public services and infrastructure if governments try to reduce budget deficits while also cutting taxes.[12]

NATIONAL TAX DIFFERENCES

The competition in laxity has been restrained by a number of EU measures, such as ceilings on aid to less developed regions, or the agreed 15 per cent and 5 per cent minimum positive rates of VAT. Fiscal competition is more likely to result in the lowering of unusually high rates of tax than in the slashing of those that are already average. For example, in 1995 France cut the high rate of social security tax on lower-paid workers so as to make labour costs more competitive. This kind of harmonization can be left to national discretion rather than needing to be imposed from Brussels. Binding EU harmonization in many kinds of tax is a long way off, and, whether or not it is desirable, the example of the US shows that it is not necessary in practice among states with a variety of tax regimes, even if it may be desirable in theory. When it comes to corporation tax, Delaware taxes are low and California tries to tax everything worldwide. The Ruding Report on the harmonization of corporation tax in the EU was shelved, and is unlikely to be revived.[13]

Two main kinds of taxes need to be harmonized for the single market to function smoothly. One is sales taxes, in other words VAT and excise duties. US experience suggests that differences of 5 per cent or so in sales tax rates between states are tolerable. The UK, together with the rest of the EU, has agreed unanimously that all positive standard VAT rates should fall between a minimum of 15 per cent (the rate in Germany) and a maximum of 25 per cent (the rate in Denmark). This still leaves reduced rates for some goods. The UK was thus able to raise its 15 per cent to rate to 17.5 per cent in the 1991 Budget, and to maintain its zero rate for food, books and newspapers and other items – although, once abandoned, it cannot be restored.

Excise duties diverge more widely than VAT rates and cause more problems. For example, total tax on a packet of 20 cigarettes in 1995 ranged all the way from 46p in Spain to £2.80 in Denmark, with the UK nearer the top end at £2.11. The UK Treasury has lost revenue and British retailers have lost sales, although the British consumer has won lower prices, from a regime in which drink and tobacco cost far less in Calais than in Dover. For example, in 1994 twenty-four 25cl bottles of Stella Artois cost £4.50 in France and £10 in the UK[14].

The other urgent form of harmonization is taxes on the income on savings, particularly bank deposits. These can vary between zero, where there is no withholding tax, and the standard rate of income tax withheld. If such differences cannot be removed, the single market in banking will be distorted by the flight of deposits to the lowest-tax areas, such as the Channel Islands and Luxembourg. The fact that banks levy charges for the use of tax havens which partly offset the distortions is hardly an argument for keeping them.

When Mrs Thatcher negotiated the Single European Act in 1985, she agreed to qualified majority voting on a wide range of matters – in the interests of British trade, of course. She drew the line at taxation, and there it remained for the next ten years: 'I was not going to have majority voting applying, for example, to taxation . . . The ability to set one's own levels of taxation is a crucial element of national sovereignty.'[15] If the single market is to prosper, the UK may have to agree to qualified majority voting on some tax matters, if only to prevent deposits draining out of British banks, as they have out of German banks, into Luxembourg and other tax havens. No country wants to surrender its fiscal independence, but in this case some pooling of sovereignty would be to the UK's advantage. Majority voting on one or two specific taxes would have only a marginal impact on total UK tax revenue.

There is a big variance among EMU members with regard to the level of both tax and public expenditure as a proportion of GDP, and the distribution of revenue between different kinds of tax and of expenditure between different budgets, see Figures 8, 9 and 10. Even if there will have to be more convergence of deficit levels, the same deficit can be the result of very different levels of tax and public expenditure. For example, in 1994, France and the UK had similar government budget deficits of 6 and 6.5 per cent of GDP. In France's case, this was the difference between 49 per cent tax and other receipts and 55 per cent spending; in the UK's case, between 36.5 per cent tax and other receipts and 43 per cent spending.[16]

In 1993, the UK had the lowest tax burden of any EU country save Portugal at 34 per cent of GDP, compared with a maximum of 50 per cent (Denmark and Sweden), and a median of 44 per cent (France). (Government receipts include items other than taxes.) It had the lowest government expenditure burden except for Ireland at 44 per cent of GDP, compared with a maximum of 73 per cent (Sweden), and a median of 55 per cent (France). The political pressures in the UK to reduce these figures still further to the much lower levels in Japan and the US might be abated if the UK were to make the more appropriate comparison with its European partners, especially its nearest neighbour, France. However, the UK is free to take its own decisions, and to follow its own route rather than that of the rest of the EU, provided that it meets the Maastricht deficit limit of 3 per cent.

The UK stands out in various ways in its tax structure. Apart from France and Portugal, it raises the lowest proportion of tax revenue in the EU from personal income and social security tax, 35 per cent. Apart from Denmark and the Netherlands, it raises the lowest proportion from corporate profits and social security tax, 18 per cent. The

Latin countries get more than others from employers' and employees' social security taxation, the UK less. Denmark and the Netherlands make up for it by financing more of their high social security spending from personal taxation. The UK raises a higher proportion of revenue than any country except Greece, Ireland and Portugal from taxes on goods and services, such as VAT, but particularly excise taxes on alcohol and tobacco. The UK is unique in Europe, but similar to Japan and the US, in getting a substantial 12 per cent share of tax revenue from property, in the shape of business rates and council tax.

The UK is also unusual in having the largest proportion of its pensions funded by private-sector schemes in the EU. Other member countries have much larger unfunded pension liabilities, which represent an obligation for future government spending and a potential source of deficits. The UK also has a more favourable demographic structure, with less of a future increase than other countries in the number of pensioners compared with people of working age. Other countries are already starting to tackle these difficulties by such expedients as incentives for private-sector pension funding, extension of the working age, and high social security contributions.

It is alarmist to suggest that prosperous European countries will be unable to maintain fiscal discipline because of liabilities falling due some decades hence, These can already be foreseen, and require to be met by sensible long-term planning rather than by panic measures within the much nearer Maastricht Treaty deadlines. The differences among countries on pensions demonstrate the good sense of continuing to allow a wide variety of tax and expenditure systems in the EU. The phrase 'pension time bomb' was coined by the most ardent partisans of the single currency, but this has not prevented it being used by its opponents as yet another spurious argument against it.[17]

These patterns are unlikely to change significantly. Different taxes should not be seen in isolation. There is less difference between countries in the total tax burden on each sector of the economy than there is in the composition of the burden.

THE MAASTRICHT FISCAL CRITERIA[18]

The main constraint on national fiscal independence is the Maastricht Treaty ban on excessive deficits. This is a convergence criterion countries have to pass if they are to be admitted into the single currency. They have to take some notice of it even if they do not want to join. Unlike the other convergence criteria, it carries on into full EMU, and is a permanent obligation on all members.

Not all economists or political leaders accept that the Maastricht criteria are sensible, and the figures on which they are based are rules-of-thumb rather than scientific calculations.[19] I argue below that they have a sound economic and political justification. The British Chancellor of the Exchequer, Kenneth Clarke, got the agreement even of Eurosceptics when he said that the Maastricht criteria were justifiable on purely domestic grounds:

I personally think the convergence criteria are sensible . . . Even the most hardened Eurosceptic, I would hope, who may be against having anything to do with EMU, would like us to choose of our own volition not to go in, rather than be rejected as a failure because we fail to get within the criteria anyway.[20]

He did in fact base his Budget strategy on achieving them. It is an unimpeachable two-way bet. If the UK does not join the single currency, it will have sound public finance. If it does, it will have the advantages of a sound non-inflationary currency as well.

The Maastricht fiscal criteria are complex and subtle, as are the means of holding countries to them. I summarize and attempt to interpret this crucial section of the Treaty. It is these criteria that will be crucial in determining the number of countries qualified to join the single currency, because by 1995 no countries save Denmark, Ireland and Luxembourg had passed them. Interpretations vary according to the nationality of the commentator and the number of countries one wishes to bring in.

The definition of the statistical concepts, which also matters, is laid down in the Treaty. Government means central, regional and local government, and social security funds, but not public sector enterprises. The deficit means the government financial deficit, so it is not reduced, though it may be financed, by the revenue from privatization share sales. Government investment means gross fixed capital formation, so does not include public capital finance for the private sector. Debt is gross consolidated government debt at nominal, not market values, and is often much higher than net debt after government financial assets are deducted.[21]

In the third and final stage of EMU, 'Member States shall avoid excessive government deficits', while in the second stage now in place they need only 'endeavour' to avoid them.[22] Already in the second stage there is to be no monetary financing of deficits, and no bail-outs of one country by another, or by EU institutions. So governments are not allowed to borrow from their central banks or, in stage three, from the ECB, which, in their turn, must not buy government debt. Governments must have no privileged access to any financial institutions, and neither the EU nor Member States must assume public sector commitments in another Member State.[23]

The EU Commission has to monitor fiscal policies with a view to identifying 'gross errors'. The two criteria, both for convergence and inside full EMU, are set as 'reference values' which are not to be exceeded by the 'planned or actual' government deficit to GDP ratio, or the government debt to GDP ratio. These values are put into a protocol as 3 per cent and 60 per cent. In Brussels jargon a 'reference value' is not a binding limit but a number to be referred to as a kind of benchmark when making a judgement. The fact that the numbers are in a protocol and not in the main text of the Treaty also gives them a less elevated status.

In both cases there are loopholes. The deficit limit applies unless 'the ratio has declined substantially and continuously and reached a level that comes close to the reference value' or 'the excess of the reference value is only exceptional and temporary and the ratio remains close to the reference value'. The debt limit applies unless 'the ratio is sufficiently diminishing and approaching the reference value at a satisfactory pace'.

If these requirements are not fulfilled, the Commission has to prepare a report, but there are more loopholes at this stage too. The report 'shall also take into account whether the government deficit exceeds government investment expenditure' and 'take into account all other relevant factors, including the medium-term economic and budgetary position of the Member State'.

The Commission's report also has to take into account 'the sustainability of the government financial position; this will be apparent from having achieved a government budgetary position without a deficit that is excessive'. This introduces a new, time-related concept itself the subject of a wide variety of interpretations.[24] It applies to the convergence criteria in stage two, presumably so as to ensure that good performance at the moment of decision is not a flash in the pan, only to slide back once the country is in full EMU.

If a country's deficit has been steadily going down by say 1 per cent a year, has reached 4 per cent of GDP, and is planned to fall to 3 per cent of GDP in the current year, the criterion might be thought to be satisfied. On the other hand, a government which announced planned deficits of 3 per cent of GDP year by year, but failed to achieve its plans every time, would not be taken seriously. This was the problem which discredited the Gramm–Rudman–Hollings balanced budget law in the US in the late 1980s; it was enough to show a planned balance, even if there was always a deficit in the out-turn.

There is something to be said for the 'golden rule' that budget deficits should be incurred only for capital spending, with a balance on current spending.[25] If a country spends over 3 per cent of GDP on government gross domestic fixed capital formation, then the reference to 'investment expenditure' would apparently allow it to exceed the 3 per cent deficit limit. In 1994, those EU countries for which figures were available mostly fell within the limit. The figure for Japan was a high 8.9 per cent. The figure for France was the highest available in the EU, at 3.4 per cent of GDP; if this figure is maintained, France could thus pass the convergence criteria with a deficit over the 3 per cent limit. In the UK the figure was only 1.9 per cent;[26] the current plans are that it should fall quite sharply, as the private sector takes over more public projects.

How is the 'medium-term economic and budgetary position' to be taken into account? Will countries in recession be allowed to exceed the deficit reference values, provided that the budget deficit averages 3 per cent over the cycle, or is within 3 per cent in a mid-cycle year of 'normal' demand conditions? Will high unemployment be taken into account, so that a cyclically adjusted measure of deficits is accepted? If the country is in a recession, has a deficit of 5 per cent, but expects to have a deficit of 3 per cent in a normal year thanks to higher tax revenue and lower unemployment spending, the criterion could be passed under one interpretation of the rules.

WHEN IS DEBT SUSTAINABLE?

A common-sense interpretation would indicate that the deficit criterion is more important than the debt criterion, because the question is whether the deficit is excessive, not whether the debt is. If the debt ratio is over 60 per cent of GDP, clearly it has to be falling and not static or rising from year to year, at least within recent and expected future experience. What is 'sufficiently', and how fast is a 'satisfactory pace'? If the deficit itself is 3 per cent or less, it seems difficult to argue that it is excessive if the debt is over 60 per cent of GDP but falling from year to year. Say the debt ratio is 100 per cent of GDP, a fall of 1 per cent a year will bring it to 60 per cent after 40 years – surely too slow. A fall of 4 per cent a year, such as Ireland has maintained since 1987, will bring it to 60 per cent after ten years – the most that can be expected from any country.

There is only a low correlation between deficit and debt levels, see Figure 11. Countries with high deficits can have low debts (France and the UK), and vice versa (Ireland and the Netherlands). The correlation between high debts and high deficits applies mainly to extreme cases such as Belgium, Greece, Italy and Sweden. However, countries with high debts must have low deficits if their debt ratios are to come down, so the positive correlation must be reversed in future years.

The 60 per cent debt and 3 per cent deficit criteria seem to have been chosen because they were close to the EU average at the time. To be on the safe side, countries might aim at a debt that was 50 per cent of GDP, and a deficit that was 2.5 per cent of GDP. If the debt/GDP ratio is to be sustainable at the 50 per cent level, that means that the debt and the GDP should increase at the same percentage rate, keeping the ratio constant. In the example in Table 15, we show the debt and the GDP each increasing at 5 per cent a year, so that the ratio stays at 50 per cent. (The increase is nominal, not real, so that real GDP would be rising by 2.5 per cent a year, and prices by 2.5 per cent, making a total 5 per cent nominal increase.)

The annual deficit is the same as the rise in the debt. If the debt is 50 per cent of GDP – 50 units in the table – and the deficit is 2.5 per cent – 2.5 units – then those 2.5 units are 5 per cent of the 50 units of debt. For the debt and the GDP both to be rising at 5 per cent, the deficit has to be only 2.5 per cent of GDP, because the debt is only 50 per cent of GDP. A larger debt/GDP ratio can be sustained at the same level with a bigger annual deficit/GDP ratio. So the debt has to be reduced to a reasonable size to avoid excessive deficits. It is not enough to say that it is sustainable, if the level is too high.

The deficit criteria are easier to reach as nominal GDP accelerates, and governments can inflate their debt away, and harder as nominal GDP slows down, and governments are denied the age-old stand-by of the inflation tax. If EMU does indeed reduce inflation to zero or a very low figure, the deficit criteria will be harder to achieve. If it boosts the rate of real economic growth, the criteria will be easier to reach. If you cannot inflate your way out of debt, you can try to grow your way out of it.

If the rate of interest on the debt is the same as the nominal rate of growth of GDP – 5 per cent in our example – then we can imagine a situation in which the budget deficit consists only of interest payments. The increase in the debt is due solely to interest on the existing debt, and the rest of the budget is in balance. This balance, before adding interest payments to government spending, is called the primary balance. In the example, a more common scenario is given, where the interest rate of 7 per cent is higher than the rate of growth of nominal GDP. There then has to be a primary surplus, because the limits on the deficit are such that it is not big enough to meet all the interest payments, and the budget has to be in surplus before adding interest payments to expenditure. If the interest rate could be reduced to 5 per cent – which is one possible aim of EMU – then some of the money now being spent on debt interest could be recycled to government welfare programmes.

Governments can reduce their gross debt below what it would otherwise have been by selling financial or physical assets and using the proceeds instead of new debt which they would otherwise have had to issue. In the former case, it makes no difference to net debt – in some ways a better figure to use than gross debt – because both financial assets and financial liabilities have gone down by the same amount. In the latter, where governments privatize public sector industries, as has happened extensively in the UK, it makes no difference to the size of the annual financial deficit, but it reduces the debt because it finances some of the expenditure which leads to the deficit. Such assets sales are one-off, and do not help long-term sustainability. They may even harm it by cutting the government's income.

The UK is due to meet the 3 per cent deficit criterion in 1997–8, with a deficit of only 2 per cent of GDP planned.[27] This is consistent with 3 per cent or less in calendar year 1997. The debt ratio is expected to peak at 51.75 per cent in 1996–7. The merits of the government's policy of moving into budget surplus after that are harder to fathom. A further reduction in the deficit, and the attainment of a surplus, would result in a fall in the debt/GDP ratio to 44 per cent by 2000–1, whereas sustainability requires it to be no more than static. This means that government receipts will have to rise from 38 per cent of GDP in 1996–7 to 39 per cent in 2000–1, while government expenditure is cut from 41 per cent of GDP to 38 per cent.

The Maastricht criteria are a good incentive to put the public finances on a stable basis, but overfulfilment may put intolerable strains on the economic and social system. The costs of meeting the criteria for countries such as Belgium and Italy with high debt ratios, if interpreted too literally, will be unthinkable cuts in real GDP and rises in unemployment such as to guarantee that it would unrealistic for them to think of entering the single currency on such a basis.[28] There is no economic miracle by which a debt of 100 per cent of GDP can be reduced to 60 in a few years while keeping inflation low and unemployment tolerable.

HOW EXCESSIVE DEFICITS WILL BE AVOIDED

The Treaty lays down an elaborate multi-stage procedure which comes into action as soon as the Commission decides that there is an excessive deficit in a member state. The early stages are already operating in stage two, but the later ones involving sanctions do not come into play until stage three and full EMU.[29] The Council has to decide whether to accept the Commission's view. This indicates that the judgement is qualitative, and does not depend only on a mechanistic application of the 3 per cent of GDP reference value. If the Council upholds the Commission's view, then it makes recommendations in secret to the member state to be carried out within a time limit. If the state takes no effective action within the limit, the Council may publish its recommendations.

So far, we are still in stage two, so there is a continuous monitoring of the convergence criteria on deficits. In stage three, compliance measures are stepped up. If the deficit country fails to put the Council's recommendations into practice, the Council gives notice of further deficit reduction measures to be carried out within a time limit, and the country has to make progress reports on a regular timetable. If the country does not comply, then a list of sanctions is available. The country may have to publish additional information before issuing bonds. The European Investment Bank may reconsider its lending policy to the country. The country may have to make a non-interest-bearing deposit with the EU, or pay fines. The Council takes all the above actions by a two-thirds weighted majority vote, excluding the country with the excessive deficit.

It is not clear what happens if the deficit country does everything that is asked of it, but the deficit goes up or stays the same instead of going down. This could happen if tax increases and public expenditure cuts push it into recession, and there is a cyclical increase in the deficit which swamps the reduction measures. Presumably the Council would take account of the medium-term situation and wait for the deficit to come down in the recovery phase of the cycle.

Countries with excessive deficits would be punished by the financial markets long before the Council got around to implementing its multi-stage procedure. They might have to pay high spreads over current rates for government bonds in the single currency, and their credit ratings would tumble. They might even have difficulty in getting banks to underwrite their bond issues at all.

The judgement of the market, however, might not be sufficient. Some Canadian provinces with high borrowing requirements pay fairly small additional interest spreads. The market may assume that, in spite of the no-bail-out clause, other EU governments could not stand by and allow the credit rating of the whole Union to be impaired by the misbehaviour of one of its members. On the other hand, the markets might assume the worst, and anticipate that a country, particularly a small one on the fringe, could be allowed to default, or even leave the single currency to revert to a national currency. (Leaving would not help if the bond was issued in the single currency, in fact it would make it harder to service the debt in devalued national currency.)

A leading bond market analyst, Graham Bishop of Salomon

Brothers, has proposed that the provisions of the Maastricht Treaty should be reinforced by detailed regulations designed to make it harder for countries to finance excessive deficits, in case market discipline proves not to be sufficient.[30] If a government's bonds are in danger of losing some or all of their market value owing to the possibility of default, the banks and other institutions holding those bonds, including possibly the European Central Bank, could suffer from the financial fall-out. Some provision therefore has to be made for risk-spreading so as to avoid systemic risk.

Such proposals stop short of amending the Maastricht Treaty to set up a new European fiscal authority, as proposed by some Germans, since this would be unlikely to secure agreement. Uncertainty about the effectiveness of either market disapproval or the Treaty sanctions has led German spokesmen, notably Dr Theo Waigel, the Finance Minister, to propose that fiscal discipline goes further.[31] He has proposed a 'stability pact', by which countries would agree to aim at budget deficits of only 1 per cent of GDP, and pay (refundable) fines of 0.25 per cent of GDP for exceeding the 3 per cent limit. Some Germans say that there should be a central fiscal organ, parallel with the ECB, to control national fiscal policies. The paradox is that such an authority was omitted from the Maastricht Treaty at the insistence of Germany, who thought that it would detract from the independence of the ECB.

Others who stick by the Treaty and nothing but the Treaty regard this as a step towards political union – which the Germans want anyway – and an infringement of national fiscal sovereignty – which it would be. If the Maastricht limits are sensible on domestic policy grounds, countries should not need to be forced into making their best endeavours to attain them. The German proposal would not go as far as a federal budget, but would impose greater central coordination on national budgets. It appears to be addressed at domestic audiences concerned that Germany will give up the D-mark too easily. As far as Germany's EU partners are concerned, it is a negotiating position designed to promote a strict interpretation of the Maastricht criteria. It remains to be seen what kind of agreement is finally reached.

FISCAL STABILIZATION WITHOUT CENTRALIZATION

The fiscal constraints of Maastricht will have to be applied with care if fiscal policy is to be allowed to play a stabilizing role. This holds whether there is a general symmetric shock, requiring a fiscal stimulus for EMU as a whole (such as another oil shock), or a particular asymmetric shock in one national region (such as German unification). There is a dilemma here. Either member states will have to accept constraints on their budget deficits (like most US states, which have to balance their budgets), and the EC central institutions will have to abandon their own balanced budget constraint in order to stabilize activity in the states (running a US-type federal deficit); or member states will have to continue allowing the automatic stabilizers to push them into cyclical deficits, while the EU itself continues to run a small balanced budget.

The automatic stabilizers are so-called because tax revenue goes up and down, and unemployment benefit down and up, as the business cycle goes up and down, as explained by the OECD.[32] So if the government sits on its hands and does nothing, the budget deficit falls or goes into surplus in a recovery, and rises in a recession; the effect is to damp down the recovery, and give the economy a boost in the recession.

Sir Donald MacDougall has drawn attention to his 1977 report proposing quite modest, but still politically unacceptable, increases in the size of the EC Budget for stabilization purposes.[33] He points out that the 1.35 per cent of GDP represented by the EC Budget still falls far short of his suggested 5 per cent, or the 20–25 per cent average of federal states. The structural funds embodied in Maastricht are there more to redistribute income to the poorer states than to achieve stabilization, which is a requirement for any state irrespective of its relative income level. Some experts cast doubt on the ability of national fiscal policies to achieve stabilization without substantial supra-national transfers, while others hold that national automatic stabilizers can do the job as long as they are allowed to operate.[34]

The OECD evidence shows that the US, the example of a federal budget often quoted, has weaker automatic stabilizers than other members, because it has a lower tax to GDP ratio. So taxation does not take such a big share of any increase in GDP, nor does a fall in taxation boost recovery so much as a result of any slowdown in GDP. The UK was in a similar position, with the budget deficit rising by only 0.33 per cent of GDP for every 1 per cent fall in GDP, and vice versa. The latest Treasury evidence is that this figure has risen to about four-fifths of 1 per cent of GDP over two years, and that the OECD estimate was too low.[35] The OECD estimate for most EU countries with higher tax ratios is about 0.5 per cent.

The OECD findings are consistent with the decentralized approach to fiscal policy adopted for EMU. If member states allow the automatic stabilizers to operate, then those suffering a loss of economic activity will pay less tax to their national treasuries just as they would pay less tax to the federal treasury under a centrally taxing federal system; only if member governments raise taxes as the cycle is slowing will the stabilization mechanism fail to take effect. Similarly, member states will automatically pay more welfare benefits to the unemployed as the cycle turns down; here the parallel with the USA is even closer, since most welfare is paid by the states and not by the federal government – all of it from 1995 onwards.

If the stabilization mechanism breaks down in a decentralized EMU, it will be because the member states are pressurized into raising taxes and cutting expenditure to reduce deficits in a recession. This would happen only if the Maastricht fiscal criteria were applied 'sado-masochistically'.[36] Full EMU will make it easier for member states to finance deficits in a unified European bond market in the single currency without exchange rate risk, although not without credit risk.

It is sometimes argued that fiscal deficits in an integrated area do not help stabilization, because of spillovers of the extra demand into imports from other states in the area. The economic arguments run both ways, and it is hard to say a priori whether a fiscal stimulus will have more impact on domestic or on imported output; much depends on the exact form the fiscal measures take. If the objective is to maintain incomes rather than output, the argument is in any case irrelevant, because it does not matter so much whether the extra income is spent at home or abroad. Factor movements of capital into, and labour out of the deficit area should eventually restore equilibrium. Fiscal deficits sometimes do and sometimes do not give rise to matching balance of payments deficits (spillovers); if they do, then capital inflows finance both deficits at once.

If a country in recession has to finance a higher deficit across its borders within the single currency area, it will not have an exchange rate risk; and may save something if interest rates are lower than they would have been for a national currency. However, it will have to finance a future stream of interest payments across its borders. This will increase its balance of payments deficit but, as we have seen, the increase will be easier to finance.

The main difference between European EMU and some federal systems will be in the smaller scale of concessionary grant-type finance from the centre to offset regional deficits, which will be limited mainly to the structural funds for poorer regions. The flows of banking and investment funds should, however, make up for this, given exchange rate stability, as they do between regions of a single country.

The Delors Report took the view that the net impact of EMU on the less developed regions of the EU would be negative, and recommended a big increase in structural funds to 'help poorer regions to catch up with the wealthier ones'.[37] It will be many years before faster economic growth per head in countries such as Greece, Portugal and Spain enables living standards to catch up with those in Northern Europe, see page 37. There are still wide regional income disparities, as there still are in the US, in spite of a much larger federal budget.[38]

The structural funds in 1995 amounted to about £20 billion (25 billion ecus), only about 30 per cent of the modest-sized EU budget, amounting to 1.2 per cent of GDP.[39] The cohesion funds set up specifically to deal with the effects of EMU were less than a tenth of this amount. Most of the structural funds were for agricultural and declining industrial areas. The regions eligible cover about half the population of the EU: the whole of Ireland, Greece and Portugal, most of Spain, most of Scotland, Wales and Northern England, the Eastern Laender of Germany, the South of Italy, and the rural heartlands of France.[40] The structural funds, while only a fraction of 1 per cent of EU GDP, account for 2 per cent or more of GDP in small lower-income countries such as Ireland and Portugal, and over 5 per cent in Greece. The areas qualifying for structural funds will increase enormously if the applicants from central Europe join the EU, but the unwillingness of the richer countries to increase their budgetary contributions will limit the amount of additional expenditure.[41]

The Edinburgh budget package agreed in 1991 provided for a 20 per cent increase in expenditure in real terms up to 1999, but this is a rise only from 1.20 to 1.27 per cent of EU GDP.[42] The big uncertainty will arise after 1999, when the new central European members will have to be fitted into the budget, and the UK's budget rebate is to be reviewed. The UK already jibs at contributing £2.2 billion net to the budget (the 1994 figure), even though the country benefits from a special reduction of £3 billion. The British preference for widening the EU over deepening it could result in the loss of the UK budget rebate in order to make a success of this very policy objective. It will be in British interests to press for private sector initiatives to stimulate faster growth in new member countries, so that extra strains on the EU budget from poorer countries do not finally make the UK rebate indefensible.

In the US, the type of expenditure undertaken centrally by the federal government is not mainly designed to stabilize the economic cycle, but has longer-term economic development aims, often influenced by political 'pork-barrel' motives. In rather similar manner, the main expansion of the EU budget will have to be for the extension of the structural funds to central Europe, not for the stabilization of the economic cycle in richer countries. The effect of EMU on economic growth and inflation should in any case be to raise the first, lower the second, and make both more stable. Any further stabilization over and above that will remain the concern of national governments.

The task of the EU fiscal authorities will be to apply the Maastricht limits in such a way as to give national governments the budgetary flexibility they need to cope with regional and national fluctuations. Otherwise, national governments will be deprived of an important tool of economic management, and EMU will deliver lower inflation, but without higher growth. Fortunately, the decisions will be taken by the governments themselves as members of the ECOFIN Council, so these dangers can be avoided.

7
The Transition to the Single Currency

PROS AND CONS OF A TIMETABLE

The single currency can be seen as an investment project. The costs are earlier in time than the benefits. The costs and the benefits are both difficult to measure exactly. The benefits must be greater than the costs, or the project would not be worth considering. If the costs are too high or come too early, and the benefits are not high enough or come too late, then the present value of the costs is higher than the discounted present value of the benefits; putting the two together, if the net present value of the whole project is negative, it is not worth going ahead. This may be so even if the benefits, when they finally occur, are higher than the costs are in the immediate future, because the benefits have to be discounted.

This framework should not be interpreted too literally. It is a metaphor to illuminate the debate about EMU. The terms of the debate are constantly changing, as views about the costs and the benefits change with the swings of events and arguments. The costs of making the transition to the single currency are not the same as the costs of being inside it once it has come about, which were discussed in chapter 5. Some costs are already being incurred and others yet to be incurred are being worked out with greater precision as time goes on. The decision to put a timetable in the Maastricht Treaty transformed the position. It became possible to work out over what period the transition costs would be incurred, and how far off the main benefits were. A project which imposed up-front costs without specifying any particular date by which the benefits would accrue could not have been taken seriously.

To express general support for EMU while saying that it will, and indeed should, take a long and indefinite period to achieve is thus unhelpful. For example: 'If the self-imposed target date of 1999 is missed does that matter so very much by comparison with the magnitude of the task being attempted and the need to get it right?'[1] The higher the costs that have already been incurred by a country or an interest group, the less sense it makes to talk about postponing the benefits, unless one decides to write off the whole investment as a bad job – not necessarily an indefensible point of view, but one that needs to be made explicit, and not dolled up as lukewarm support. The fact that considerable costs have already been sunk, even if they were higher than expected, improves the cost-benefit analysis from the present time onwards, provided that the remaining costs decline as the target date approaches, and the benefits are achieved.

The nature of the cost-benefit calculation changed fundamentally as a result of the two crises in the Exchange Rate Mechanism (ERM) in 1992 and 1993. Up to that point, the EU Commission was able to argue that countries had already incurred a major cost by linking their exchange rates, and the additional costs were modest enough to justify going ahead as quickly as possible:

Stage I yields already substantial benefits in terms of exchange rate and price stability and also implies the main cost of EMU, i.e. the loss of the exchange rate as an adjustment instrument . . . Since going beyond Stage I would not involve any costs this implies that beyond Stage I there are only benefits.[2]

Unfortunately, some countries felt unable to go on incurring the mounting interest rate costs of exchange rate stability – notably Italy and the UK – while others continued to incur them, but at a lower level thanks to the flexibility given by the new wider 15 per cent exchange rate bands after August 1993, and to the fall in German interest rates. Countries which left the ERM are not anxious to begin incurring the costs of rejoining the ERM, but those which remained, particularly France, do not want to go on incurring costs longer than they have to, and want to see the benefits of the single currency in return for the losses in economic growth and employment that they feel they have already accrued. This is why EMU has a much higher priority in France than in the UK.

There has always been tension between countries which wanted to speed up the project to get the benefits quicker, and those which wanted to slow it down because they did not want to incur the transition costs, or they were doubtful about the benefits. The first camp, known as the 'monetarists',[3] led by France, argued that monetary union would lead to economic convergence. The second, the 'economists', led by Germany, wanted economic convergence to be a precondition and not a consequence of monetary union. This is also known as the 'coronation' theory, because the single currency comes at the end to crown the economic edifice. The Maastricht Treaty was a compromise between the two. The Germans got their convergence criteria, but the French got their timetable.

The Single European Act of 1986 succeeded because it had a time-table, going to the end of 1992, during which the various directives setting up the single market had to be carried out. Even if some were not implemented by the due date, the majority that were would never have been agreed so quickly without a timetable. The Maastricht Treaty also allowed a timetable of five to seven years.

The 'monetarists' regarded the Maastricht timetable as too leisurely and argued that over even a seven-year period financial speculation could wreck the ERM, as indeed it did before the Treaty had even been ratified. The 'economists' thought it was not long enough to give all EU countries time to satisfy the convergence criteria. They are likely to be proved right about this, even though the approach of the deadlines has been a powerful incentive to some countries to improve their economic performance.

The Treaty has two deadlines, of which the first has been missed.[4] Full monetary union could have gone ahead with a majority of EU member countries on 1 July 1997, had a decision been taken by 31 December 1996. This was impossible, because a majority of countries cannot by then pass the convergence criteria. So if the Treaty is adhered to, the final stage of monetary union will begin on 1 January 1999 even if only a minority of countries qualify, as confirmed by the Madrid summit in December 1995. A decision on which countries should join must be taken by 1 July 1998; the Madrid summit brought this forward to 'early 1998'. A different date for the start could have been chosen by the end of 1997. This was meant to allow for a date earlier than 1 January 1999; the letter if not the spirit of the Treaty would have allowed a later date to be set.

The paradox of the timetable is that a minority of countries might have been ready by the end of 1996 to take a decision to go ahead in mid-1997, but would not have been able to because they would not have been a majority. Yet by 1998, a majority, though probably not all, of the EU members may be ready to enter the final stage. So the provisions allowing only a minority to go ahead may prove redundant.

The decision to go ahead in 1999 was criticized by John Major, the British Prime Minister, because it could lead to 'division and recrimination' if a minority of countries were to go ahead into EMU without the others.[5] Yet if unanimity had been the rule, the pace of the slowest would have been unbearably slow. The argument for letting some countries join the single currency before others is threefold. First, it may be easier to organize logistically, and thus have a lower cost, albeit for a lesser initial benefit. Second, countries unwilling to join may be spurred to do so by fear of the penalties of being left out. Third, countries unable to satisfy the convergence criteria by the first deadline will be given more time.

All three attitudes are present in the UK, which secured an 'opt-out' from the third stage of EMU (it is strictly speaking an 'opt-in'), as did Denmark. 'Unless the UK notifies the Council that it intends to move to the third stage, it shall be under no obligation to do so.'[6] The UK need not decide whether to join until others take their decision, and can then come in at any later time. The difference between these two countries and their partners was bridged by a compromise summed up by M. Jean-Claude Trichet, now Governor of the Banque de France, as: 'No veto, no coercion, no arbitrary exclusion.'[7] In other words, the UK cannot stop others going ahead (although it sometimes looks as if the British Government is doing its best to do so); the others will not force the UK to join (if it says, like Groucho Marx, 'I wouldn't want to join a club that would have me as a member'); and the UK will be allowed to join as long as it passes the convergence criteria.

The transition takes two forms. First, there are the three stages needed to get to the single currency, which were adopted by the Maastricht Treaty from the Delors Report. Then there are the three phases in which the Euro itself is introduced, see Figure 12. After the report to the EU Commission by the Maas committee of experts, the phases were introduced in the Commission's green paper of May 1995, and developed in more detail in the November 1995 paper by the European Monetary Institute.[8]

CONVERGENCE IN STAGE TWO

The Maastricht Treaty goes into great detail about stage two.[9] Stage one began on 1 July 1990, with almost universal freedom of capital movements. Stage two began, as laid down, on 1 January 1994, even though the ERM had taken two major steps backwards. Since then the ECOFIN Council has been coordinating members' policies, laying down guidelines, monitoring their implementation, and making recommendations, which can be published if a majority agrees. The IMF operates in a similar way, but the ECOFIN deficit sanctions will go further, see page 122.

Economic policy coordination will focus on convergence. The convergence criteria cover four indicators: inflation rates, government budget deficits, exchange rates and long-term interest rates. They are explained in greater detail in the appropriate chapters of this book. They were thought to be a test of whether countries were ready for full monetary union, and as a sort of 'dry run' for the real thing. About half the then twelve EU countries were already meeting the convergence criteria in 1990 and 1991[10] – only they had not at that stage been specified as such.

The boom induced partly by the single market programme generated a momentum towards the single currency needed to complete and complement it. Inflation rates did not rise in the boom as on previous occasions – except in the overheated UK – and economic growth brought about a cyclical reduction in budget deficits. The ERM was keeping exchange rates stable after apparently ending a series of realignments in 1987, and long-term interest rates converged to reflect the low perception of exchange rate risk.

The chance to make a dash for monetary union was missed. Germany's attention was distracted to the much higher domestic political priority of German Economic, Monetary and Social Union (GEMSU); and the recession in the US and the UK, and then in continental Europe, made the convergence variables diverge again. The foreign exchange markets became disillusioned after the Danish referendum in May 1992, and exchange rate convergence came apart too. The unification of Germany pushed the unification of Europe into second place for some years, but made it all the more important because of the need to fit a larger Germany into a larger Europe.

Stage two, and the economic recovery that went with it, saw a painful rebuilding of convergence by most countries, see Table 16. We take the EU Commission May 1996 forecasts for 1997, the year when countries must achieve the convergence targets. The forecasts assume policies unchanged as of May 1996, but clearly policies can and do change. We assume that countries that have already planned policies to reduce their budget deficits to less than 4 per cent of GDP by 1997 will be able to go the extra kilometre and reduce them to 3 per cent, or pass the criteria by having reduced their deficits 'close to the reference value', in other words between 3 and 4 per cent.

We also assume that if the debt ratio is diminishing, as it normally would if the deficit was coming down, even countries with debt ratios over 60 per cent will pass. This is the area in which governments may have to interpret the Treaty so as to admit more members to the single currency, and override an alternative interpretation by the Bundesbank designed to restrict membership. There is nothing in the Treaty itself to say how some of the key phrases should be interpreted, and one legal opinion is as good as any other. The Treaty as it stands is neither strict nor permissive. Decisions on which countries pass the convergence tests will be made by a qualified majority of the Council on the basis of reports from the Commission and the EMI.[11] So countries may be admitted even in the event of one or two of the others wishing to interpret the criteria so as to exclude them.

Inflation, once thought to be the most important and the most difficult target, is proving relatively easy. Twelve out of the fifteen EU countries look like meeting the inflation targets, and two others may come very close. This will be a good performance in absolute as well as relative terms. The three lowest-inflation countries are forecast to have an average of 1.6 per cent, slightly below the current level. The limit would then be 3.1 per cent, and the UK would be well within it, and right on the domestic target limit of 2.5 per cent. Devaluing countries such as Italy, Portugal, Spain and the UK had smaller rises in domestic inflation than had been expected after such sharp exchange rate falls. However, it still seems likely that Italy and Spain will just fail to meet the target, even after meritorious efforts.

Budget deficits are turning out to be much harder to control than inflation. The recovery did not bring them back to their level of the late 1980s, because of the long-run trend for structural deficits to rise on account of the pressure of welfare spending and the unwillingness to raise taxes. The current recovery may run out of steam by the late 1990s and bring about another cyclical rise in deficits. So multi-annual deficit reduction programmes may fail to give the exact results predicted. Countries have to take care that their anti-deficit measures are not so Draconian as actually to increase deficits by inducing recession.

All the countries which pass the inflation criterion also pass the deficit criterion, with the exception of Austria, Belgium, Portugal, Sweden and the UK – in other words, seven countries. Greece and Italy are expected to have deficits of 5–7 per cent of GDP; even though they are coming down, there is little chance that they will reach 3 per cent by 1997, or even come close to it. The UK's drastic deficit reduction programme may not quite meet the Maastricht criteria by 1997.

There is some doubt over whether France will achieve its target of a 3 per cent deficit by 1997, in spite of a firm commitment by President Chirac. It appears to be incompatible in the short-run with his other commitment to tackle unemployment. If France cuts interest rates to boost job creation, the franc could lose its hard-won stability in the ERM. The strikes of late 1995 raised fresh doubts, which were not entirely dispelled by the outcome. If France does not pass this key criterion, there will be no monetary union worth having; there will be little point in a mini-union of Germany and the Benelux countries.

If France does not qualify, the UK will be 'off the hook', and will not need to make up its mind whether to opt in, much to the relief of many political leaders. In the end, France is 'condemned to succeed'; the Franco-German relationship at the heart of Europe might not survive a failure on the part of one or other country to go ahead with EMU. The consequences for the whole of Europe would be severe, both politically and economically.

The countries with deficits forecast to be between 3 and 4 per cent could well reach 3 per cent with further efforts, although they would have to persuade the others that their fiscal positions were sustainable after entry into the single currency, and not just a flash in the pan. They are Austria, Belgium, Portugal, Spain, Sweden and the UK. The number of countries passing the inflation and the deficit criterion would then rise from seven to twelve, excluding Spain because it fails the inflation test.

The long-term interest rate criterion has not been taken as seriously as the others, partly because it is expected to be achieved if the other three are. If a country has a low inflation rate, a small budget deficit, a stable exchange rate and the intention of going into a monetary union, it is hard to see why its long-term interest rate should be more than 2 per cent above that of the three best performers. A divergence of the long-term interest rate usually means that financial markets can see that one of the other convergence variables is going off the rails. Long-term interest rates have been volatile, and rise at times of crisis, as bond market prices fall. The use of an annual average to measure convergence should iron out this kind of volatility.

It is no coincidence that the three Mediterranean countries and Sweden are forecast to fail the interest rate test in 1997 – and doubtless 1998 as well – because financial markets expect them, rightly or wrongly, to fail the inflation and the deficit criteria. It is disturbing that even in countries which pass these criteria long-term interest rates are forecast to be as high as 5 per cent in real terms, over and above the rate of inflation. The benchmark set by the three lowest-inflation countries would be 6.7 per cent, and the UK would be within a 1.2 per cent spread of this figure. In this case convergence is in an upwards, not a downwards direction. High real interest rates are the price exacted by the financial markets for continuing political and exchange rate uncertainty. They will come down only once the single currency is a reality, see chapter 3. This is the argument for going ahead as fast as possible, rather than dragging out the interest rate cost of the transition.

Because the Maastricht Treaty was drafted before the two ERM crises, exchange rate stability is enshrined in it as one of the convergence criteria to be met before a country can enter EMU. The criterion in article 109j of the Maastricht Treaty is:

The observance of the normal fluctuation margins provided for by the ERM of the EMS, for at least two years, without devaluing against the currency of any other Member State.

This is explained in the Protocol on the convergence criteria:

The criterion . . . shall mean that a Member State has respected the normal fluctuation margins provided for by the ERM of the EMS for at least the last two years before the examination. In particular, the Member shall not have devalued its currency's bilateral central rate against any other Member State's currency on its own initiative for the same period.

These provisions could be taken to mean that a member state could revalue its currency during the two-year period without this counting as a devaluation of any other currency; or that the devaluation of a currency on the initiative of the EU Monetary Committee and not the country affected would not infringe the criterion; or that a general realignment of all ERM currencies could take place without infringing the criterion.

As long as the normal bands remain at the 15 per cent set in August 1993, rather than the previous 2.25 per cent, it is a fairly easy criterion to pass. The EMI Council 'considers it advisable to maintain the present arrangements',[12] so it is unlikely that there will be any return to narrower bands in the ERM. Yet in another way this target is more difficult, because it has to be achieved over two years, instead of in the previous year only, like the other three.

We assume that countries which stay within the ERM without changing their central parities on their own initiative will pass this test. This comprises Austria, Belgium, Denmark, France, Germany, Luxembourg and the Netherlands (which has uniquely remained within the original 2.25 per cent bands). If they pass the other convergence tests, they make up a seven-nation 'hard core' of countries expected to go into the single currency in 1999, as long as Denmark reverses its earlier decision to opt out.

Countries in the ERM which devalued in 1992–5 have a chance to maintain their central parities for the two years 1996 and 1997, which will determine the outcome of the test. Ireland is likely to do so, and will then join the hard core. Portugal and Spain may also do so, but it will depend on whether they pass the other convergence tests.

It is also hard to see how countries such as Italy and the UK, which have left the ERM, and are unlikely to rejoin, could be said to be even within 15 per cent bands as long as they have not rejoined the ERM, however stable their exchange rates may be. The same could be said of Finland and Sweden, which are members of the EU without having joined the ERM. According to the UK version of the Madrid summit in December 1995, it was agreed that ERM membership was not essential to passing the exchange rate stability criterion, because the ERM no longer existed in its original narrow band form assumed by the Maastricht Treaty. This would allow the UK to opt into the single currency in 1999 without rejoining the ERM, provided that it could give other evidence of exchange rate stability. It would also make it easier for Finland, Italy and Sweden to pass the convergence tests without being in the ERM.

Exchange rate stability could be measured by seeing how far a currency's exchange rate deviated from an average value in 1996 and 1997, and whether the trend of that average was level over the period. It might be difficult to lay down the rules in advance, but a judgement could be made in early 1998 by looking back at the record. Countries would have to make some attempt to manage their exchange rates rather than let them float freely, but this is usually implicit in monetary policy anyway.

The pound could well be fairly stable in 1996 and 1997, particularly if it was thought that the UK was going to opt into the Euro, and might even bounce back to an average value of DM2.50, which would then become the rate for entry into the single currency. Allowance would have to be made for the usually short-term instability likely to accompany the general election that has to be held during these years.

Italy's prospects of a stable exchange rate will also depend on whether it looks like entering the single currency, and on its rather unstable political situation. Finland should be able to achieve stability without joining the ERM. Sweden will have to decide whether it actually wants to join the Euro, whatever the outlook for its exchange rate; again, the problem here is political more than financial.

The convergence criteria are to be measured on the basis of the 1997 statistics, so decisions on who qualifies for the single currency will be taken at the Council of Heads of Government meeting in early 1998, deciding by qualified majority vote. At the same time decisions will have to be taken about the countries 'with a derogation' which do not yet qualify, see chapter 8. Elections in the major countries fall during this crucial period: Italy and Spain in 1996; the UK in 1996 or 1997; France and Germany in 1998. However, the fact that the main parties in these countries do not differ substantially from each other on EMU makes it unlikely that governments will abandon convergence programmes ahead of elections to catch votes.

If the 'hard core' of seven, plus Finland, Ireland, Portugal and Sweden, reach the convergence targets by early 1998 and decide to go ahead at the beginning of 1999, the UK will have to decide whether to opt in and join them. The Government will have the advantage of having an election behind it, so will have freedom of manoeuvre. If the UK and Denmark opt in, there will be twelve countries going into the single currency in 1999, with three-quarters of the EU's population and GDP. Far from dividing Europe, a partial EMU of this size would act as a magnet to the Mediterranean countries to improve their economic performance so as to qualify. By 2002, two more countries may catch up on the convergence criteria and come in – Italy and Spain – leaving only Greece as the laggard. The UK could be the 'swing' country, not in making up the legal majority – an irrelevant point in 1998 – but in giving EMU the critical mass to make it irresistible to countries that have not yet joined. We explore the UK position further in chapter 9.

THE QUEST FOR 'REAL' CONVERGENCE

The transition scenario set out here falls between two extremes, which were characterized earlier in this chapter as the 'monetarist' and the 'economist' approach to EMU. The first, put forward by the Belgian Professor Paul de Grauwe,[13] is that convergence is more easily achieved after monetary union than before, and that it would be better to drop the criteria in favour of strengthening the monetary and fiscal regime of the single currency. This is an intellectually attractive and defensible position, which in effect says about the Maastricht Treaty what the Irishman said when asked the way to Dublin: 'I wouldn't start from here if I were you.'

For better or for worse, the Maastricht Treaty has to be the starting point, and we must make the best of it. De Grauwe makes the additional point that the application of the criteria will split Europe. I have argued that the split could be limited to the Mediterranean countries if the UK does not worsen it by refusing to join, and that they could be brought in soon afterwards. There could be a worse split if these countries agreed to stringent additional criteria for EMU which they were not able to observe.

At the other extreme is the view often expressed in the UK, for example by the CBI,[14] that 'real' convergence criteria are needed in addition to the Treaty criteria, 'such as unemployment, current account balances, and GDP growth'. To these Labour Party representatives have added productivity and competitiveness. The suggestion is that the Treaty criteria are all 'nominal', and thus in some way less important. The addition of such 'real' criteria might mean that the single currency was placed beyond reach for ever.

Other indicators mentioned in the Treaty that have to be taken into account in reports by the EU Commission and the EMI on whether countries can join EMU are the development of the ecu, the results of the integration of markets, the situation and development of the balances of payments on current account, and an examination of the development of unit labour costs and other price indices.[15]

There is no unemployment criterion for convergence and no mention of unemployment in any Treaty sub-text. Bringing in a new unemployment criterion looks suspiciously like a delaying tactic. Unemployment varies widely among countries, and is more likely, in line with De Grauwe's argument, to improve after the single currency has brought real interest rates down. Convergence in GDP growth (see page 36), is the last thing needed if lower-income countries are ever to close the gap with their more prosperous northern neighbours. If convergence in GDP per head is required, this would mean excluding the Mediterranean and, even more, the central European countries from EMU for the foreseeable future.

It is also wrong to harp on 'competitiveness' as an additional criterion, as though this was something self-evident. The UK has in fact become extremely competitive in terms of the level of export prices and unit labour costs. So much so, that French and German industrialists accuse their British counterparts of competitive devaluation (see page 47). Unit labour costs have tended to move in line with consumer price inflation, so if a country passes the inflation test it is unlikely to be suspect on grounds of rising unit labour costs, and if it passes the exchange rate stability test it is unlikely to be accused of unfairly cutting its unit labour costs.

If by competitiveness is meant something deeper than price and cost levels, which are very sensitive to currency changes, then of course the UK lags behind some other countries in some industries in terms of productivity, but this is on the whole made up for by lower pay and employer social security payments. The kind of long-term improvement in economic performance that seekers after 'competitiveness' hanker for is more likely to be achieved by joining the single currency than by hanging around on its margins. The ultimate test of competitiveness is the ability to pay one's way in the world while increasing living standards, and here the balance of payments is relevant.

Nine out of the fifteen EU countries are forecast by the EU Commission to have surpluses in their balance of payments on current account in 1995. Germany and the UK are forecast to have deficits of less than 1 per cent of GDP, Austria and Spain of 1.7 per cent of GDP, Greece and Portugal around 3 per cent of GDP. Payments imbalances will in any case be no problem in the short run thanks to free capital flows and the end of exchange rate risk within the Euro currency area. However, any country that ran a persistent and widening balance of payments deficit within EMU would be in danger of building up a crippling external debt burden, albeit in its own domestic currency – the Euro.

THE THREE PHASES OF THE EURO

The stages are concerned mainly with economic and monetary convergence, while the phases are more a matter of currency logistics. The Treaty hardly began to tackle the detailed problems of introducing a new Europe-wide currency, and allowed too little time. Stage three, the final one of the EMU, was originally divided in people's minds into 3a and 3b, the first with irrevocably fixed exchange rates, the second with a single currency. Then it was divided into phase B and phase C, with a gradual transition rather than a clean break.

Phase A, the preparation for the single currency, will begin not more than a year before stage three. The Madrid summit in December 1995 laid down that the decision on which countries should enter the single currency would be taken in early 1998, thus leaving nearly a year for phase A, although countries which look certain to enter will have started preparations before then. Phase B covers stages 3a and 3b, because it combines the single currency for large transactions with irrevocably fixed exchange rates for smaller ones, and will take a maximum of three years – which may also turn out to be a minimum. It is thus likely to last from 1 January 1999 to 1 January 2002. Phase C will mean the universal introduction of Euro banknotes and coins over a period of six months in the first half of 2002. So the new currency will not be fully in being until mid-2002.

The Maas Report concluded that there were four possible scenarios for the changeover:

1. *Big Bang* The introduction of the Euro in bank deposit and note and coin form simultaneously for all purposes at the beginning of stage three.

2. *Delayed Big Bang* Exchange rates would be irrevocably fixed at the beginning of stage three, then the Big Bang, as in 1, would take place after three or four years.

3. *Pragmatic Big Bang* The Euro would be introduced at the beginning of stage three only for monetary policy operations between the ESCB and the commercial banks, then in bank deposit form when the banks were ready, and more gradually in note and coin form.

4. *Minimal approach* The Euro would be used only for monetary policy purposes from the beginning of stage three, with further options left open under a regime of irrevocably fixed exchange rates.

The solution adopted by the EMI is a combination of 2 and 3. The Euro would be used from the beginning of stage three for monetary policy operations. Financial markets would be encouraged to switch to it as soon as possible in bank deposit form, thus building up a critical mass of transactions. National currencies would continue to exist for retail banking purposes. Their irrevocable fixing would be secured by the closing of foreign exchange markets, and the substitution of a system of conversion at par rates guaranteed by the ESCB. To give time for the printing and minting of Euro notes and coins, they would be introduced in a Big Bang, probably at the beginning of 2002.

Phase A, like stage one, is preparatory, covering the year 1998. It is a recognition that a new currency cannot be introduced 'like a thief in the night', even though that might be the most efficient way of doing it if the logistics permitted. When the London Stock Exchange decided in October 1983 to reform itself, it left three years of preparation before the 'Big Bang' in October 1986, so one year is a very short time. It would be too short were preparations not already taking place in the two years 1996 and 1997, and had the idea of a Euro Big Bang not been replaced by a more gradual scenario.

Phase A includes: the setting up of the ECB and the ESCB, which will have to be operational from the first day of 1999; the legal frame-work for the Euro;[16] national bodies to coordinate its introduction (on the lines of the UK Decimal Currency Board); and planning details of the conversion for banks, businesses, shops and the general public, as consumers, investors and taxpayers. The public sector itself will have major conversion tasks that have hardly even been thought about in the UK; the national accounts, government finance, local government, social security and the tax system will all have to undergo rapid and complex changes, which may not be completed until the end of phase B.

Phase B, like stage two of EMU, is a period of transition, when the Euro is gradually introduced over a widening range of transactions. It is expected to last for three years – a compromise between those who are impatient to do it in two and those who reckon they need four. Different banks and businesses could move at different speeds, although too much of a 'market-led' approach could end in tears unless similar organizations using common financial data and joint settlement procedures agree to move at the same pace.

During phase B, there will still be different national currencies, but they will in effect be different denominations of the same currency – the Euro. There will be a single monetary policy run by the ECB and the national central banks in the ESCB, so the macroeconomic advantages of low inflation and low interest rates should appear early on. But the savings in transactions costs cannot be fully realized until the national currencies have been phased out.

Exchange rates will also need to be 'irrevocably' fixed during phase B, until the single currency can physically be introduced. This raises different kinds of problems from those of running the ERM as a fixed-rate system during stages one and two. Financial markets will have to be convinced that no national currency can withdraw from EMU as long as it still exists in some form. It will be far more difficult and expensive, but not impossible, for countries to withdraw from the single currency itself once it is fully in being.

The plan is to have a 'critical mass' of transactions in Euro almost from the start of phase B. Commercial banks' dealings with the central banks and with each other, and perhaps with large corporate customers, will be in Euro. So the new currency may soon account for 90 per cent of transactions by value, but only 5 per cent by number, as all lower-value retail transactions involving individuals and small and medium enterprises will still be in national currencies. There will have to be a frontier within the banking system where money moves at fixed conversion rates between Euro and national currency. The banks want as far as possible to avoid dual running, because of the high cost of putting all amounts in both Euro and national currency.[17] It will be better to use one or the other (with conversions shown).

It was agreed at the Madrid summit that from the start of phase B all new government debt issues traded on secondary markets would be denominated in Euro (there are already some such issues in ecu, which will presumably be converted into Euro). This will contribute to the critical mass of Euro instruments. In deference to Germany, non-traded government debt issues can still be made in national currency until the end of phase B. There will be strong market pressure on governments to convert existing issues of traded debt from national currency into Euro as early as possible during the transition period; otherwise they will tend to trade at a discount (with the exception of German D-mark government 'Bund' issues) and form small illiquid market pockets.

It will be vital to reassure people that there is no possibility of national currencies being devalued or leaving the system during this crucial period – one reason for making it as short as is feasible. Foreign exchange markets between national currency components of the single currency will close, because there will be no losses or profits to be made, and all large-value transactions will in any case already be in Euro. Banks will nevertheless have to convert sums between national currencies or between them and the Euro, and may charge a small fee for doing so if they are allowed to, see page 42. Bureaux de change will still be needed to change one country's national notes and coins into another's for travellers. The Euro will be a currency in its own right, but it will be a bank deposit currency only. There will also be bank deposits in national currencies, and all notes and coins will still be in national currencies.

Alarm has been expressed about the possibility of currency substitution during phase B.[18] What is to stop other countries changing all their money into D-marks if they become impatient waiting for the Euro? In theory, nothing. In some ways it would be cheaper and simpler to make the D-mark the single currency of EMU, but it would be politically unacceptable, even to the Germans. In practice a number of things would happen to bring the process to a halt. The ECB would seek to control monetary growth in the Euro currency area. If there was a big expansion in the supply of D-marks, which the Bundesbank would be obliged to meet, other national central banks would have to reduce the supply of their currencies. Banks would make conversion charges, and interest rates would diverge, with low rates on D-marks and high rates on other currencies. The cost of gambling against an outcome guaranteed by governments would become too high.

All through phases A and B, the mints and printing presses would be producing the huge supply of new coins and banknotes needed to re-place national currencies. It would not be particularly helpful to release them gradually, as the demand might outstrip the supply. Phase C, starting at the beginning of 2002 and lasting six months, would see the introduction of Euro notes and coins, and the withdrawal of national notes and coins. Phases A and B would have given banks, shops and other businesses, and public administrations, four years to prepare their systems for the use of the new currency by the general public. Phase C thus corresponds to what was originally thought to be stage three, the introduction of Euro notes and coins from the start. It will complete stage 3b of full use of the new currency, following the stage 3a of irrevocably fixed exchange rates now included in phase B.

In the UK, £20 billion of notes and coins will have to be replaced: 17.5 billion coins and 1.25 billion notes. About 20,000 cashpoint machines will have to be changed and innumerable slot machines and telephone coin boxes. The new notes and coins will go in a 1–2–5 sequence. We use c for a hundredth of a Euro (probably a cent), and E for Euro. The coins will be 1c, 2c, 5c, 10c, 20c, 50c, E1 and E2, all similar in value to the current British coinage, including the new £2 piece to be introduced in 1997. The notes will be E5, E10, E20, E50, E100, E200 and E500; the first four will be similar in value to the current Bank of England issue, and the three new higher-value notes will correspond to the kind of notes in use in some continental countries. (At the time of writing a Euro is worth 83p, so all the above amounts should be multiplied by 0.83; the exact conversion will not be known until some time in 1998.)

PLANNING A MEGA-PROJECT

This is a mega-project. Careful planning and popular involvement are essential to its success. A compromise has been reached, with more details being filled in all the time. On the one hand, it will take time to accustom people to the new currency and to carry out the reprogramming of bank computers and the printing and minting of notes and coins. On the other hand, a speedy operation and a clean break with the past will avoid the expense and confusion of a long period of dual running with two different currencies.

There are few precedents for the replacement of up to fifteen national currencies by a single new currency. The lack of popular support in some countries, and the indecision of governments in others, makes it more difficult than it needs to be. In an ideal world, governments would jointly decide some years ahead to introduce a new currency with popular support, and use the intervening time to educate businesses and the general public about the details.

Some countries and some banks and businesses are already taking a chance by investing management resources in the single currency. If it does happen in their country, they will enjoy a competitive advantage; if it does not, they will write off an investment that is still modest. Some governments are calling for a market-led approach, in other words expecting the private sector to take the initiative. Most private sector operators, however, are waiting for governments to give a lead. Money is a public utility, which functions more efficiently if it is part of a single network than if competing systems are set up, of which only one is in the end universally adopted.

If the UK does not decide whether to opt in until early 1998, British banks and businesses which play a waiting game will have barely a year in which to prepare for the single currency at the beginning of 1999. Their rivals in other countries likely to join will have spent the previous two years getting ready. If the Euro is going to be set up as the main currency of continental Europe, British banks and businesses will need to get ready for it anyway, as a major foreign currency, if not yet as the domestic currency. So there will be much to gain, and little to lose, if the private sector anticipates a government decision. To this extent, 'market-led' pressure could push the Government into making up its mind. Much of the planning will still depend on details in which official participation is essential.

Decimalization in the UK is a useful recent experience.[19] It was simpler than the move to the Euro, because the basic unit of currency, the pound, did not change, and only one currency was involved. Even so, it took almost five years from the announcement of decimal currency in March 1966 to the introduction of the new coins in February 1971. Not until the passage of the Decimal Currency Act in July 1967 was it certain that the pound and not ten shillings would be the basic unit, so the effective time for conversion was three and a half years. The two final years were used for intensive education and training for schools, businesses and the general public. The conversion from two units of coinage, the shilling and the penny, to one, the new penny, at fractional conversion rates, was tricky. The old units were soon forgotten, however, and there is no evidence that traders used the changeover to increase prices. At least the UK has a decimal currency, as all its EU partners do, so to that extent the move to a Euro with 100 subdivisions is easier.

Decimalization shows that fractional conversion rates have one advantage over changing the number of zeros. The old equivalents are not easy to convert back to mentally. When France adopted the new franc for 100 old francs in 1958, many French people continued for decades to think in terms of the old units, adding on a couple of 00s or taking them off. (France abandoned the LSD system at the time of the Revolution.) In 1994 Brazil successfully redenominated its currency at a rate of 2750 to 1.[20]

Experience of metrication in the UK shows the pitfalls of allowing both systems to continue side by side for too long. The retention of double counting in gallons, fahrenheit and feet and inches made it too easy for people to go on thinking in these measurements rather than discarding them and adjusting to litres, centigrade and metres. The final phasing out of the old measurements in shops in October 1995 came as a shock to many people at a late stage in the process of change.

The conversion to Euro will affect every aspect of daily life. The education campaign will be made more difficult because the value of the Euro in pounds will not be known until about a year before the UK enters the single currency. At present a Euro is worth about 83p, and a pound is worth about 1.20 Euros; the British are lucky in that their national currency unit is closer in value to the Euro than any other, and could even drop to a one-for-one parity, if the Government does not join at the first opportunity.

The basic amounts that people will have to convert include: prices in the shops, bulk purchase contracts, pay packets, tax and national insurance payments, insured values of contents and houses, bank statements, loan amounts, mortgage debts, and so on. Mortgages will be particularly complex. The principal of any mortgage loan repayable after 1 July 2002 will be redenominated in Euro. The interest rate should come down in percentage terms as inflation and real interest rates fall (see page 65). However, the principal repayment may be larger in terms of borrowers' salaries because it may not have been devalued so much by inflation. This effect will not be due specifically to the Euro; it would happen under any financial regime which reduced interest rates and inflation. A particular problem will arise where mortgage rates have been fixed beyond 2002, since they will not then fall; borrowers should already be taking care not to get caught.

There will not be such problems for most traded bonds, because the value of bonds in the secondary market goes up and down with supply and demand. When a bond goes up, the interest rate (called the yield) goes down, because it has been fixed as a percentage of the original par value. When a bond goes down, the yield goes up. So if gilt-edged sterling bonds are thought by the markets to be a better investment once they are converted into Euro, their market value will rise, but their interest yield will go down. Bond markets will thus be strongly influenced by whether national currencies are expected to enter the single currency. The main problem will be in the case of existing ecu bonds. Their value should also increase if they are converted into Euro bonds at 1-for-1, because the ecu has been weaker than the D-mark. But if they are still contractually based on the old basket ecu, it may weaken against the Euro. There will be work for the lawyers.

CHOOSING A NAME

The name of the new single currency has been an object-lesson in protracted national bickering. The Maastricht Treaty refers to it as the ecu, which is the name of the currency basket widely used in bond and banking markets. It was thus assumed that the ecu (an old French coin), would develop further during stage two, and become more widely used as training for the single currency, after becoming familiar as a common parallel currency. The ecu had several disadvantages. It fell out of favour in the financial markets when the 1992 and 1993 ERM crises resulted in its devaluation. It had no central bank of issue, no manifestation in the form of notes and coins, and no central bank to back it. It was an extra currency, not a substitute for existing national currencies, and thus an additional source of exchange rate instability rather than a way of eliminating it.

Germany insisted on a last-minute amendment to the Treaty, substituting ECU for ecu throughout, which had to be inserted on a correction slip. ECU is a description, not a name. It stands for European Currency Unit and leaves it open what the name of the unit should be. The Germans insisted against French opposition that the ECU should not be called the ecu. The ecu has gone down in value against the D-mark and is thus discredited in the eyes of the German population that has to be persuaded to accept the new currency as being as good as the D-mark. It also happens to sound rather like the German word for cow, *die Kuh*.

Dr Theo Waigel, the German Finance Minister, tried to placate the French by suggesting in 1992 that the ECU should be called the Franken, an old German as well as the current French currency.[21] This was quietly dropped when it turned out that the Spanish translation would have to be Franco. Mr Kenneth Clarke, the UK Chancellor of the Exchequer, suggested the florin, an alternative name for the Dutch guilder, and a pre-decimal British coin, and received the support of the *Financial Times*. Most existing names have translations in different European languages, so cannot be the same everywhere. Even the ecu translates into Italian as *lo scudo*, and into Portuguese as *o escudo*, which is, confusingly, the name of the existing currency.

The name Euro, adopted at the Madrid summit in December 1995, has the advantage that it is invariant across languages, and symbolizes the idea of Europe. (It is said to denote a kind of wallaby, but this might be a better image than that other Antipodean creature, the emu.) It was accepted as a lowest common denominator, to which no country has strong objections. If the word for each national currency is added, as proposed by Dr Klaus Haensch, the President of the European Parliament,[22] then once again it varies, and there could be a problem trying to use a Eurofranc note in Germany instead of a Euromark note, even if it were possible to tell whether it was a Belgian, French or Luxembourg Eurofranc. There is a similar problem in using Scottish banknotes in England, even though they are part of the same currency. One poll showed that people would prefer a different name for the new currency and would only be confused by the retention of the old name. The £1.5 billion Scottish banknotes, which are issued by the Scottish commercial banks, will presumably be phased out along with Bank of England notes, unless they are redenominated in Euro, and backed by ECB notes.

Different national symbols, if not national suffixes, could be used on notes and coins if it was thought important to gain popular accept-ability for the new currency. No doubt slang terms such as 'quid' will be switched from the national currency to the Euro. The monarch's head has always been on one side of British coins, but has appeared on Bank of England notes only since 1960. National heroes are commonly used on notes in most countries, but one can imagine British notes with the Duke of Wellington being accepted with dif-ficulty in France. The cost of repatriating Euro notes with national symbols back to the country of issue would reduce the transactions advantages of the new currency. To avoid this, they should be small enough not to affect the similarity and interchangeability of Euro notes and coins.

As Lord Lawson discovered when he was Chancellor of the Ex-chequer, 'the British are healthily conservative over coinage, objecting to almost any conceivable change'.[23] In April 1983, the pound coin was introduced for the first time. In Novenber 1984 Lawson announced the phasing out of the pound note, which 'led to the most tremendous outcry, including a campaign by the *Sun* newspaper which issued large numbers of lapel badges featuring a picture of my face and the legend: "Hands off our nickers" . . . the initial outcry proved to be a storm in a teacup; the pound note disappeared (except in Scotland).'[24] It should not be too difficult to design a new European currency superior to the British, in which notes of different values are so alike in colour that they are constantly confused. It will have to be introduced with con-siderable marketing skills against the worst that the *Sun* newspaper can do. The moral of Lord Lawson's tale is that new notes and coins generate short-term excitement which is soon forgotten.

EURO CONVERSION RATES

Another important point will be the exchange rates of existing national currencies against the new Euro. This is important both to start the new currency on a level playing field, where prices are at a reasonably competitive level across the European single market, without too drastic subsequent adjustments, and to effect an easy transition in the minds of business people and consumers. Stage two was meant to accustom people to stable values for their national currencies against the ecu, as they were locked into ever tighter bands, but now the ERM and the basket ecu are no longer essential features of the preparations for the Euro. National currencies can and do fluctuate within their 15 per cent bands, thus provoking fewer speculative attacks, and there is no longer a unique set of central conversion rates on which the system is converging.

The members of the single currency must, according to the Treaty, 'adopt the conversion rates at which their currencies shall be irrevocably fixed at which irrevocably fixed rate the ECU shall be substituted for these currencies, and the ECU will become a currency in its own right. This measure shall by itself not modify the external value of the ECU.'[25] The decision has to be unanimous by the EU Council at the beginning of the third stage. On examination this clause seems virtually unworkable as it stands. When it is decided in late 1997 or early 1998 which countries are to join the single currency, they will want to know at what exchange rate they will merge their national currencies into it. Phase A requires up to a year of advance preparation to set up the ECB and so on. Anything could happen to exchange rates during this year. Speculators could force the D-mark up, and make membership at an overvalued rate unattractive to Germany. So it would be better to fix exchange rates well in advance too.

It was assumed by the drafters of the Treaty that ERM exchange rates would converge on their central parities within the narrow 2.25 per cent bands, and that these would be the conversion rates for the ECU at the start of stage three. Financial markets have moved rates away from their central parities, and they could move even further away within the 15 per cent bands without any central parity changes. There is a choice about conversion rates. They could be market rates, central parities or a set of rates chosen by other criteria. There is an infinite set of available rates that satisfies the Treaty requirement of no change in the external value of the ecu; if some market rates are lowered, others then have to be raised to keep the external value the same.

I give an example in Table 17 of a set of conversion rates that would fulfil two requirements. First, currencies that had become misaligned by market movements could be realigned to achieve a better starting level of competitiveness in the single currency. Second, round-number conversion rates could be chosen so as to make the new Euro user-friendly, instead of the market rates to several places of decimals. The exact choice of rates would be made nearer the time of decision; some currencies may by then have been devalued. Once the new rates were announced, central banks would be committed to them, and financial markets could be expected to converge on them.

The table shows how the ecu basket is made up from fixed amounts of twelve national currencies, and how its value in terms of the dollar and the pound can be calculated. It then shows the market rate of each currency against the ecu itself, and the nearest rounded rate. The key rate is the proposed new D-mark rate of 2 to the Euro, which would popularly be known as the 'Doppelmark', or double mark, worth exactly twice as much as the Mark.[26] The pound, already closest in value to the ecu among the EMU currencies, would move to an easy rate of 80p to the Euro, or £1.25 to the pound. It would be a good chance to re-establish parity between the British and Irish pounds during the transition period; they are currently only 2 per cent apart, but conversion charges take 5 per cent or more off the large number of travellers across the Irish Sea.

The rounded rates devalue the D-mark by 6 per cent and its other hard currency ERM associates by slightly less, thus correcting the overvaluation that has made German industry barely competitive. They revalue the pound and the lira upwards by 3–5 per cent, thus meeting the charge made by other countries of excessive competitive devaluation, although this has not been judged by the EU Commission to justify compensation measures, see page 49.

COSTS OF THE CONVERSION

The European Banking Federation and the British banking associations have put forward similar estimates of the costs of converting to the new currency, and the time taken.[27] The Federation has estimated 8–10 billion ecus (£6.4–8 billion), and the British associations £914 million. In both cases, this would be about 2 per cent of operating revenues over a three-year period; some of the continental banks believe that they would need four rather than three years. These costs are based on the (now abandoned) assumption that there would be a 'Big Bang' six months after the start of stage three, when both bank deposit money and notes and coins in the new currency would be introduced. Other assumptions, such as the more gradual approach of the Commission's Green Paper, would mean higher costs. However, the postponement of part of the cost well into stage three might mean that the net present value of the costs at the start of the process did not rise by much.

Table 18 gives some idea of the breakdown of UK costs both by function and by product, and of the pervasive nature of the conversion operation, stretching right through every banking activity. More is involved than simply giving all the software a 'global replace' command to substitute E for £, and convert the numbers by 1.25 or whatever the factor is. The cost of changing IT systems is estimated at £436m, nearly half the total, but every other function is affected too.

Costs in non-banking corporations will generally not be as high as in banks. There has been less systematic study of what they will be. Long-term insurance and pension funds will be particularly affected, because many of their assets and liabilities will mature after 1999, in other words in Euro and not in pounds. The legal basis for the change in the currency in which their long-term contracts are expressed will have to be carefully thought out.

The costs of conversion for whole economies will be much higher than those for the banks. The rest of the private sector, and the public sector, will each have costs to bear. To the internal costs must be added the costs of educating schoolchildren and the public generally. Governments may be persuaded to meet some of the costs, particularly for training in small and medium enterprises, and special courses in the education sector. It would be surprising if the total cost came to less than 0.35 per cent of GDP, spread over three years, say 0.15 per cent, or about £800 million a year. This would be the same as the transactions costs savings in only one year from abolishing exchange rates, see page 39, which would be permanent, while the transition costs would drop away. The macroeconomic benefits would be much higher, though harder to measure.

Denmark has the same status as a state with a derogation, while the UK has a status all on its own. What we say about states with a derogation therefore applies to Denmark, but not to the UK. All non-participants continue to try to meet the convergence criteria, as in stage two, except that Denmark and the UK will be doing so for their own sake, unless and until they opt to join the single currency.

The states with a derogation and Denmark will have to accept the stage three obligation to avoid excessive deficits under article 104c1, while the UK will still only have the stage two duty to 'endeavour' to avoid excessive deficits under article 109e4. Both the countries with a derogation and the UK will be subject to the peer group pressure of the excessive deficits procedure already being followed in stage two under article 104c, but they will both escape the stage three provisions for timed deficit reduction programmes imposed by the Council and the accompanying sanctions under paragraphs 9 and 11 of that article.

Both the states with a derogation and the UK will abstain from the key monetary provisions of stage three linked with the establishment of a single monetary policy and a single currency by the ECB. The Treaty provides for a General Council of the ECB, in which central bank governors from EU countries outside the single currency take part. They become members of the General Council, but not of the Governing Council. The General Council is excluded from all the major monetary policy decisions to be taken by the Governing Council.

All non-participants, including the UK, will be in the invidious position of having to go on trying to meet the convergence criteria, including exchange rate stability, without having any say in the management of the single currency or its monetary policy. Countries which do not join the single currency will thus be excluded from decisions which might have a profound effect on their economies.

It is understandable if some of these countries, such as Italy, wish to delay the whole project until they are ready, so as to avoid second-class status for an indefinite period. If a country such as the UK already fulfils the convergence criteria, there will be more to lose by staying out than by going into the single currency. As over half British exports go to other EU members, Britain has a vital interest in arguing from the inside for well-balanced anti-inflationary growth policies among its trading partners so as to enlarge the size of their markets for its exports. Membership of the ECOFIN ministerial council gives the UK a say in economic policy, but it will be excluded from a say in monetary policy if it does not join the single currency. Since economic and monetary policy are closely linked, a half-in, half-out status for the UK would be anomalous and, in the long run, untenable.

The ECB and the Monetary Committee will in any case have to work out exchange rate arrangements for those EU members who will not or cannot join the single currency at the beginning of stage three. The importance of such arrangements was underlined in the June 1995 meeting between Mr John Major, the British Prime Minister, and President Chirac of France. Following this, the EU Commission made an interim report to the Madrid summit, which called for full reports by the Commission and the EMI.[2]

France and the UK have opposite reasons for wanting to study the matter. France is one of the countries most concerned at the potential disruption to trade and investment from 'competitive devaluation' by countries outside the single currency, especially those not in the ERM (see page 47). The UK is worried by the danger that the single currency will split the single market and leave EU members outside it isolated, and by the difficulty of running EU institutions designed for one Community to meet the needs of an inner and an outer group. France tends to focus more on exchange rate arrangements, while the UK's concerns range rather more widely. The UK believed at the end of 1995 that only a minority of countries would enter the single currency, leaving a big problem for the majority outside; this was some progress from its earlier view that hardly any country would be ready. The arithmetic of convergence (see chapter 7) indicates that the single currency countries may be in the majority, which would put pressure on the UK to join it. Otherwise, the UK could find itself in a second tier consisting of a minority of existing EU members, in a group soon to consist mainly of new members from southern, central and eastern Europe.

M. Yves-Thibault de Silguy, the member of the Commission dealing with EMU, has proposed a 'stability pact' between the ins and the outs to prevent disruptive exchange rate changes.[3] Its details can be expected to emerge in the final version of the Commission's report. Meanwhile, Mr Major raised so many questions about the relationship between the two groups of countries that he appeared to be trying to delay the single currency altogether to avoid having to answer them, while denying that this was his motive. It was not so much the substance of Mr Major's questions that worried the other European leaders, as the negative stance which seemed to inspire them.

Mr Major put his questions as follows:[4]

We need to consider how having some countries in a single currency and others outside it would affect the way the Community takes decisions. What would stop the members of a single currency voting en bloc against the interests of other members? . . . And how would those outside a single currency protect their interests?

We also need to recognize the possible tensions in containing the Community Budget. What if some of the less competitive regions within a single currency demand further aid to cope with the loss of jobs they may suffer? What if the weaker countries outside demand ever higher pay-outs from the Community to help to develop their economies to join a single currency?

The strongest advocates of a single currency see it as a step towards closer economic and political integration. So what if those inside the single currency decide to speed up the process from the start? What signal would that send to countries outside the initial single currency block – including new members from the young democracies of Eastern Europe?

What does this mean for Europe's greatest success, the Single Market? If only a small group of countries join a single currency, they may fear the consequences of those outside devaluing their currencies to gain competitive advantage. That fear could lead to protectionist measures which damage free trade. It would be folly if the drive to a single currency served only to destroy the Single Market.

His concerns attracted a terse response at Madrid from the French Minister for Europe, M. Michel Barnier: 'If Britain is worried about the ins and outs it should be in.'[5]

A NEW LOOK FOR THE ERM

The Commission's interim report to the Madrid summit makes out the case for using the ERM to stabilize exchange rates between single currency countries and the non-participants. Article 109m says that the exchange rate policy of each state is a matter of common interest, and article 109j defines the convergence criterion of exchange rate stability in terms of ERM membership (see page 135). However, the report leaves open the possibility of an alternative exchange rate arrangement, which it defines as follows:

1. It should provide a framework for non-participating countries to prepare for entry into the single currency, including new members who have not yet entered even stage one of EMU.
2. It should not disturb financial markets or interfere with the ECB's single monetary policy, since this is designed to bring price stability to non-members as well as to members of the single currency.
3. It should have an institutional framework designed to provide exchange rate stabilization policies and the pursuit of other convergence criteria, so that it is credible and sustainable in the financial markets.
4. It should be managed as part of the European Community, because the single currency would be at the centre of the arrangement, and the Community is already coordinating economic policy through ECOFIN.

The Treaty leaves it open what kind of exchange rate arrangement non-members of the single currency should have. The ERM will not be able to go on as an unchanged currency basket, because some of the currencies in the basket will have merged into the single currency. In theory, the basket ecu could continue. 'The currency composition of the ecu basket shall not be changed,' the Treaty says,[6] but the Euro would necessarily have to be substituted for the currencies merging into it if it were to survive the beginning of stage three.

Right from the outset in 1979, the role of the basket ecu in the ERM did not work out as intended. Intervention has always been judged on the basis of the bilateral grid of parity limits of national currencies against each other, and not on the basis of the divergence indicator against the ecu.

The Euro would increase the continuing dominance of strong against weak currencies in the basket as their relative value rose. The D-mark is one-third of the total; the Dutch guilder has a greater weight than the pound; and the Belgian franc a greater weight than the lira! The weight of the seven 'hard core' currencies most likely to join the single currency is 75 per cent of the basket. This would be unsatisfactory. The basket is in any case already out of date. The weights of the existing currencies can no longer be changed; it was not enlarged to include the currencies of Austria, Finland and Sweden when they joined the EU on 1 January 1995, and it will not include the currencies of future EU members.

After the two major crises in the ERM in 1992 and 1993, it is hard to see a new version of it regaining much credibility in financial markets. The difficulties of the ERM show that it would be better for as many currencies as possible to join the single currency from the outset than to try to enter a damaged vehicle with loose steering for a long-distance rally over difficult terrain. It has survived thanks to the adoption of 15 per cent bands, but those countries aiming at exchange rate stability have tried to remain well within those bands. While flexibility is needed, some rather stronger requirement for stability needs to be incorporated.

For countries with higher than average inflation rates seeking convergence, such as new members from central Europe, some kind of real exchange rate convergence, such as that proposed by John Williamson in his 'Proto-emu' proposal, might be appropriate.[7] Countries would then be allowed to devalue their currencies within the system in line with relative rises in prices or unit labour costs in order to retain constant competitiveness.

BETTER A PEG THAN A BASKET

A new version of the ERM is possible, where the Euro would take the place of the ecu in the existing ERM, and non-member currencies would be pegged to it at fixed but adjustable rates within bands of 15 per cent. It will be easier for non-members to peg their currencies to the single currency itself, rather than to a basket diluted by the addition of currencies that are by definition weaker (because they are too weak to join the Euro). If satellite currencies are pegged to a central currency, their exchange rates can vary against each other by twice as much as each can vary against the central currency. So if non-members had to limit their fluctuations against each other to 15 per cent bands as required by the convergence criteria, they would have to peg to the Euro with 7.5 per cent bands.

If non-member countries make good progress in meeting convergence targets for inflation, long-term interest rates and budget deficits, they should be able to remain within their bands against the Euro without devaluing. To make the arrangement credible, there would have to be mutual commitments from both the non-members and the ECB to defend the parity limits as long as convergence was continuing. Devaluations would not be excluded, and have indeed already been required during stage two by some of the likely non-members, but they would be kept in reserve for exceptional circumstances.

One alternative would be to have a more flexible code of conduct governing exchange rate relations, rather than continuing the ERM. 'This would establish principles according to which the exchange rate policies of both the upper and lower tiers would be conducted and a framework of rules setting target zones for exchange rates or permissible degrees of exchange rate movement in a given period.'[8]

Such solutions would not necessarily apply to countries which did not want to become members of the single currency at any particular date, even if they continued to retain the right to opt into it in some distant future. Each of these countries is a special case. Denmark has remained within the ERM in spite of not wanting to join the single currency, and would no doubt stay within any new ERM; it would be the only country in the new ERM which had passed the convergence criteria, and might see little to lose in joining the single currency after all, rather than being grouped with weaker countries in the new ERM.

The UK case is different. Britain has not rejoined the ERM so far, even though it may need to do so to qualify to opt in to the single currency (see page 136). If it decides not to opt in to the single currency, rejoining the ERM just to stabilize the pound against the Euro will become even less attractive. The pound might in practice remain within wide bands around a notional central parity. But there would be no reason for the ECB to take on a commitment to defend the pound, even if the UK had passed all the other convergence criteria. The pound might be subject to damaging speculation outside the single currency, particularly if it was the only major European currency in that position, after speculation between other currencies merging into the Euro had to end as they were phased out of existence.

Lack of exchange rate discipline between members and non-members of the Euro would damage the European single market in many ways. Even those who do not accept that one market needs one money may come to see that many monies moving in different directions can lead to many markets. Opting out of the single currency is a form of Europe à la carte. It offends against the principle that members of the EU should obey all its rules and not only the ones that suit them. A 'two-speed' concept is quite different, because it implies that the members that have been left behind are committed to catching up as soon as they can.

The UK opt-out is the most extreme form of the 'free rider' problem posed by the two-tier approach to the single currency. The countries setting up the Euro will have paid the convergence costs of reaping the benefits of a stable currency area over a large part of the EU; non-member countries will also get some of the benefits, particularly if they succeed in pegging their exchange rates to the Euro, but without paying the full costs. UK companies with operations in the Euro currency area will be able to trade and invest in it as a true single market, without their own government joining it. Even if the UK is not in the end better off than the others, their inveterate suspicions of Britain as a 'Trojan horse' will fuel political divisions, when the single currency, if it has a political dimension, ought to be knitting the EU closer together.

It is quixotic of the British Government in these circumstances to accuse the other countries, perhaps a majority of them, of dividing Europe, when it is the possibility of an opt-out by the UK that will have precisely that effect. The high priority which the British Government puts on the enlargement of the EU should make it all the more important to avoid chaotic currency relationships over an even wider area extending into central and eastern Europe.

NON-EUROPEAN UNION COUNTRIES AND THE SINGLE CURRENCY

Of the four EFTA members which have decided against joining the EU, Switzerland is a case apart. It refused to join even the European Economic Area, as Iceland, Norway and Liechtenstein did.[9] Its geographical position in the EU is that of 'a hole with a mint in it'.[10] The Swiss franc will be a major international currency competing with the Euro. Swiss banks are the fifth biggest international lenders after those of Japan, Germany, France and the US (in that order!), see Table 20. Swiss foreign exchange market intervention has traditionally aimed to control the domestic money supply and not the exchange rate. The Swiss franc has shown strength against the D-mark when doubts have arisen over EMU, and may similarly be in demand as a safe haven currency from the Euro, as from the US dollar, at future periods of uncertainty. Swiss membership of the ERM is out of the question, and the most that can be expected is some kind of informal 'non-aggression pact' between the ECB and the National Bank of Switzerland.

Norway was associated with the European currency snake in the 1970s, but dropped out. Its krone is more of a 'petrocurrency' than any other in Europe. Oil and gas are a larger part of its national output than they are of the UK's. Norway would be sympathetic to any arrangement linking it with its Nordic neighbours; Norway and Iceland have asked to join them in a 'Schengen' type agreement for free movement of persons. In view of the uncertain prospects for the Swedish krona joining the ERM or the Euro, Norway is unlikely to make any move, and will wait for Sweden, even though Denmark may decide to opt in to the Euro before Sweden joins.

There is some way to go from EU to ERM membership or to full EMU and the single currency. Candidate members of the EU are not necessarily expected to join the ERM, or a recycled version of it, at the moment of EU entry. However, there is a question-mark over whether countries can join the EU without also signing up for EMU at some future date, since the Maastricht Treaty has become part of the Rome Treaty. The three new members who joined the EU in 1995 each took a different course.

Austria joined the ERM because it already had an informal currency link with the D-mark of many years' standing. Finland did not join the ERM, but announced that it would do so at a suitable time with a view to converging and entering full EMU. Sweden not only did not join the ERM, but made a declaration that it would reach a separate decision about EMU after several years, subject to parliamentary ratification. There is thus a range of different precedents. However, the EU Commission maintains that there can be no UK-style opt-outs from EMU for new EU members.[11]

There is some merit in the idea of an ecu zone (to be rechristened a Euro zone?) for central Europe, to provide the same kind of anti-inflation discipline as the ERM did in western Europe in the early 1980s.[12] Some countries may follow the example of Estonia's link with the D-mark, and adopt shock therapy to reduce inflation rapidly. Others may prefer either periodic devaluations against the Euro, or a crawling peg, but in such a way as to prevent their currencies from falling by as much as the full difference in inflation rates between themselves and the Euro area.[13] Since some other candidates see EU membership as a way of stabilizing their high-inflation currencies, they would hardly welcome being kept out of EMU. But they would need time to adapt to it, like their Western European counterparts.

The three stages of the Maastricht Treaty look like a suitable apprenticeship for the central European countries even more than for those who originally signed up to it. These countries have lower living standards than the poorest existing EU countries; that in itself is not a barrier to membership, if they are able to grow their economies fast enough eventually to close at least part of the gap. The legacy of Communism will still make it difficult for them to meet the convergence criteria for inflation and deficits, and to remain competitive within the single market they will be joining.

ERM membership, with capital controls, wide bands and adjustable exchange rates, should be seen as a prelude to the three stages of EMU for these countries. Stage one begins with freedom of capital movements, for which the Czech Republic (though not other candidates) may be ready. Stage two consists of convergence policies on inflation and budget deficits, and coordination of monetary and exchange rate policies. This would be the real test for new members. At the end of it they would hope to qualify to join the single currency as full members. ERM membership plus the three stages could well take ten years or so from the time of joining the EU, so they might not complete their entry into the single currency until 2010.

Some countries in central Europe have used the dollar rather than the D-mark as a currency peg, notably Poland, because dollar banknotes have been used there as currency for many years. The use of the Euro as a peg would more accurately reflect their trading patterns, as they do more trade with Europe than with the US. It would be a more logical preparation for full membership of the EU, and would represent a political as well as a commercial choice.

The Euro would become a currency magnet for a diverse set of former Communist countries. The Czech Republic, Hungary and Poland are likely to be the first to join the EU, by about 2002. The three Baltic republics will not be far behind, particularly now that Finland and Sweden have joined the EU. Bulgaria, Romania and

Slovakia may be about five years behind. The republics of former Yugoslavia should all be considered as long-run candidates for EU membership once lasting peace is restored to the area, with Slovenia ready sooner than the others. If economic integration is a way of avoiding wars, it is surely needed in the Balkans even more than in western Europe. There is little sense in having Greece as a member of the EU and not the countries between it and the rest of the area.

This bird's eye view of enlargement makes it clear that not just a two-speed but a multi-speed approach to both EU and EMU membership is needed; yet the eventual destination must be the same. If the UK insists on sitting out EMU and the single currency, this could be a disastrous signal to central and southern Europe for each country to go its own way and cherry-pick à la carte. Although the British Government wants enlargement, it is resisting the extension of qualified majority voting that will be needed if it is to be viable. 'A majority maintains that the enlarged union would appear to require the extension or even the generalization of the qualified majority, for reasons of efficiency, in order to prevent the paralysis of the enlarged union when taking decisions.'[14] Widening the Union, far from being an alternative to deepening it, requires deepening as a precondition of success.

Enlargement could be expensive for the higher-income countries already in the EU, with the first four central European entrants adding two-thirds to the existing EU Budget, on the now rather dated assumption that the existing criteria are applied unchanged and immediately to the new members.[15] Since most of the Budget is spent on agriculture and certainly would be so in central Europe under present criteria, Mr Franz Fischler, the EU Agriculture Commissioner, has declared that there can be no enlargement without a reform of the Common Agricultural Policy.[16] The EU cannot be expected to pay even a fraction of such a bill unless there is an economic, monetary and political pay-off. The countries of central Europe will not provide growing markets for Western European trade and investment unless they can be guided into the path of non-inflationary economic growth and fit into a stable political and security framework. A single currency could play a vital role in this process, even if the transition to it has to be gradual.

The former Soviet republics are another proposition. It was inevitable that the rouble area would break up when the political foundations of the Soviet Union crumbled (see page 83). It might be better to put the pieces of the rouble monetary area and the Soviet common market back together again than to attempt to integrate them into the EU. Otherwise, Ukraine and Belarus might be tempted to seek a link with the EU and leave Russia isolated. The idea of economic and monetary integration between Russia and the EU is even more far-fetched than such a link between the US and the EU. A line has to be drawn somewhere. Russia and the other former Soviet Republics might benefit more from following the example of western and central Europe than from seeking to join it.

THE EURO AS A WORLD CURRENCY

The Euro would become a major world currency, even more important than the D-mark is today. Its importance would depend on how many currencies joined it, particularly the British pound. The advantages are of three kinds. The first consists in seignorage gains and transactions cost savings of the kind that accrue inside the EU; the second in advantages to the European financial services industry in the international banking and bond markets; the third in monetary relationships with the other major currencies, the US dollar and the yen.

The dollar now enjoys the advantages of being a world currency. The Euro would to begin with do no more than take on the combined size of the D-mark and the other currencies joining it. It might then compete away some of the advantages of the dollar. It may do no more than accelerate the gradual trend of recent years away from the dominance of the dollar towards a multi-currency world, as the yen and the D-mark increase in importance.

One clear advantage is that of seignorage, see page 17. The more governments can finance their deficits by issuing banknotes, the less they have to pay in interest on bills and bonds. Two-thirds of all dollar banknotes are estimated to be held outside the US, or about $200 billion in mid-1993.[17] At bond rates of 6 per cent, this is a saving to the US Treasury of $12 billion a year. Euro banknotes held outside the EU might gradually build up to a similar level, far higher than that of the D-marks now in use in central Europe and the Balkans, some of which are issued locally and thus do not benefit the German public finances.

The Euro would become an attractive foreign currency in all non-member European countries. Its use in banknote form might be only marginally at the expense of the dollar. Currencies such as the French franc and the pound, no longer much used abroad in banknote form, would be able to share in this seignorage revenue by merging into the Euro. If $100 billion in Euro notes were held outside the single currency area, this would be worth $6 billion a year in interest saved at 6 per cent, of which about $1 billion (£650 million) might accrue to the UK.

The US has used the dollar more widely than this in order to finance continuing balance of payments deficits by issuing dollar bank deposits and securities to foreign governments and private sector holders. The EU has a balance of payments surplus at present on current account. Were this to swing into deficit because of a faster rate of economic growth, the Euro could be used to finance it, and at lower rates of interest than those that have to be paid by the individual currency components. Being able to borrow in your own domestic currency is a privilege granted to few countries; most have to borrow in dollars or currencies stronger than their own, thus incurring exchange rate as well as interest rate risk.

The Euro would be widely used as an invoicing currency for trade. Up-to-date figures on trade invoicing are lacking, but the general picture is clear.[18] The dollar is used to invoice about 90 per cent of US trade and a large part of world trade. It is used for about two-thirds of Japanese trade, for a large part of world trade in oil and primary commodities, and for much developing country trade. Other major countries use their own currencies to invoice their trade, more on the export than on the import side; these currencies, in order of the extent of their use, are the D-mark, the pound, the French franc and the lira. Their home countries use the dollar for their trade with the US and their commodity imports. They use each other's currencies for trade among themselves in the single European market; this would all be done in Euros.

The EU Commission estimates that about 10 per cent of EU trade might switch from being invoiced in dollars to being invoiced in Euro, i.e. domestic currency, leading to a fall in the dollar's share from about 20 to about 10 per cent.[19] This would save about 0.05 per cent of EU national income, $3.5 billion for the EU as a whole and £350 million for the UK alone. For the trade external to the EU, which goes on being invoiced in dollars, there will be a saving on the transactions costs on Euro/dollar foreign exchange deals compared with those on deals between the dollar and individual European currencies, see page 40.

This is an example of the additional cost savings on foreign exchange transactions, the great majority of which are unconnected with trade. At present, the US dollar is used on one side or the other of 83 per cent of all foreign exchange deals, giving it a 41.5 per cent share of the market, see Table 22. Transactions between most pairs of currencies, say French franc into Spanish peseta, go through the dollar, because the dealing costs for two currencies against the dollar are generally less than the costs of dealing between the two currencies direct. Once dealing costs between the Euro and each currency are no higher than those between the dollar and the same currencies, the dollar will drop out as a third-currency intermediary, over a period.

THE EURO IN WORLD FINANCE

The potential importance of the Euro as an international financial currency is shown in Table 20. If the component currencies are put together, it will account for a third of all international bank loans, compared with two-fifths for the dollar, and 15 per cent for the yen. The dollar is already less important as a domestic currency lent abroad out of New York than are the combined European currencies lent abroad from their home bases. It is the greater use of the dollar in euro-markets for loans out of one non-US country into another that gives it the edge at present. Growing use of the Euro in loans between non-European countries is likely eventually to raise its share to equal or surpass that of the dollar.

The Euro and the dollar each have a 3 percentage point higher share in the international bank deposit market than in the loan market, because of the lower share of the yen, with only 9 per cent. Again, it is eurodollar rather than domestic deposits which put the dollar ahead. The Euro may come to equal the dollar's share of deposits as its world role turns out to be more than that of the sum of its component currencies.

The reason for expecting the Euro to increase its share of the international bank lending market is that this market is already dominated by banks owned by EU countries. If all fifteen EU countries join the single currency, Euro banks by nationality of ownership will have half the world market, Japanese a quarter, American only a tenth. The American banks lost share heavily after their disastrous ventures into developing country lending, and their rediscovery of their home market. If the market in loans in Euros increases, the market in deposits in Euros will also rise, as banks fund their loans in a matching currency.

The Euro would also become a major currency in world bond markets, see Table 21. Its share of the international market would equal that of the US dollar at 37 per cent, three times the current share of the D-mark. The international market, which is used by corporate borrowers and minor governments, is only 11 per cent as big as all domestic bond markets, which are used by all governments as well as by corporates. Domestic bond markets are themselves heavily traded internationally. Here the size of the US Treasury market gives the dollar a 44 per cent share, compared with 32 per cent for the EU currencies and 20 per cent for the Japanese yen.

The US dollar still dominates as an official foreign exchange reserve currency with 63 per cent of the total, see Table 22. The D-mark is the runner-up with 16 per cent; this rises only to 22 per cent when other minor reserve currencies such as the pound and the franc are added to make up the future share of the Euro as a reserve currency. (The basket ecu is not strictly speaking a reserve currency, because it is held by EU countries only as part of a swap arrangement against reserves in dollars and other currencies.) The Euro would be held as a reserve currency not by EU countries – domestic currency cannot be a foreign exchange reserve – but by other countries seeking to diversify out of dollars. Over time, the shares of the dollar and the Euro might each come to be over one-third of the total, with the yen's share rising to one-fifth.

In the London foreign exchange market, deals between the EU currencies, and thus the Euro, and the US dollar are just over half of total turnover, see Table 3; the leading 22 per cent share of DM/dollar business is twice that of £/dollar business. But intra-EU deals now accounting for 12 per cent of the London market turnover would disappear from the market, so the share of deals with the Euro on one side could rise to nearly three-fifths. However, some of the present business between European currencies and the dollar masks triangular trades between pairs of European currencies going through the dollar (see page 40), so the turnover between the Euro and the dollar might after all remain at about half.

The share of EU currencies in the world market as a whole is smaller than in the London market, see Table 22. That of the Euro would be 35 per cent, in other words 70 per cent of all currency deals would have the Euro on one side. The share of the Euro would drop because deals with EU currencies on both sides would cease, but the share of the dollar would also drop, because it would no longer be used as an intermediary between EU currencies. These two effects might roughly cancel out and leave the shares unchanged in a smaller total market.

The pound has lost importance as the London foreign exchange market has gained it. The pound and UK-owned banks account for only about 5 per cent of the international banking market, compared with three times that much for the D-mark and German banks. The same figures apply to the respective shares of the pound and the D-mark in foreign exchange dealings. The UK domestic bond market, mainly government gilt-edged stocks, is only just over 2 per cent of the world market; the eurosterling international bond market, used mainly by British corporate borrowers, is 7 per cent. The Swiss franc is level pegging with the pound as an international banking currency, but the pound is still ahead of the Swiss franc in bond markets. The pound would be dwarfed by the Euro, where it is now well behind the D-mark, and comparable in size of markets with the French franc and the lira.

The existing basket ecu has marked time since the 1992 ERM crisis. It accounts for 3 per cent of the international banking market, and 4.5 per cent of the international bond market. While the ecu has pioneered the way for the Euro, the importance of the Euro is that it will replace the national currencies of Europe as well as the ecu.

THE ROLE OF THE CITY OF LONDON

The single currency is of vital importance to financial services and to investment income, where the City of London has a comparative advantage. The City would have a better chance of playing a leading role in the new Euro markets if the pound was part of the Euro. Business lost in the foreign exchange market could be regained in the Euro money market covering the whole single currency area, which would replace the intra-European foreign exchange markets as the conduit for the flow of funds around Europe. The City will be missing a great opportunity if the UK does not join the single currency because much financial and investment business using the single currency may migrate to its home territory on the Continent. The City can hope for only a limited share of this market if it remains offshore.

The Euro will dwarf the pound, and even the D-mark, and rival the dollar as a world currency, see Table 23, which sums up the findings of Tables 20–22. By comparison with shares of GDP, the Euro will punch about equal to its weight, where the pound punches below its weight, and the dollar well above. The US and the EU have roughly equal shares of industrial country GDP at 36–7 per cent, but the dollar share of many markets is higher. The Euro's share of markets is likely to increase if the City joins the single currency and uses its global presence to win share from the dollar.

The City is the leading international financial centre in Europe, but so far has never managed to oust Frankfurt, Paris and other European centres from their well-protected domestic patches. City bankers differ on whether to give priority to pushing the City in Europe's new and barely open single financial services market, or to exploiting their traditional advantages in the fast-expanding rest of the world.

The City, like island Britain, has in the past benefited from being off-shore. Self-regulation, the English language, the time-zone straddling New York and Tokyo, and the clusters of interacting financial specialists have attracted banks from the US, Japan and continental Europe to come and set up international operations that would fall foul of domestic regulation back home.

Most of the City's market now belongs to foreign banks, and British customers for its services are in a minority. It creates 800,000 jobs. The financial and business services sector of which it is the hub accounts for 22 per cent of Britain's gross domestic product. Ever since the City got going again after the Second World War, its prosperity has been independent of the fluctuating pound sterling and the arthritic British industrial sector. By the same argument, many in the City maintain that it can continue to do well whether or not Britain and the pound opt in to the single European currency.

As Stanislas Yassukovich, Chairman of the City Research Project, says: 'What is the relevance of the currency of the realm to the success of an international financial centre? In my opinion, there is virtually none.'[20] He is contradicted by Sir Nicholas Goodison, a former Chairman of the Stock Exchange and then Chairman of the TSB bank: 'It will do us no commercial or financial good to be left out.'[21] The Bank of England, as can be expected, sits on the fence. Alastair Clark, a Deputy Director, says: 'The Single Market programme has brought real and important gains, which will continue and grow irrespective of whether or when the UK joins a monetary union.'[22]

The City is in any case having a hard time coming to terms with Brussels regulations designed to create a level playing field for financial services, on top of the already costly new structure of self-regulation set up in 1986 by the Financial Services Act as a result of the Big Bang on the London Stock Exchange. The securities firms in the City are particularly restive at capital adequacy regulations designed to suit German universal banks which do banking and securities off a single capital base. The single monetary policy that goes inescapably with the single currency will require harmonization in money markets, including a uniform system for bank reserves, and the end of many features peculiar to the City, such as the discount houses' monopoly of money market operations with the Bank of England (see page 79).

The importance of the single currency to the City will vary by market sector. The City is number one in the world in foreign exchange, with a market share of 30 per cent in April 1995 compared with 27 per cent in April 1992. New York has 16 per cent, Tokyo 10 per cent, Singapore 7 per cent, and Hong Kong and Zurich 6 per cent each. Of the continental markets, Frankfurt has only 5 per cent and Paris 4 per cent, see Table 22.

Equity markets will still remain nationally based for a time, because of differences in corporate accounting, even when all shares are quoted in the single currency. A Europe-wide stock exchange will need some harmonization of accounting standards. London has claimed 64 per cent of all cross-border stock exchange dealings; this will increase if the UK joins the single currency, and fall if it does not. In the longer run, London should be able to build on its lead in international equity dealing to dominate the European single currency-based stock market once the accountants and the regulators can agree on common standards.

Bond markets are already dominated by London in the corporate eurobond sector, and City banks arrange 75 per cent of all eurobond issues. The big change will come in European domestic government bond markets. Once they all switch to the single currency, spreads will be based only on credit and not on currency risk, and will narrow dramatically, so that British and German bonds, for example, become closer substitutes. The single currency will account for 32 per cent of all domestic bonds and 37 per cent of all international bonds, and many of these will be issued and traded in the City. It is hard to see the City getting a big share of the pan-European bond market if Britain opts out of the single currency, in spite of the hopes of LIFFE (London International Financial Futures and Options Exchange), the main City derivatives market now leading in German bund contracts.

Success in the European financial market has been elusive for the UK; continental banks from Germany and Switzerland have done better in London than their British counterparts have in Frankfurt and Zurich. Deutsche Bank has taken over Morgan Grenfell, and Swiss Bank Corporation, S. G. Warburg. If the City increases its market share in Europe, albeit through continental-owned banks operating out of London, this need not prevent it continuing to exploit its comparative advantage in other parts of the world.

More of the 50 per cent of all international bank lending done by banks of EU national ownership may become concentrated in the City, which is now the leading international banking centre in the world, with 16 per cent of total bank loans. City banks also lead the world in mergers and acquisitions (50 per cent of the total) and institutional fund management (81 per cent).[23]

The City's à la carte approach looks doomed to failure. Either Britain will have to come into the single currency and try to get the kind of monetary policy operation that suits the UK banks, or the City will find itself effectively shut out of the single market in financial services, to the benefit of Frankfurt and Paris, which are trying to win market share from London.

Optimists argue against this that the City will continue to provide offshore markets for financial instruments in the single currency with greater efficiency and less regulation than the onshore centres. The City would like to play the part that New York plays in the US system, with the Bank of England as the Federal Reserve Bank of New York acting in the financial markets as the operating arm of the central bank headquarters in Frankfurt or Washington. To make the analogy exact, the City would have to be within the single currency area, however.

EXCHANGE RATES STILL A GOVERNMENT PRESERVE

National governments will retain one important power in EMU, through their membership of the ECOFIN Council, and that is to decide exchange rate policy between the single currency and other currencies such as the dollar and the yen.[24] This is a power which governments, including the German Government, all have at present, even when their central banks are independent. It is possible that there will be no exchange-rate policy, and that the Euro will float freely against the dollar and the yen in a manner determined by the independent interest-rate policies of the world's three main monetary areas. However, the size of the EMU will make it more feasible than it is even for Germany at present to manage floating currencies by coordinating interest rates, or even to return to target zones as in the 1987 Louvre Agreement.[25]

Many commentators have looked forward to a tripolar world, in which the dollar, the yen and the Euro would be the three major currencies, each supreme in its own vertical third of the world, and coexisting in an orderly and stable relationship. The Maastricht Treaty leaves this possibility no more than open.[26] It provides for an exchange-rate system linking the Euro to other non-EU currencies, and for the adoption, adjustment or even abandonment of the central rates within this system. In the absence of such a system 'general orientations' can be formulated for exchange-rate policy.

The ECOFIN Council decides on exchange-rate policy, acting on recommendations from either the Commission or the ECB, but as a sop to the ECB the primary objective of price stability is to be maintained. The ECB's job is to conduct foreign-exchange operations and to hold and manage the official foreign reserves of the Member States.[27] This corresponds to the existing division of labour in many European countries, by which the central bank is responsible for monetary policy and the finance ministry for exchange-rate policy. There is an unresolved potential conflict between domestic monetary policy, aimed at stable prices, and international monetary policy, aimed at stable exchange rates.

If the ECB intervenes in the markets to keep the Euro's exchange rate from rising against the dollar, it has to sell Euros and buy dollars. This increases the Euro money supply, lowers Euro interest rates, and may lead to inflation. If it does not intervene, the Euro rises against the dollar, and prices and exports fall in Europe, which may lead to deflation. If the ECB intervenes to keep the Euro's exchange rate from falling against the dollar, it has to sell dollar reserves and buy Euros, causing a cut in the Euro money supply and a rise in Euro interest rates, which may lead to deflation. If it does not intervene, the Euro falls against the dollar, and prices and exports rise, which may lead to inflation. It looks like a case of 'damned if you do, and damned if you don't'.

If ECB interest rates are too high against dollar and yen rates, single currency members could become uncompetitive against the rest of the world, and low inflation would be at the cost of higher unemployment. If ECB interest rates are too low, single currency members could have an export-led boom and a rise in primary import prices which could raise the inflation rate. Exchange-rate policy is too important to be ignored. The Economic and Financial Committee of ECOFIN, which will be the main forum for discussion of external exchange rates, can be expected to cooperate closely with the ECB and heed its advice.

In an area as large as the EU, domestic price stability must be the first objective. The exchange rate against the dollar and the yen has less effect on prices and foreign trade than it does for any individual EU country. Only 36 per cent of EU trade – 8 per cent of EU GDP – is done with the rest of the world outside the EU. This does not mean that the EU should follow the example of the US and follow a policy of 'benign neglect' of the Euro's exchange rate. The idea of target zones for world exchange rates was raised at the time of the 1987 Louvre Agreement and pursued with mixed results. It was revived by the Bretton Woods Commission on the 50th anniversary of the IMF in 1994.[28] If it is to work, it needs policy coordination not just on exchange rates but also on interest rates and budget deficits, as provided for in the Maastricht Treaty.

World trade and economic growth would benefit from stable exchange rates. They would benefit even more from a single world currency, but this is a long way off. The formation of a single European currency is as much as can be managed for the time being. If it is successful, the experiment could be broadened. In the meantime, it is better to search for a stable set of exchange-rate linkages than to write off international monetary cooperation as impossible. At least the formation of a European currency will protect Europe against some of the fall-out from world currency turbulence. As Prime Minister Mahathir of Malaysia says: 'When elephants fight, it is the grass that gets trampled.'

Europe's currency orientation is bound to pay more attention to the dollar than to the yen. The dollar and not the yen is the main currency in world finance. The dollar and not the yen is undervalued to the point where US exports, and those of Far East countries linked to the dollar, sell at prices which seem to many Europeans unfairly competitive.

The Euro is nevertheless likely to be torn between the dollar and the yen. When the dollar is weak, the yen is strong, so the Euro could be rising against the dollar but falling against the yen. European exchange-rate policy may thus be to seek a sustainable rate against the dollar – one Euro to the dollar would be a simple benchmark, compared with one Euro to about 80 US cents at present – but not go all the way with the dollar when it moves against the yen.

From the point of view of a single country such as the UK, entry into a world currency such as the Euro makes it possible to have more influence over world exchange rates and monetary policies than as a middle-ranking power with declining international financial influence. The pooling of official reserves has for many years been one of the key points of monetary union schemes. Jean Monnet proposed a European Bank and Reserve Fund, pooling a part of national reserves, in 1958. It was endorsed by the European Heads of Government in 1972.[29] It is a good example of how sovereignty can be more effective shared than exercised separately. The UK reserves were inadequate to deal with a crisis such as the attack which forced the pound out of the ERM in September 1992. They could be better used as part of a bigger reserve pool by the European Central Bank than by the Bank of England spitting into the wind on its own.

Short of world monetary union, the best way forward for the EU would be to seek policy coordination with the US and Japan that would be wider in scope than exchange-rate stability. The first aim should be to persuade the US and Japan to accept the Maastricht criteria for fiscal deficits as a permanent long-run objective, which is in fact in line with what they are doing anyway for domestic reasons. (In 1994 the US, in recovery, had a general government deficit of 2 per cent; Japan, in recession, 3.5 per cent.) This would guarantee low long-term interest rates. EMU's efforts to lower its high real interest rates by reducing government deficits will be even more successful if the other major currency blocs are following the same policy.

9
The Economic and Political Case for UK Membership

THE CASE FOR THE SINGLE CURRENCY

A frequent conclusion of objective economic studies is that there are strong arguments for and against the single currency, which are finely balanced, with not much to choose between them. The arguments tip more clearly in favour of membership for a 'hard core' of continental countries than for the UK, but even in the case of the UK they seem to point towards membership on certain conditions and when the time is right – not necessarily at the same time as the start by the 'hard core'. A good example is the recent Chatham House study by Christopher Taylor, the former European Adviser to the Bank of England:

On these assessments, the fundamental economic case for this country's joining EMU seems tentatively favourable. Provided the UK economy has converged securely in real terms, and strong doubts remain about an independently run monetary policy, the macroeconomic arguments point on balance to joining.[1]

A stronger conclusion was reached by the Action Centre for Europe working group under the chairmanship of Lord Kingsdown, a former Governor of the Bank of England:

The balance of the evidence and of the arguments which we heard seems to weigh clearly in favour of the case for British participation in Economic and Monetary Union in Europe.[2]

On the evidence of this book, the balance of argument is more heavily in favour of the single currency, and of Britain's joining it, than has so far been generally acknowledged. Enthusiasts for British entry often argue for it on political grounds and take the economic arguments from experts who do not always share their enthusiasm. The economic case in favour is put forward by sane, objective, methodical analysts, who are anxious to protect their professional reputations by acknowledging the case against as well. Both the political and economic case against British entry into the single currency, or further involvement of any kind in the European Union, are generally put by dedicated Eurosceptics, who use facts and figures selectively to support their gut feelings.

The economic case for entry into the single currency will not be widely heard, much less accepted by public opinion, if it is not put forward with as much crusading zeal as the case against. If the analysis of the preceding chapters is accepted, the economic case for going in is clear. It now needs to be put forward robustly, without too many ifs and buts, and without harping on how much there is to be said on the other side.

There is no certainty in economics, whether about the past, the present, or the future. It would be as absurd to claim that the case for entry into the single currency is certain as to claim that the case against is certain. In these circumstances it can be tempting to stay with the devil you know rather than the devil you don't. Yet the British economy is already past the peak of a slow and weak recovery, unnoticed by the majority of home-owners, consumers and voters. There is increasing disillusion with the status quo.

The argument against radical policy changes is that they involve unmeasurable risks for the sake of unquantifiable benefits. A typical British attitude was that put by Mr Malcolm Rifkind, the Foreign Secretary, after the Madrid summit. He said that the burden of proof should be on those who wanted to join the single currency, to justify giving up more national sovereignty.[3] However, the British economy looks as if it could benefit from a number of policy improvements, if the stop–go pattern of recession and recovery is to be converted into steadier, higher, longer-run growth.

New Labour is probably sensible in not offering the radical policy changes which lost its predecessors the last three general elections. Entry into the ERM was a radical policy change forced upon Mrs Thatcher by those who soon succeeded her. Its failure could have been avoided, had her advice been taken, see page 3. Its main lesson is that the old-style ERM was not such a good introduction to the single currency as had been hoped.

Entry into the single currency offers the next British Government the chance to make a successful radical change of economic policy. The

general election has to be held by May 1997. The decision whether to
opt in may have to be taken within nine months of that date. One
appeal of the single currency is that it provides a framework into which
so many other policies, more widely agreed than it is, can be pursued
with a greater chance of success than at present. They include increased
trade in goods and services, lower interest rates, including mortgage
rates, faster economic growth, falling unemployment, lower inflation,
sustainable public finances, and greater bargaining power in the world
economy. For the Labour Party, they also include social policy improvements by acceptance of the Social Chapter of the Maastricht
Treaty.

One aspect of the economic case difficult for some British officials
and politicians to accept is that its success depends on closer cooperation with their continental counterparts, and on closer integration of
the UK economy and economic policy with those of our EU partners. It was a right-of-centre American academic, James Buchanan,
who invented the 'public choice' theory to explain why people
always want to hang on to and benefit from the power they have in
government.[4] To those in power, it often seems preferable to pursue a
'Britain first' policy, even if it may be second best. A first best policy
may be shunned because it means pooling power and accepting
others' influence on UK policy in return for British influence on
their policy.

The opt-out has jeopardized the UK's chances of successful pooling
of economic policy, because it has raised wider questions about how
committed the UK is to EU economic policies ranging wider than the
single currency itself. British officials in the European Commission are
not as numerous, influential or supportive of its policies as their counterparts, particularly the French. Bank of England officials have played
a full part in preparing for the single monetary policy at the European Monetary Institute, but it remains to be seen how much influence
they can have if it is assumed that the UK will not join the European
Central Bank (opening up in 1998) as a full member.

As soon as the UK notifies the EU that it does not intend to enter
the third stage of EMU, it loses its 'right to participate in the appoint-
ment of the President, the Vice-President and other members of the
Executive Board of the European Central Bank'.[5] Even if the UK were
to change its mind and join later, a commitment not to opt in until

2002 or later would amount to a loss of voting powers at a crucial time.

We have shown (see page 43) that it pays a relatively small country to join a relatively large monetary area once it exists – whether or not it was a good idea in the first place. Members of the single currency will get advantages from which the UK is excluded. Worse still, once the UK is outside, it will be far more advantageous to the UK to join the single currency countries than for them to admit the UK, because the merger would give them access to a much smaller extension of their monetary area than the UK would get by joining them. In theory, the door should be open to the UK, but entry would have to be negotiated, possibly on worse terms than if the UK joined at the outset.

THE ECONOMIC ARGUMENTS

The strongest of all the economic arguments is that real interest rates under a single currency could fall from 4 per cent to 3 per cent, and nominal rates from 6.5 per cent to 4.5 per cent as inflation falls from 2.5 to 1.5 per cent. For British business, this would mean cheaper finance and more capital investment; for the British householder, it would mean lower prices in the shops, cheaper mortgages – and at fixed rates – and a revival of house prices. It would raise the UK's potential rate of economic growth from 2.5 per cent to 2.75 or possibly even 3 per cent, and the actual rate of growth would be higher as spare capacity is brought into use.

Faster economic growth would create more jobs, both in manufacturing and in services, and reduce unemployment on a permanent basis. It should be possible to reduce unemployment from just over 8 per cent to about 6 per cent. This cannot be done on present policies before entry into the single currency. The sooner Britain joins, the better the news for the over two million unemployed.

Table 24 brings together the rough estimates from various parts of the book into a hypothetical profit and loss account for the single currency's effect on the UK economy. Transactions costs savings and seignorage from the new currency come to 0.5 per cent of GDP, extra net exports to 0.2 per cent, and net interest rate savings, including mortgages, to 1.0 per cent, making a total gain in GDP level year after year of 1.7 per cent. Costs are incurred mainly by banks and building societies, which lose 0.3 per cent of GDP on lower profits from foreign exchange dealing and on the spread between deposit and lending rates. There is thus a net gain of 1.4 per cent of GDP, or £10 billion, the equivalent of a 5p in the pound cut in personal income tax.

There are much greater potential gains from a rise in the rate of economic growth following on lower interest rates. An increase of 0.5 per cent would accumulate to 6 per cent after ten years, worth £42 billion. Even if half of this could be consolidated into a permanent increase of even 0.25 per cent in the growth rate, its net present value would be seven times annual GDP, or £5,000 billion.

If long-term interest rates fell from 7 to 5 per cent, there would be an annual saving of £7 billion, or 1 per cent of GDP, on interest on the net debt of the public sector. Most of this is paid to UK life insurance and pension funds, and will be switched either into reducing the national debt, or, more likely, into spending on government programmes for education, health, infrastructure and social security. It will thus be a redistribution of income within the UK rather than an addition to GDP.

The one-off conversion costs would be about £2.5 billion, spread over three years. They would not be a loss to GDP, because they would consist of internal transfer payments within the UK to computer programmers and equipment manufacturers. It seems a small enough price to pay for the potential benefits.

The interest-rate savings will come from a process of mutual monitoring among EU members. Because there is a global capital market, in which huge sums move freely around the world, it is impossible for a country the size of the UK to achieve lower real interest rates on its own. Even if it manages to reduce its budget deficit, this will be little help in lowering British interest rates.

As many EU countries as possible need to reduce their budget deficits so as to increase public savings and bring interest rates down for one and all. The UK has just as much interest in seeing that French, German and Italian budget deficits are kept down as in tackling its own. The single currency goes with a fiscal policy mechanism to ensure that budget deficits and thus interest rates are lowered on a long-run basis.

The other major economic advantage of the single currency is that inflation will be kept low by means of a common monetary policy run by the European Central Bank. Stronger competition when all prices are expressed in the single currency will also lower inflation. Low inflation will make loans cheaper and less of a burden in the early years. It will make economic decisions about purchasing and pay bargaining more rational by getting rid of money illusion. It will help savers and people living on fixed incomes, and will reduce the amount that needs to be put into pension funds to provide against future inflation.

The single currency will rival the dollar as a world currency, and outclass the yen. This will bring advantages to the UK as well as to the other members. Exchange rates between the single currency, the dollar and the yen could be managed so as to avoid the costs of instability now that Europe has so many separate currencies. The City of London will benefit from the single currency if the UK joins, in its dealings both with Europe and with the world as a whole. The City could increase its dominance as a world financial centre by becoming the main marketplace for all single currency markets: in money, foreign exchange, banking, bonds, equities, derivatives and insurance. If the UK does not join, the City will lose much of the share it might have had in these markets to continental financial centres in the single currency area.

If the UK joins the single currency, it will find it easier to promote the policies that it wants in other areas, such as trade, competition, financial deregulation, the Common Agricultural Policy and its own EU Budget rebate. If it does not, it will be accused of dividing the single market and will not get the cooperation it seeks from its partners on other issues.

Contrary to a recent statement by Mr Malcolm Rifkind, the Foreign Secretary, the single currency is not a matter for variable geometry. It is an essential part of the European Union:

Variable geometry is already well-established. . . . Sometimes one hears this described as a potential two-speed Europe. But that is unwise. It implies a common destination arrived at in different timescales. That is certainly appropriate to enlargement but may not be appropriate to social policy or to a single currency.[6]

Monetary policy cannot be kept in a separate compartment from financial and commercial policy for long. If the UK stays out of the single currency, the single market will not make progress, and could unravel.

Giving up an independent monetary policy will help the European

Central Bank to achieve lower inflation and lower interest rates than the independent policy could have delivered. Giving up devaluation of the nominal exchange rate against other European countries will mean that a policy which has been a mark of past failure is no longer needed. The UK will still be able to change its real exchange rate by means of relative pay and price movements, and the single currency's exchange rate against the dollar and the yen will still be able to change.

The economic advantages of the single currency will not have major political costs. The power of the House of Commons to take tax and expenditure decisions will remain, and will have to be more actively exercised. The limits on tax changes will be no more than those already needed to make the single European market work. The curbs on budget deficits are already accepted as right in domestic policy terms. The loss of monetary sovereignty will be felt less, because there is little democratic check on decisions now made by the Treasury and the Bank of England. The loss of national coins and banknotes is a sentimental matter of no economic significance. The decimal currency was an improvement on the LSD currency, and the single currency will be an improvement on the present British currency. It will be better designed, will be usable over six times as wide an economic area, and will keep its value longer.

THE POLITICAL CASE FOR THE SINGLE CURRENCY

The economic case stands. There is also a political case, which is in some respects related to the economic case, in other ways independent of it. There is a political case for setting up a United States of Europe, which would, like the United States of America, be one country, though structured as a federation. But the single currency does not need a single government for its success. Nor does the political case which I accept include a United States of Europe. The USE is a bogeyman used by Eurosceptics to discredit the other side.

There is a positive and a negative aspect to the political case. The positive aspect is that the single currency will help to keep the European Union countries together, and in the last resort make it impossible for them to fight each other again. Success with the single currency could lead to progress with the other two pillars of the Maastricht Treaty, covering the common foreign and security policy, and justice and home affairs. The single currency should help to make a success of the enlargement of the Union in central Europe by creating closer links with the new members. The single currency will also help to bind the new larger Germany in with the rest of the EU, as long as the Germans can be given a sufficient political union counterpart to monetary union. Such political union will include the points just mentioned, but not a United States of Europe.

If France and Germany cannot agree on a monetary-political union bargain by 1998, there will be no single currency. This would be against the political and economic interests of both the UK and Europe as a whole. The foundations of post-war Europe would crumble away instead of being built on. The British should not be standing on the touch-line, expressing *Schadenfreude* – joy at the misfortune of others – every time France or Germany seems to be in danger of not meeting the Maastricht budget deficit targets. They should be actively participating in the process of policy coordination designed to ensure that as many countries as possible meet the criteria. If there is no single currency to join, it will be even worse news for the UK than if there is a single currency that the UK does not join.

The current attitude of many people in Britain is to wait and see if France and Germany agree, thus postponing the decision whether to opt in until 1998. There will be a strong political case for the UK to join then if they go ahead, as well as the economic case. There will also be a strong negative case that the UK would suffer political damage by being reduced to second-class status in Europe if it did not then join. Even waiting in order to join after about 2002 would be dangerous, because most of the rules of the club would have been written in the interests of France and Germany. In any case, the UK may cease to pass the convergence criteria as a result of the loss of confidence in existing policies by foreigners and by the British themselves.

There is no doubt that nationalism has become a stronger force, for both good and evil, in Europe since the collapse of Communism. It has led to many countries in central Europe, and the Baltic States, regaining their independence and rediscovering their national pride. It has also led the republics of former Yugoslavia, and some of those of the former Soviet Union, into ethnic wars.

If Britain follows the trend and takes a nationalist stance over European economic, monetary and political union, it will not be difficult to arouse popular support among British voters. But it will be to Britain's disadvantage, and set a bad example to France, Germany and other European countries. Britain can no longer make Europe safe by a nineteenth-century 'balance of power' among rival nation-states. Nations are still a focus for loyalty and enthusiasm, but they can achieve their potential only by working together in a wider European framework. The British still seem to think that European citizenship will detract from, rather than add to British citizenship. According to the Reflection Group on the IGC, referring to the EU Member States:

In most of them the concept of citizenship increased the feeling of belonging to the Union, in some, by contrast, there was a failure to put across the idea that citizenship of the Union is not intended to replace national citizenship but actually to complement it.[7]

The UK belongs to the latter category.

WHAT SHOULD THE BRITISH GOVERNMENT DO?

There is little point in arguing about whether the UK should announce its decision to opt in as soon as possible. It would be a welcome gesture, but neither of the two biggest political parties is likely to do so. The decision cannot be finally taken until it is known, in early 1998, whether the UK and enough other countries have passed the convergence criteria to make the single currency worth setting up. The parties could announce in advance of this that they intended to opt in if these convergence conditions were fulfilled.

What is not helpful is for even the Europhiles in the two parties to announce that they will opt in if not only the convergence conditions in the Treaty but other 'real' convergence indicators, mentioned in the Treaty but not yet fully specified, are favourable. These include, on different occasions, competitiveness, unemployment, economic growth, unit labour costs and the balance of payments. We have tried to show that there is no economic justification for any of these extra criteria (see page 138). The UK should not impose on itself additional criteria which do not hold for other countries. This is unilateral decision-making on a multilateral matter agreed by Treaty and ratified some years ago. It looks like a smokescreen to avoid being committed in advance to a firm decision.

Even Mr Kenneth Clarke, the Chancellor of the Exchequer, and a supporter of UK entry into the single currency, sometimes puts too much stress on extraneous criteria. He said in February 1995:

We should not lose sight of the need to address the deep-seated structural differences within Europe's economies. The Maastricht Treaty itself refers to indicators which reflect these: trade balances on the current account; the integration of markets; the development of unit labour costs. As the Governor of the Bank of England has also pointed out, there must be concern about the possibility of on-going differences in rates of productivity growth and relative flexibility in labour markets.[8]

The British Government is likely to satisfy the convergence criteria as well as any of its prospective partners in the single currency. By 1998 there will be a recently elected government in the UK. The governments of France and Germany will look on enviously. They will be facing elections, the first in March, the second in October 1998, but they will still have to take major decisions on going ahead with the single currency. The new British Government should not need more than six months to get its feet under the desk. It should not plead that it wants to spend a few more years assessing the merits or demerits of an independent monetary policy before deciding whether to join. It should use its electoral support to take a decision which may be controversial, but should be proved right before the following election early in the twenty-first century.

Above all, a government which decides to go in to the single currency must persuade the voters of its economic and perhaps also some of its political advantages. It would be an abdication of responsibility for a government to say that it could not make up its mind, but wanted to see what people thought. Neither public opinion polls nor a referendum would be worth much in these circumstances. If the Government, with all the expertise at its disposal, cannot make up its mind, how can it expect the voters to do so? As the Kingsdown Enquiry pointed out: 'Britain's right to opt out . . . has in fact had the effect of postponing a sensible debate in Britain.'[9] The Maastricht Treaty was not properly explained to the people, who did not get a chance to vote on it in the UK.

If one major political party was in favour of the single currency and the other against it, the matter could be settled by a general election.

The divisions within each of the biggest parties are such as to ensure that this will not happen. The Liberal Democrats, however much they may be in favour of the single currency, are unlikely to increase their support in an election by campaigning in favour of it. It is important that neither of the biggest parties announces that it will not opt in in advance of an election, thus tying its hands for the life of the 1997–2002 Parliament during the crucial years when the single currency may be set up.

After the election, the Government, if its hands are not tied by a pre-election pledge not to opt in, needs to run a massive popular campaign to explain the issues, and why it is in favour of joining. If it gets support in Parliament and in the opinion polls, a referendum may not be needed. The referendum in 1975 to endorse British membership of the EEC on renegotiated terms was held to seek approval for a clear policy adopted by the then Labour Government. A referendum held in a policy vacuum, with private sector yes and no campaigns, and the Government sitting on its hands, would produce only confusion. If a referendum is held, it should be to seek popular approval for a positive government policy on the single currency. It would be better still if a party won a general election with a clear policy, and then implemented it without needing a referendum.

The importance of educating the public was stressed in the EU Commission's Green Paper:

There is a need to explain to Europe's citizens the real value of their new money, and to convince them that it is an element of stability, growth and the future well-being of our continent. This will need a determined communications effort which is simple, continual and transparent.[10]

Other countries are well ahead of the UK in their popular education campaigns, because their governments have already made up their own minds. A Single Currency Board, on the lines of the Decimal Currency Board, needs to be set up as soon as possible to supervise the transition, and explain how it would affect different kinds of people. The single currency needs to be marketed like any other new product. Banks and financial institutions have enormous experience of marketing financial products; they should use their expertise to add some sex appeal to the rather unpromising name, Euro.

The low level of public support for the single currency among the

British population could be raised if the Government were to put the case for it. No government should passively follow public opinion or actively ignore it in determining its policy. Leadership is needed, not to impose a new currency on a hostile population, but to persuade them that it will improve their lives. Here indeed is a policy to fire people's imagination, and to mark the millennium.

10
Conclusions

I take the UK's ten dangerous illusions about EMU at the end of chapter 1, and see how they may be dispelled by contradicting them in the light of the main findings of the book.

1. *It is likely to happen.* The Madrid summit at the end of 1995 was a turning point. The British Government and people suddenly realized that, as Mr Kenneth Clarke put it, the chances of the single currency going ahead in 1999 were 60–40. It became clear that France and Germany were determined to pay the economic and political price to fulfil the conditions laid down in the Maastricht Treaty. The strikes of late 1995 showed that the French Government was determined to achieve convergence by 1997. Both the French and German Governments are totally committed. Britain would do better to help them on and join too than to indulge in *Schadenfreude* from the sidelines. Conflict between France and Germany has involved Britain in two world wars. It is a prime British interest to help the two countries move closer together.

There will be room for doubt about how many, and which countries, are ready to enter the new world of the Euro in time for the beginning of the new millennium. Forecasts are always uncertain, but the determination of most governments, including the British Government, to follow convergence policies is certain.

The convergence criteria are achievable for most countries. We are already in a world of low inflation, but not low enough in the UK and a number of other countries to bring decisive advantages. Current inflation rates provide a suitable platform from which to launch into a new era of even lower inflation, of a more permanent kind than Britain has known since the Second World War. Britain and other countries are tackling their budget deficits in spite of rearguard actions by disaffected groups, and sound public finance will bring lower real interest rates to the benefit of private investment and public expenditure. Exchange rate instability has become less of an issue since the ERM stopped taking heavy casualties in full frontal assaults on it, but can only be finally tackled by setting up the Euro.

2. *It is vital to have a timetable.* The single European market, which was backed by the UK, became a reality only because of the end-1992 deadline. The EMU timetable had two starting dates. The first, 1997, has been missed. The second, 1999, allows enough time, especially with the new notes and coins not due until 2002. A timetable prevents governments postponing difficult action to curb budget deficits. The lack of a timetable would prolong uncertainty about EMU, which carries a high cost in terms of interest rates and exchange rates. The sooner the UK accepts the 1999 deadline, the quicker it will reap the advantages of the single currency.

The passing of the 1996 deadline for an early start was only realistic, but so was the firm decision at Madrid to adopt the 1998 deadline written into the Maastricht Treaty as an obligation rather than an option. It was better to concentrate convergence policies into the few years leading up to 1997, while political and economic circumstances were favourable, rather than letting each country go at its own pace, and finding that their economic cycles start diverging again. The shorter the transitional pains, and the sooner the benefits of the single currency, the better. Business optimism about the single currency should make the convergence criteria easier to meet in the time allowed.

If the chances of the UK going in to the Euro in 1999 are 60–40 or better, this justifies immediate preparations in British banks, companies, government departments and schools. Banks have already made estimates of their costs, which are bearable, and are being given a timetable. Preparations should go on through 1996 and 1997, because if the UK decides to join in early 1998, there will be less than a year left before the new currency begins to be introduced, with irrevocably fixed exchange rates.

Consumers, shops and small businesses will have another three years, until the first half of 2002, to prepare for the new Euro notes and coins. Six years from the Madrid summit to the new notes and coins is not a rushed timetable, if good use is made of it by advance planning. People need to know what happens when. Leaving it to chance or 'the market' is a recipe for chaos.

3. *It will do immense harm to wait and see.*   Waiting longer will not help us to make up our minds. It will widen the rift between Britain and the single currency countries, which will move ahead fast and write their own rules without taking British interests into account. It will be like Britain's refusal to sign the Rome Treaty in 1957. It may be many years before we join, and then it will be on their terms and not on ours.

The consequences of the UK staying out of the first group of countries would be adverse, in terms of a lower exchange rate and economic growth rate, and a higher inflation rate and interest rates. The problem of ins and outs would be much worse if the UK was one of the outs; the European Union would be split commercially, economically and politically. The economic effects could be so dire as to destroy hopes of the UK continuing to achieve convergence with the single currency members.

Once outside, the UK would have no share in exercising pooled sovereignty over the European Central Bank's monetary policy, or the choice of its executive board, and would have far less influence over a wide range of policy issues affecting its interests, such as agriculture, the EU Budget, competition, enlargement and international trade. It would become the leader of a motley group of countries on the fringes of Europe, including an increasing number of former Communist economies in central Europe.

The fortunes of the single currency without the UK would be no indication of its prospects with the UK. If Britain joined, other borderline countries would make the extra effort needed to do so, and this momentum would give it a greater chance of success. A narrow monetary union would not bring such great advantages to its members as a wider one, and would disadvantage non-members. By retaining for a further period the option to let the pound depreciate, the UK would ensure that it was forced to use it.

4. *We do not need to become more competitive before joining.*   The British economy is as competitive as it will ever be, thanks to the low exchange rate it has had since leaving the ERM in 1992. It will be lucky to be able to join the single currency at a similarly low exchange rate. UK industries have nothing to fear from those on the Continent. They may have lower productivity levels in some areas, in spite of rapid increases in the last decade, but they make up for this with lower labour costs.

Asking for an extra convergence criterion called competitiveness is just another excuse for not joining the single currency. UK performance will benefit more from joining than from not joining.

The addition of more criteria to the existing list for entry into the Euro makes it more difficult for countries to enter; that may be the object. Most of the additional criteria are not needed to establish whether a country is fit to join the single currency. They are all objectives of economic policy which would be better served by joining than by staying outside. They include unemployment, competitiveness, productivity, economic growth and the balance of payments. The UK's chances of improving performance in these areas would be less if it were to exclude itself from the single currency.

The EU is already an optimum currency area in terms of free movement of capital, and had better not become one in terms of free movement of labour, because wage levels can and should diverge for many years to come in different countries with varying productivity levels.

The UK economy still has weaknesses, but they could be dealt with as part of a policy package with the single currency at the centre, including also lower interest rates, higher business investment and more international competition. The UK is not such a poor performer that it could not survive in full EMU without devaluation, but not such a good one that it could afford to stay outside like an offshore Switzerland.

Europe's other major economies have different strengths and weaknesses, and the UK is well able to compete against them, particularly since the overvaluation of the pound in the ERM was corrected. Entry into the single currency should bring a once-for-all increase of £12 billion, or 1.7 per cent of GDP, in foreign exchange and interest rate savings; more important, it could raise the GDP growth rate by 0.5 per cent for some years, and by 0.25 per cent permanently.

5. *We will be worse off outside.* Some British interests believe that the future lies in the Far East and not in Europe, and that Britain should model itself on low-public-spending economies like Hong Kong. It should not be trying to move downmarket to compete with the low labour cost economies of Asia, but upmarket to compete with the high labour cost economies of the Continent. The UK and other European

economies have felt the competition of cheap products from the Far East. This does not mean that the UK can pursue a radically different path from its neighbours by opting out of the social chapter and lowering labour costs so as to level-peg with Hong Kong and Taiwan. The UK cannot compete against low-cost imports from other countries, but it can persuade them to buy its high-value exports, as do other European countries. The UK should turn its back on the temptation to solve its balance of payments problems by devaluation, and instead try to improve the non-price competitiveness of its high-technology exports.

The City of London does more business with the rest of the world than with Europe. That shows what unrealized potential there will be once the City is allowed to compete on equal terms in the single European market for finance – to which the single currency is essential. It is a myth that the City has better prospects outside than inside Europe. On the contrary, it has some catching up to do on the Continent, and can be the main financial centre in Euro markets – as opposed to euro-markets – only if it is in the Euro area. The UK is already committed to European regulation in financial services, and no longer has the option of being an unregulated offshore haven. Neither Hong Kong, nor Norway, nor Switzerland are appropriate models for the UK, which is a major European power.

There is little freedom at present for the UK to run an independent monetary policy, because it can control its own interest rates only to a limited extent. The cat-and-dog ménage of the Chancellor of the Exchequer and the Governor of the Bank of England is unlikely to give as good results as an independent British or, better still, European Central Bank. There are diminishing returns to devaluation as the UK becomes more integrated into the EU, and it is a confession of failure rather than a recipe for success. If it does not join the Euro, it will have no say over the rules, the management or the policies of the European Central Bank. It will have more influence in European and world monetary affairs if it is part of the Euro and the ECB. Other EU countries still actually value the UK's contribution to policy-making, in spite of the worst efforts of British politicians to keep them at arm's length.

6. *The single market needs a single money.*   The single European market exists, but would function much more effectively with a single currency.

Separate exchange rates increase the costs of foreign trade and invest-ment, add a risk premium to interest rates, and disrupt trade and prices by unpredictable revaluations and devaluations. NAFTA is not a single market, only a free trade area. The US is a single market, and could only function with a single currency. Currency and other uncertainties have already caused a 60 per cent real terms drop in the annual inflow of foreign direct investment into the UK since 1989, see page 60.

The UK cannot fully obtain the benefits of the single European market, which it played such a big part in creating, unless it joins the single currency. The competitive devaluation feared by other countries has already distorted flows of trade and investment, reduced the will to remove more trade barriers, and slowed down economic growth in the EU. Further exchange rate misalignment in the future could cause the single market to unravel, to the detriment of British interests. The single money is needed for the single market, not just to make it work better, but to stop it fragmenting. It is not the single currency, but its absence, which threatens to destroy the single market.

Only when transactions costs and exchange rate premia on interest rates are eliminated will trade and investment in the EU be boosted by lower prices and lower interest rates. There cannot be a single market if prices differ in each country because they are in a different currency. Interest rates, the price of money, diverge so much because of exchange rates that there cannot be a single market for money and banking until they are all quoted in the same currency.

7. *Ordinary people will accept it.* No government has ever tried to sell the idea of a single currency to the British people. They have been sub-jected to a torrent of anti-EMU or, at best, polite Eurosceptic rhetoric. Few people understand the issues at stake, and even supposed defenders of the single currency often sell it short. The 1975 referendum cam-paign showed that people can be won over by pro-Europe arguments – but only if the main parties put their weight behind them. Even so, polls show that between a third and a half of the British people support the single currency, especially young people on whom the future of the nation depends.

Splits in the political establishment have prevented governments from either understanding the advantages of the single currency them-selves or putting them over to the electorate. The popular tendency to see the pound as a symbol of national identity is mistaken, and has no basis in history. Public opinion polls show majority support for British entry into the Euro from business, but only minority support from the population as a whole. There is evidence that when the Euro is explained to people, they become more favourable, and if they think Britain might be left out while France and Germany go ahead, a majority is for going in.

A huge popular education campaign is needed if the Euro is to be successfully introduced, as happened when the pound was decimalized in 1971. The German people are unwilling to give up the D-mark, but this has not prevented the German Government from pursuing the objective for good economic and political reasons, and persuading the voters to follow its leadership. A referendum would make sense only as a way for a government to seek popular endorsement of entry into the single currency after parliamentary approval. It would be an opportunity to put the arguments before the public, but only one among many. The process of public education about the Euro has to last far longer, and go far deeper, than a referendum campaign ever could.

8. *It need not divide Europe.*   The Maastricht Treaty always allowed for a two-speed single currency. This was to let some countries catch up with convergence if they were not ready in time. It looks as if at least ten out of the fifteen EU countries will be ready to go ahead in 1999, and if Britain and Denmark join, there will be twelve, see page 138. This would create enough momentum to spur the laggards to converge within a short time. If Britain refuses to join in spite of passing the convergence criteria, this will divide Europe into two much more equal camps, and other countries may be encouraged to stay out. If Britain does not join, it will still have to abide by all the obligations of stage two of EMU, without getting the benefits of stage three. It will also be responsible for dividing Europe far more than the countries which go ahead according to the Treaty, which all have signed and ratified.

It is unlikely that every EU member will join the single currency. It will not be easy to set up a new Exchange Rate Mechanism to link the Euro and the currencies of non-members, which will include those of EU countries either unable or unwilling to join, and those of new members from central and southern Europe. If Britain joins the single currency, there will be far less of a problem.

The exchange rate of a pound outside the Euro will be speculative and difficult to control, while the currencies of smaller countries on the verge of entry into the Euro will be easier to handle. A majority of EU countries is likely to be ready to go ahead in 1999. If a minority is accused of dividing Europe, it is more likely to be a minority of non-participants than a minority of participants. Britain will be making the split worse if it sides with the minority of non-participants when it is entitled to join the majority of participants. If the only non-participants are countries keen to join as soon as they meet the convergence criteria, there will not be a serious split.

The single currency is not a suitable subject for variable geometry, so that it does not matter who chooses to join and who not. It is an integral part of European Union, and the monetary component of Economic and Monetary Union. If too many areas of policy are left to variable geometry, and if the UK is on the outside of most of them, not only will Europe be divided, but Britain will be in the outer tier and unable to influence the inner tier on matters of vital national interest.

9. *It will make enlargement meaningful.* The UK, like other EU members, wants enlargement to extend to the former Communist countries of central and eastern Europe for political reasons. However, if enlargement results in a loose group of disintegrating countries rather than a closely linked Community of integrating countries, it will be politically counterproductive, as well as being economically unproductive. These countries will not be ready for EU membership for some time, or for convergence of the kind required to join the single currency. Each group will move at a different pace.

The timetables are such that even the most promising candidates for enlargement are unlikely to join the EU until after the single currency has been set up in 1999–2002. By this time, the existing EU must decide at the Inter-Governmental Conference starting in 1996 on measures which are a precondition of the success of enlargement: reform of the Community institutions, the EU Budget and the Common Agricultural Policy, and qualified majority voting. The single currency, far from being an obstacle to enlargement, will be needed as an anchor of monetary stability for the new central European members.

The European Union has no choice. It must be widened and deepened. Widening without deepening will result in a loose and unruly group of up to thirty separate nation-states, not to say nationalistic states. Deepening without widening will restore the Iron Curtain in an economic dimension. On the present timetable, the single currency will be completed before enlargement. The reforms to the Common Agricultural Policy and the EU Budget, which are preconditions of enlargement, are far less advanced than EMU, and will take longer to work out. Once the single currency is in place in the existing EU, the new members in Central Europe will benefit from the convergence disciplines and, eventually, full membership of it.

10. *It will not mean the end of the nation-state.* There is no intention, and no necessity, even in the minds of the keenest integrationists, to replace the UK and other nation-states with a single state. Political union of a limited kind is needed to persuade Germany to give up the D-mark, and to make the European Union work better. It covers topics like democratic parliamentary control, majority voting so that small countries cannot block progress, and closer cooperation in areas such as foreign and security policy, immigration and crime, where individual nation-states are manifestly unable to cope on their own. Far from being a price that has to be paid for the single currency, political union in this sense will serve British interests. The UK was isolated in the reflection group on the 1996 Inter-Governmental Conference, which reported at the end of 1995. It must not risk becoming isolated in the reality of the European Union.

The single currency means pooling sovereignty for monetary policy through the European System of Central Banks and accepting limits on government deficits and debts. Apart from this, governments will still be free to maintain different levels of tax and expenditure, and to divide them up as they wish among different kinds of tax and purpose. They will have to use tax and spending policy more actively to run their own economic policies, as they will have less control over monetary policy. It is a fallacy that a big increase in the EU Budget will be needed to offset the effects of the single currency, since this is already done by the automatic stabilizing effect of national budgets.

The institutions of the European Union are or will be mostly federal in character, because this allows for the decentralization of as much power as possible to national governments, and the centralization of only as much as is necessary to the supranational institutions. This does not mean that there is a hidden agenda for the creation of a single European nation-state of the United States of Europe. The United States of America, which is a single nation-state, has a federal structure of government, but this does not mean that a European Union of many nation-states cannot also have federal institutions. The single currency does not require a single nation-state.

The Euro, with the UK inside it, will become a world currency alongside the dollar and the yen. Britain can thus retain, or even regain, some of its status as a world economic and financial power without giving up its national identity. Britain can avoid German domination of Europe only by joining France, Germany and other European countries as partners in an integrated Europe. For Britain to stay outside a policy as crucial as the single currency is to make German hegemony on the Continent inevitable. This would be as unwelcome to the Germans as to the other peoples of Europe.

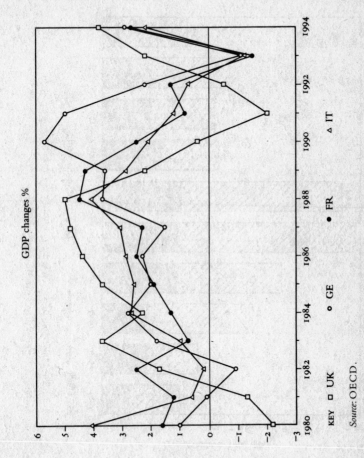

GDP changes %

KEY □ UK   o GE   • FR   △ IT

Source: OECD.

Figure 1. Annual growth rates, 1980–94

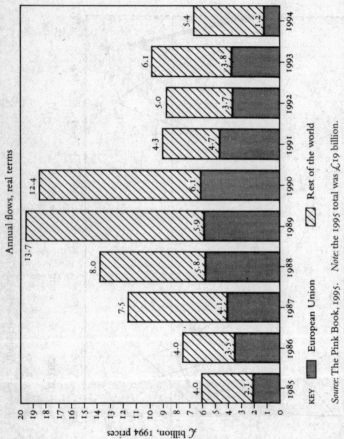

Annual flows, real terms

KEY ▓ European Union ▨ Rest of the world

Source: The Pink Book, 1995. *Note:* the 1995 total was £19 billion.

Figure 2. Foreign direct investment in the UK

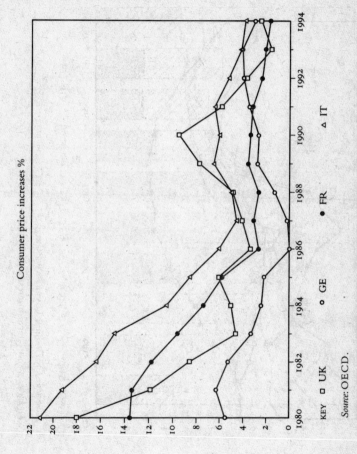

Consumer price increases %

KEY □ UK   ○ GE   ● FR   △ IT

Source: OECD.

Figure 3. Annual inflation rates, 1980–94

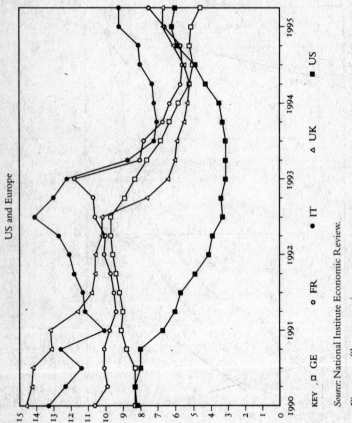

US and Europe

KEY □ GE   o FR   • IT   ▵ UK   ■ US

Source: National Institute Economic Review.

Figure 4. Short-term interest rates, 1990–95

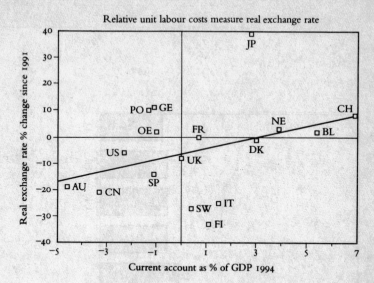

Source: OECD.

Figure 5. Current account and real exchange rate

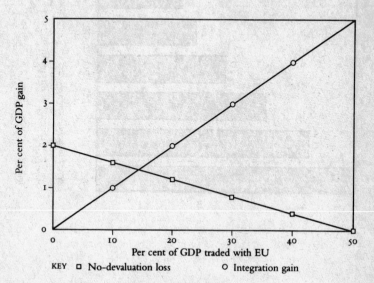

Figure 6. Costs and benefits of EMU

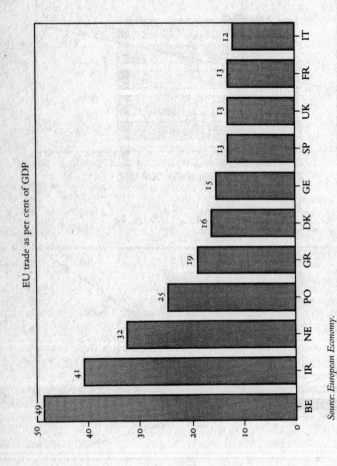

Source: *European Economy.*

Figure 7. Degree of integration, 1994

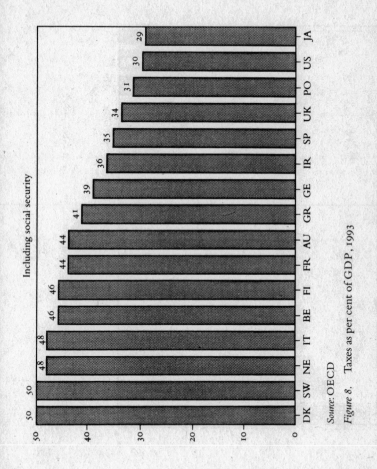

Including social security

Source: OECD

Figure 8. Taxes as per cent of GDP, 1993

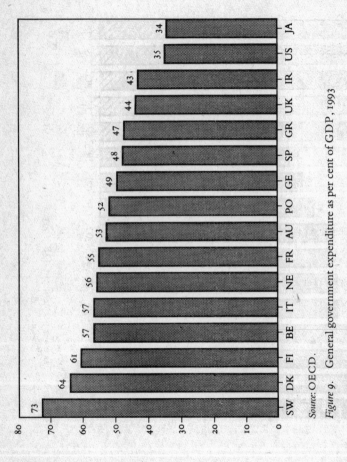

Source: OECD.

Figure 9.   General government expenditure as per cent of GDP, 1993

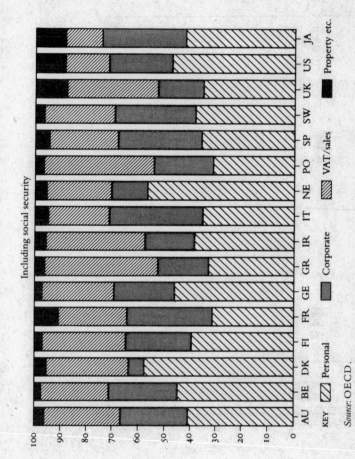

Source: OECD.

Figure 10. Taxes as per cent of total, 1993

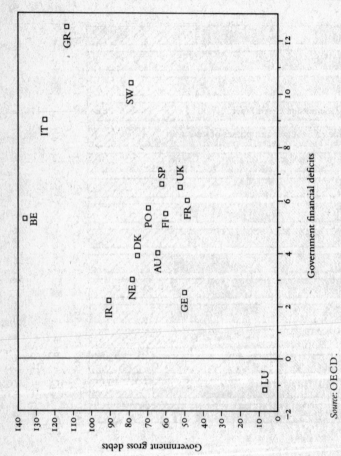

Source: OECD.

Figure 11. Deficits and debts as per cent of GDP, 1994

1990 1991 1992 1993 1994 1995 1996 1997 1998 1999 2000 2001 2002

Half 1

Maastricht Treaty:

Stage one ——————— Stage two ——————— Stage three ———————

EU Commission Green Paper: Phase A Phase B ——————— Phase C

Figure 12.   Stages and phases of transition

Table 1. In and out of the snake and the ERM

The snake		
Country	Entrance	Exit
Belgium	April 1972	
France	April 1972	January 1974
	July 1975	March 1976
Germany	April 1972	
Italy	April 1972	February 1973
Luxembourg	April 1972	
Netherlands	April 1972	
Denmark	May 1972	June 1972
	October 1972	
UK	May 1972	June 1972

The ERM		
Austria	January 1995	
Belgium	March 1979	
Denmark	March 1979	
France	March 1979	
Germany	March 1979	
Ireland	March 1979	
Italy	March 1979	September 1972
Luxembourg	March 1979	
Netherlands	March 1979	
Spain	June 1979	
UK	October 1990	September 1992
Portugal	April 1992	

Table 2.   Economic growth in EU, 1980–94

	Annual average growth per cent 1980–94	GNP/ head 1993 PPP EU = 100	Output gap 1995 (Potential – actual)
Big four:			
Germany	2.2	109	–0.9
France	1.9	110	–2.8
Italy	1.9	102	–3.0
UK	1.9	100	–2.1
Catch-up four:			
Ireland	3.9	73	0.3
Spain	2.3	78	–2.6
Portugal	2.6	69	–2.7
Greece	1.5	64	–2.4
EU	2.0	100	–2.0
US	2.3	144	1.8

Source: OECD, *Economic Outlook*, June 1995; 'UK Business in Europe', table 3.2.

Note: PPP= purchasing power parity.

Table 3. Foreign exchange market in London
(Daily turnover April 1995, spot and forward)

	Per cent of total	$ billion	Spread per cent 13–19 Oct 1995	Transaction cost	
				$ million Daily	×200 Annual
EMU/non-EMU:					
D-mark/$	22	102	0.020	20.72	4144
£/$	11	51	0.029	14.60	2919
French franc/$	5	23	0.020	4.62	923
Italian lira/$	3	14	0.047	6.60	1320
Spanish peseta/$	2	9	0.034	3.16	633
Other EMS/$	6	28	0.048	13.36	2673
Ecu/non-EMU	2	9	0.039	3.62	724
£/non-EMS non-$	1	5	0.070	3.25	650
EMU/non-EMU total	52	241	0.029	69.93	13986
Within EMU:					
D-mark/£	3	14	0.049	6.82	1364
D-mark/other EMS	6	28	0.050	13.92	2784
Other intra-EU	3	14	0.050	6.96	1392
Within EMU total	12	56	0.049	27.70	5540
Rest of the world:					
Japanese yen/$	17	79	0.045	35.26	7052
Swiss franc/$	5	23	0.042	9.63	1926
Canadian $/US$	2	9	0.015	1.42	284
Australian $/US$	2	9	0.014	1.29	258
Other	10	46	0.050	23.20	4640
Rest of world total	36	167	0.042	70.80	14159
Total	100	464	0.043	168.43	33685

Sources: *Bank of England Quarterly Bulletin*, November 1995; *Financial Times.*

Table 4.   Changing £100 into French francs
(Waterloo station, 27 September 1995)

	Pounds	Rate	Francs
Mid-rate 8.19–7.54	100	7.865	786.50
Minimum commission	-2.50		
Sell rate at Bureau	97.50	7.54	735.15
Loss on exchange	6.53		51.35
Percentage loss	6.53	4.13	6.53

Commission 1.5% or £2.50, whichever is greater.

Table 5.   Competitive devaluations?

	1992	1993	1994	1992	1993	1994
	Exports to EU as % of GDP			Imports from EU as % of GDP		
France	10.9	9.7	9.9	10.7	9.3	9.6
Germany	12.8	11.3	11.7	12.4	10.4	10.4
Italy	8.4	9.0	9.1	9.0	8.2	8.2
Spain	7.9	8.2	8.9	10.5	9.7	10.0
UK	10.2	10.2	10.1	11.1	11.0	10.7
				Changes in percentage points		
France		-1.2	0.2		-1.4	0.3
Germany		-1.5	0.4		-2.0	0.0
Italy		0.6	0.1		-0.8	0.0
Spain		0.3	0.7		-0.8	0.3
UK		0.0	-0.1		-0.1	-0.3
	Balances: exports–imports			Exchange rate changes v. DM % Jan 1992–Jun 1995		
France	0.2	0.4	0.3			
Germany	0.4	0.9	1.3			
Italy	-0.6	0.8	0.9		-33	
Spain	-2.6	-1.5	-1.1		-25	
UK	-0.9	-0.8	-0.6		-21	

Source: European Economy, no. 58, 1994, from tables 40 and 44.

Table 6.   Long-term interest rates, 1980–94

| Country | Long-term real interest rate | | Dividend yields |
| | Nominal | Real inflation-adjusted | |
	1980–94 averages		Sep 1995
United States	9.5	4.5	2.5
Japan	6.3	4.1	0.8
Germany	7.7	4.5	1.9
France	11.1	5.1	3.1
Italy	14.0	4.1	1.6
UK	10.8	4.3	4.0
Average	9.9	4.5	2.3

Source: OECD *Economic Outlook*, June 1995, tables A18, A39; *Financial Times*.

Table 7.   Business investment as percentage of nominal GDP

Country	1960	1995	Peak
US	10	12	14(1982)
Japan	17	14	21(1970)
Germany	14	13	14(1960)
France	14(1963)	11	14(1963)
Italy	16	10	16(1960)
UK	8(1963)	10	14(1989)

Source: OECD *Economic Outlook*, no. 57, June 1995, fig. 10, p. 29.

Table 8. EU share in UK overseas earnings
(£ billion 1994)

Type of income	From EU	Total	EU %
Goods exports	70.8	134.5	53
Services:			
Non-financial	6.3	20.2	31
Financial	1.2	4.7	24
Other business	4.3	14.5	29
Total services	11.7	39.5	30
Investment income	28.1	78.2	36
Total invisibles	43.7	123.0	35
Total credits	114.4	257.5	44

Note: Net EU Budget contributions = £2.2 billion.

Source: The Pink Book, 1995.

Table 9. Major country inflation

	Consumer prices Annual rise 1980–94 percentages	Purchasing power of currency in 1994 as percent of 1979
US	4.9	49
Japan	2.1	73
Germany	2.9	65
France	5.7	44
Italy	9.2	27
UK	6.4	39

Source: IMF.

Table 10. Inflation and borrowing costs

Year	1	2	3	4	5	6	7	8	9	10	Total
1: 10% interest, 5% inflation											
Principal										10,000	10,000
Interest	1,000	1,000	1,000	1,000	1,000	1,000	1,000	1,000	1,000	1,000	10,000
Discount rate	0.91	0.83	0.75	0.68	0.62	0.56	0.51	0.47	0.42	0.39	
Discounted payment	909	826	751	683	621	564	513	467	424	386 / 3855	10,000
% of repayment	9.1	8.3	7.5	6.8	6.2	5.6	5.1	4.7	4.2	3.9 / 38.6	
2: 5% interest, 0% inflation											
Principal										10,000	10,000
Interest	500	500	500	500	500	500	500	500	500	500	5,000
Discount rate	0.95	0.91	0.86	0.82	0.78	0.75	0.71	0.68	0.64	0.61	
Discounted payment	476	454	432	411	392	373	355	338	322	307 / 6,139	10,000
% of repayment	4.8	4.5	4.3	4.1	3.9	3.7	3.6	3.4	3.2	3.1 / 61.4	

Notes: 1. Loan: £10,000, bullet repayment after 10 years. 2. Discount rate $= (1/(1 + r))^t$, where r = interest rate, t = time in years.

Table 11. How interest rates could fall

	Nominal interest	Inflation	Real interest
Starting position	6.5	2.5	4.0
Effect of:			
a) Exchange rate abolition	5.5	2.5	3.0
b) Stable price regime	4.5	1.5	3.0

Table 12. Major currency changes against D-mark

Units of national currency:	value in D-marks			percentage change	
	1965 average	1979 average	1995 Sep	1965–95	1979–95
US $	4.00	1.83	1.49	−63	−19
Japan 100 yen	1.11	0.83	1.75	+58	+110
France franc	0.82	0.43	0.29	−65	−33
Italy 1000 lire	6.41	2.20	0.93	−86	−58
UK £	11.20	3.88	2.31	−79	−40

Source: IMF.

Table 13. Types of devaluation

	UK import prices		UK home prices	UK export prices	
Starting point:	DM	£	£	£	DM
£ 1 = DM 2.00	200	100	100	100	200
DM 1 = £ 0.50					
10% nominal devaluation:					
£ 1 = DM 1.80					
DM 1 = £ 0.555					
Case 1	180	100	100	100	180
Nominal and fully real					
Case 2	200	111	111	111	200
Nominal but not real					
Case 3	190	105.5	105.5	105.5	190
Nominal and partly real					
Case 4	190	95	95	95	190
Real but not nominal					

Table 14.   Degree of integration in European Union, 1994

	1 Goods & services trade % of GDP	2 Trade with EU % of total goods trade	3 $=\frac{1 \times 2}{100}$ Degree of integration	4 Ranking of 3
Belgium–Luxembourg	66.0	73.6	48.6	1
Denmark	31.8	51.4	16.3	6
France	21.9	58.7	12.8	10
Germany (West)	28.0	54.5	15.3	7
Greece	29.5	64.5	19.0	5
Ireland	59.4	68.7	40.8	2
Italy	23.1	51.8	11.9	11
Netherlands	48.9	66.4	32.4	3
Portugal	33.2	74.1	24.6	4
Spain	21.6	62.1	13.4	8
UK	26.0	50.1	13.0	9
Average	28.0	57.8	16.2	

Note: Cols 1 and 2 = average of imports and exports.

Source: *European Economy*, no. 58, 1994.

Table 15.   Sustainable debt arithmetic

Year	1	2	3	4	5
Units of currency:					
GDP nominal 5% growth	100.0	105.0	110.3	115.8	121.6
Debt year-end 5% growth	50.0	52.5	55.1	57.8	60.8
Interest 7% average debt	3.4	3.6	3.8	4.0	4.2
Deficit: rise in debt	2.4	2.5	2.6	2.8	2.9
Primary surplus: interest – deficit	1.0	1.1	1.2	1.2	1.3
Percentages of GDP					
Debt	50.0	50.0	50.0	50.0	50.0
Interest	3.4	3.4	3.4	3.4	3.4
Deficit	2.4	2.4	2.4	2.4	2.4
Primary surplus	1.0	1.0	1.0	1.0	1.0

Note: A hypothetical case.

Table 16.   Convergence forecasts for EU countries in 1997 (in percentages)

P = pass F = fail	Consumer price inflation	Govt long-term interest rate	General govt deficit: GDP	General govt debt: GDP	Exchange rate stable 1996-7
Austria P	1.6	6.6	3.1★	74★	Yes
Belgium P	1.8	6.8	3.7★	131★	Yes
Denmark P	2.4	7.5	0.6	69★	Yes
Finland P	1.5	7.3	1.6	63★	Yes
France P	1.6	6.8	3.0	58	Yes
Germany P	1.6	6.3	2.9	62	Yes
Greece F	7.0★	n.a.★	6.9★	111★	No
Ireland P	2.4	7.7	1.6	77★	Yes
Italy F	3.5★	10.4★	5.2★	123★	No
Luxembourg P	2.1	6.5	−0.3	7	Yes
Netherlands P	2.0	6.3	2.9	79★	Yes
Portugal P	3.0	n.a.	3.7★	72★	?
Spain F	3.2★	9.7★	3.7★	68★	?
Sweden P	2.5	8.8★	3.1★	80★	Yes
UK P	2.5	7.9	3.7★	56	Yes
EU 15	2.6	7.6	3.4	75	
Three best	1.6	6.7			
Limit	3.1	8.7	3.0	60	

★ = fails test

Note: It is assumed that countries with a deficit forecast of less than 4 per cent will be able to achieve or come close to 3 per cent by means of additional policy measures, and that debt ratios of over 60 per cent will be accepted if they are falling. Inflation figures are consumer price deflators. Some countries outside the ERM are assumed to pass the exchange rate stability test according to a similar standard.

Source: EU Commission forecasts, May 1996, columns 1, 3 and 4. *OECD Economic Outlook* forecasts for 1997, December 1995, column 2.

Table 17. From basket ecu to user-friendly Euro

Currency	Amount in basket	$ rate 4.10.95	$ value	£ rate 4.10.95	£ value of basket	Ecu rates against currency			Rounded $ rate	Rounded $ value of basket
						Market 4.10.95	Rounded	Change %		
	1	2	3 =1/2	4	5 =1/4	6	7	8	9 =7/1.3093	10 =1/9
Deutsche Mark	0.6242	1.436	0.4346	2.272	0.2748	1.880	2.00	-5.98	1.528	0.4086
French franc	1.332	4.962	0.2685	7.848	0.1697	6.493	6.50	-0.11	4.964	0.2683
Dutch guilder	0.2198	1.609	0.1366	2.544	0.0864	2.105	2.20	-4.30	1.680	0.1308
British pound	0.08784	0.632	0.1389	1.000	0.0878	0.828	0.80	3.53	0.611	0.1438
Belgian franc	3.301	29.54	0.1118	46.72	0.0707	38.67	40.00	-3.34	30.55	0.1080
Italian lira	151.8	1610	0.0943	2547	0.0596	2111	2000	5.56	1528	0.0994
Spanish peseta	6.885	124.0	0.0555	196.1	0.0351	162.3	160	1.45	122.2	0.0563
Danish krone	0.1976	5.574	0.0355	8.816	0.0224	7.295	7.50	-2.73	5.728	0.0345
Irish pound	0.008552	0.620	0.0138	0.980	0.0087	0.812	0.80	1.48	0.611	0.0140
Portuguese escudo	1.393	150.4	0.0093	237.8	0.0059	196.8.	200	-1.61	152.8	0.0091
Greek drachma	1.44	233.9	0.0062	369.9	0.0039	306.2	300	2.07	229.1	0.0063
Luxembourg franc	0.13	29.54	0.0044	46.72	0.0028	38.67	40.00	-3.34	30.55	0.0043
Ecu: theoretical			1.3093		0.8278	1.0000				1.2834
Ecu: market value			1.2892		0.8150	0.9846				

Source for rates: Financial Times, 5 October 1995.

Table 18.   UK banks' costs of transition to single currency

Function	Cost £m	%	Product	Cost £m	%
Systems	437	48.0	Notes and coin	74	8.1
Marketing and PR	153	16.8	ATMs	38	4.2
Legal	21	2.3	Cards	107	11.7
Audit and security	67	7.4	Payment systems	120	13.2
Accounting and			Forex and treasury	92	10.1
management	35	3.8	Loans	62	6.8
Staff training	44	4.8	Deposits	64	7.0
Stationery	132	14.5	Capital markets	63	6.9
External reporting	4	0.4	Correspondent banking	8	0.9
Other	18	2.0	Branch accounting	211	23.2
Total	911	100.0	Bancassurance	47	5.2
			International	23	2.5
			Other	2	0.2
			Total	911	100.0

Source: APACS/BBA.

Table 19.   Categories of countries not members of the single currency

Members of the European Union:

Want to join but may not qualify
Greece
Italy
Portugal
Spain

May qualify but not want to join
Denmark
Sweden
UK

Members of European Free Trade Area:
Iceland
Liechtenstein
Norway
Switzerland

Expected candidate members of EU:

Bulgaria
Cyprus
Czech Republic
Estonia
Hungary
Latvia
Lithuania
Malta
Poland
Romania
Slovakia
Slovenia

Other European countries:

Albania
Bosnia
Croatia
Macedonia
Montenegro
Serbia

Rest of the world – some key countries:

Belarus
Japan
Russia
Turkey
Ukraine
US

Table 20.   The Euro in international banking
(Billions of US$ equivalent outstanding: end-March 1995)

| | External positions of banks in industrial countries | | | | | | Percentage shares | | By nationality of bank ownership | |
| | Domestic currency | | Foreign currency | | Domestic and foreign | | Domestic and foreign | | | |
	Loans	Deposits	Loans	Deposits	Loans	Deposits	Loans	Deposits	$bn	per cent
Deutsche Mark	272	239	653	722	925	961	16	16	1,111	15
French franc	160	163	129	160	289	323	5	5	780	11
British pound	103	158	124	139	227	297	4	5	390	5
Italian lira	52	54	125	111	177	165	3	3	396	5
Ecu	178	158	179	181	179	181	3	3		
Other EU			75	111	253	269	4	4	972	14
Euro total	765	772	1,285	1,424	2,050	2,196	34	37	3,649	50
US dollars	490	740	1,879	1,809	2,369	2,549	40	42	768	10
Japanese yen	666	281	237	262	903	543	15	9	1,942	26
Swiss franc	109	88	140	184	249	272	4	5	482	7
Other	4	7	382	448	386	455	6	8	535	7
Total	2,034	1,888	3,923	4,127	5,957	6,015	100	100	7,376	100

Note: 15 EU currencies and ecu are combined under 'Euro'.

Source: BIS International Banking and Financial Market Developments.

Table 21.   The Euro in the world bond market
(Billion US$ equivalent outstanding; end-December 1994)

| | Publicly traded bonds in issue | | | Percentage shares | | |
	Domestic	International	Total	Domestic	International	Total
Deutsche Mark	1,722	242	1,964	10	12	11
French franc	766	125	891	5	6	5
British pound	360	142	502	2	7	3
Italian lira	910	46	956	6	2	5
Ecu	63	93	156	0	5	1
Other EU	1,395	104	1,499	8	5	8
Euro total	5,216	752	5,968	32	37	32
US dollars	7,266	757	8,023	44	38	43
Japanese yen	3,361	308	3,669	20	15	20
Swiss franc	136	95	231	1	5	1
Other	492	99	591	3	5	3
Total	16,471	2,011	18,482	100	100	100

Note: 15 EU currencies and ecu are combined under 'Euro'.

Source: Salomon Brothers, IMF.

Table 22. The Euro in world foreign exchange

	Official reserves $	Per cent	Use in foreign exchange deals Per cent
Deutsche Mark	159	16	18.5
French franc	22	2	4.0
British pound	39	4	5.0
Italian lira			1.0
Ecu			
Other EU	5	1	6.5
Euro total	224	22	35.0
US dollars	649	63	41.5
Japanese yen	87	9	12.0
Swiss franc	11	1	3.5
Australian $			1.5
Canadian $			1.5
Other	52	5	5.0
Total	1025	100	100.0

	Foreign exchange market turnover $bn/day	per cent of EU	per cent of world
Frankfurt	76.2	10	5
Paris	58.0	7	4
London	464.5	59	30
Milan	23.2	3	1
Other EU	170.9	22	11
EU total	792.8	100	50
US	244.4		16
Tokyo	161.3		10
Zurich	86.5		6
Singapore	105.4		7
Hong Kong	90.2		6
Other	91.6		6
Total	1572.2		100

Source: IMF, BIS.

Table 23.   Market shares of the single currency, the pound, and the dollar

Percentage shares	Single currency	Pound	Dollar
International banking:			
Currency	34–7	4–5	40–2
Nationality	50	5	10
Bond markets:			
Domestic	32	2	44
International	37	7	38
Foreign exchange:			
Reserves	22	4	63
Currencies used	35	5	42
Markets	50	30 (London)	16 (NY)
OECD GDP	37	6	36

Source: Other tables, OECD.

Table 24. Single currency gains and losses for UK

	£ billion	% of GDP
Gains in level of GDP		
Transactions savings on foreign currency		
Business	2.25	0.32
Tourism	0.25	0.04
Transactions savings by switch from $	0.35	0.05
Seignorage from issue of Euro notes	0.65	0.09
Extra net exports of goods and services	1.5	0.21
Lower personal interest rates	5.0	0.71
Lower corporate interest rates	2.0	0.29
Total	12.0	1.7
Losses in level of GDP		
Bank foreign exchange losses	0.3	0.04
Bank and building society profit squeeze	1.7	0.24
Total	2.0	0.3
Net change in level of GDP	10.0	1.4
Annual gain in GDP growth rate of 0.5%	3.5	0.5
Cumulative after 10 years	42	6.0
Net present value of permanent 0.25% increase in GDP growth	5000	714
One-off costs		
Bank conversion costs	1.0	0.14
Other conversion costs	1.5	0.21
Total conversion costs	2.5	0.36
Transfer payments		
Public sector debt interest saving	7.0	1.0

Notes

Note: References given by name of author or title only are given in full in the bibliography.

Preface

1 See 'Legal tender' by Angela Redish in *The New Palgrave Dictionary of Money and Finance* vol 2 (London: Macmillan, 1992).
2 Delors Report (1989), p. 18–19.

Chapter 1   Introduction – the UK's position

1 The single currency is often referred to as the ecu (the name of an old French coin), or, as the Germans prefer, the ECU, which stands for European Currency Unit, a description rather than a name. The ecu (or ECU) is the forerunner of the single currency, which is to be called the Euro.
2 Jean Monnet, *Memoirs* (London: Collins, 1978) p. 451.
3 See Giles Radice MP, *Offshore: Britain and the European Idea* (London: I. B. Tauris, 1992).
4 Christopher Johnson, 'The UK and the Exchange Rate Mechanism' in Johnson and Collignon (1994). See also Ray Barrell, Andrew Britton and Nigel Pain, 'When the time was right? The UK experience of the ERM' (London: National Institute of Economic and Social Research, December 1993).
5 Margaret Thatcher, *The Downing Street Years* (London: HarperCollins, 1993) p. 723.
6 Sarah Hogg and Jonathan Hill, *Too Close to Call* (London: Little Brown, 1995) pp. 187–8.
7 Speech to the Royal Institute of International Affairs on 25 January 1989. See also Lawson (1992), pp. 892–4.
8 Speech to the European Movement by Rt Hon. Kenneth Clarke, Chancellor of the Exchequer, 9 February 1995 (HM Treasury: Press release 16/95 para 47).

9 See the reference to evidence by Dr Wolfgang Rieke, a former Bundesbank official, in *Kingsdown Enquiry* (1995), p. 19. ('He believed that more effective arrangements were needed to control fiscal policy at the European level.')

10 See *Reflections on European Policy* by the CDU/CSU parliamentary party (London: Konrad-Adenauer Stiftung, 1994).

11 In a talk at the Royal Institute of International Affairs in the summer of 1995.

12 Maastricht Treaty (1992), article 3b.

13 Connolly (1995), p. xvi. Robin Gedye, 'Kohl warning of war if EU rejects monetary union', *Daily Telegraph*, 17 October 1995.

14 Gallup for Association for the Monetary Union of Europe, *European Companies and Monetary Union* (Paris: Faits et Opinions, 1989). Ernst & Young and National Institute for Economic and Social Research for AMUE, *A Strategy for the Ecu* (London: Kogan Page, 1990) figure 1, p. 28. CBI European Monetary Union Working Group, *European Monetary Union: a Business Perspective* (London: CBI, 1989). *Building on the Single Market* (London: CBI, 1993). *The Single Market and the Future Development of European Union* (London: CBI, 1994). MORI for BBC Money Programme, *British Business and the European Single Currency* (London: MORI, 1995). MORI, *Business in Europe* (London: CBI and BCC, 1995). Harris for OMLX, *EMU City Survey* (London: OMLX, The London Securities and Derivatives Exchange, 1995). Richard Brown, *The Single Currency and SMEs*, (London: British Chambers of Commerce, 1995). 'Business warms to Europe' in *Management Today*, September 1995. *The Impact of European Economic and Monetary Union on UK Industry* (London: Andersen Consulting, 1995). *Ecu Poll/Eurobarometer* (Brussels: EU Commission, 1994). *Europinion no 5* (Brussels: EU Commission, 1995). MORI for *Financial Times*, *Attitudes to the EU* (London: MORI, 1995). Social and Community Planning Research for Granada Television, *Europe Deliberative Poll* (London: SCPR, 1995). Jim Northcott, *The Future of Britain and Europe* (London: Policy Studies Institute, 1995). Peter Kellner, 'Nation turns Eurosceptic to keep the pound in its pocket', *Sunday Times*, 17 December 1995.

15 J. S. Mill, *Principles of Political Economy* (Fairfield NJ: Kelly, 1987) p. 613.

16 *Observer*, 30 April 1995.

17 Margaret Thatcher, *The Downing Street Years* (London: HarperCollins, 1993) p. 653.

18 *The Economist*, 25 September 1993.

19 *The Times*, 6 October 1995.

20 Speech at Royal Institute of International Affairs, 21 September 1995.

21 Mr Major's speeches at Madrid were reported on BBC1 news, in the *Observer* and in the *Sunday Telegraph* of 17 December 1995.

22 This section is adapted from a speech by the author to the annual conference of the European Movement, London, 25 November 1995.

Chapter 2 The History of Monetary Unions

1 Marc Bloch, *Mélanges Historiques* (Paris: SEVPEN, 1963) 'Economie-nature ou économie–argent', vol II, pp. 869–71.

2 William Tate, *The Modern Cambist* (London: Effingham Wilson, 1868) p. 4.

3 For an account of the gold standard, see Panic; James Foreman-Peck, 'The gold standard as a European monetary lesson' in Driffill and Beber (1991); Marcello de Cecco, 'Gold standard' and Michael Bordo, 'Gold standard: theory' both in *The New Palgrave Dictionary of Money and Finance* (London: Macmillan, 1992).

4 'Inflation over 300 years', *Bank of England Quarterly Bulletin*, vol. 34, no. 3, May 1994, p. 157, chart 1.

5 Panic (1992) Table 2.5, p. 64.

6 'Of the balance of trade' in *Essays* (London: David Hume, Grant Richards, 1903) pp. 316–33.

7 See Emerson and Huhne (1991), Table 7, p. 52.

8 James Truslow Adams, *The Epic of America* (Boston: Little, Brown, 1933) p. 214.

9 Martin Feldstein, 'Europe's monetary union' in *The Economist*, 13 June 1992.

10 HM Treasury, *An Evolutionary Approach to EMU* (London: HMSO, 1989).

11 Lawson (1992), p. 892.

12 For a rather optimistic prospective analysis see Leslie Lipschitz and Donogh McDonald (eds.), *German Unification: Economic Issues* (Washington DC: International Monetary Fund, 1990).

13 For the official explanations of what went wrong in September 1992, see Collignon *et al.* (1994), chapter VI, 'Official policies for the EMS and their shortcomings'. For a wider range of views, see Temperton (1993).

14 Connolly (1995), p. 327.

15 See Lord Cobbold, 'A rethink for the ecu?' in Johnson and Collington (1994), pp. 184–8.

16 Quotations from Morris Perlman, *In search of monetary unions* (London: London School of Economics and Political Science, Financial Markets Group special paper no. 39, 1991).

17 See Susan Howson and Donald Moggridge (eds.), *The Wartime Diaries of*

Lionel Robbins and James Meade 1943–45 (London: Macmillan, 1990) p. 82 and *passim*.

18 See Robert Solomon, *The International Monetary System 1945–1981* (New York: Harper and Row, 1982).

19 For accounts of the snake and the ERM, see Connolly (1995), Dyson (1994), Gros and Thygesen (1994), Ungerer and others (1990).

Chapter 3   EMU Makes You Grow Faster

1   Delors Report (1989), p. 22 para. 29.

2   Commission of the European Communities (1990), *One Market, One Money*, chapter 3 and annex A.

3   Association Cambiste Internationale, *The Single Currency in Europe: a Working Paper* (Paris: ACI, 1995) pp. 17–18.

4   1995 interim reports, Barclays, Lloyds, Midland, NatWest.

5   'The foreign exchange market in London', *Bank of England Quarterly Bulletin*, vol. 35, no. 4, November 1995.

6   *The Blue Book 1995* (London: HMSO, 1995), table 5.7.

7   House of Lords Select Committee on the European Communities, *Cross-Border Credit Transfers* (London: HMSO HL 69, 13 June 1995) p. 6.

8   Emma Tucker, 'Brussels moves on bank transfers', *Financial Times*, 14 September 1995; *Single Market News* no. 1, November 1995, p. 8.

9   Emerson and Huhne (1991), p. 39, table 2.

10 *One Market, One Money* (1990), p. 63.

11 Institute of Directors, *A Single European Currency* (London: Director Press, 1995). British Chambers of Commerce, *Businesses are Citizens of Europe* (London: ABCC, 1995).

12 *Implementation of a Single European Currency: Report on a Survey of UK Banks and Building Societies* (London: Association for Payment and Clearing Services and British Bankers' Association, 1995). *Survey on the Introduction of the Single Currency: a First Contribution on the Practical Aspects* (Brussels: Banking Federation of the European Union, 1995).

13 For a formal treatment of network advantages, see Kevin Dowd and David Greenaway, 'Currency competition, network externalities and switching costs: towards an alternative view of optimum currency areas', *Economic Journal*, vol. 103, no. 420, September 1993, pp. 1180–9.

14 'Banks dream of "electronic wallets" for every shopper', *The Times*, 22 November 1994.

15 'Electronic money', *The Economist*, 26 November 1994.

16 Guy de Jonquières, 'Price flaws undermining EC's single market hopes', *Financial Times*, 3 August 1992.

17 Kevin Done, 'Ford blames price variation on currencies', *Financial Times*, 18 June 1993.

18 Emma Tucker, 'Car price differences widen in EU', *Financial Times*, 25 July 1995.

19 Address to the Association for the Monetary Union of Europe conference, Brussels 31 May 1995 (Paris: AMUE, 1995) p. 43.

20 Commission of the European Communities, *The Impact of Currency Fluctuations on the Internal Market* (Brussels: Communication from the Commission to the European Council COM(95) 503 final, 31 October 1995).

21 Group of Ten, *Saving, Investment and Real Interest Rates* (London: Bank of England, October 1995).

22 Christopher Taylor, *EMU 2000? Some Questions and Answers* (London: Royal Institute of International Affairs briefing paper no. 22, July 1995).

23 'A leap into the unknown', *The Economist*, 8 January 1993, p. 99–100.

24 John Kay, 'More competition, more consolidation', *Financial Times*, 20 October 1995.

25 Penelope Rowlatt, *Convergence criteria and Maastricht*, seminar paper, November 1993. David Miles, 'Fixed and floating-rate finance in the United Kingdom', *Bank of England Quarterly Bulletin*, vol. 34 no. 1, February 1994, table G p. 41. Fionnuala Earley, 'The development of fixed rate mortgages and annual review schemes', *Housing Finance*, no. 24, November 1994, pp. 17–24, and various other issues.

26 Gavin McCrone and Mark Stephens, *Housing Policy in Britain and Europe* (London: UCL Press, 1995), figure 12.2, p. 242.

27 Hamish McCrae, 'Low rates? Tell that to grandpa', the *Independent on Sunday*, 17 December 1995.

28 Lionel Barber, 'Emu "will trigger wave of banking mergers",' *Financial Times*, 25 November 1995.

29 Association Cambiste Internationale, *The Single Currency in Europe: a Working Paper* (Paris: ACI, 1995) p. 24.

30 These numbers, like those used by the European Commission, are plausible orders of magnitude, not precise forecasts. See Richard E. Baldwin, 'On the microeconomics of the EMU' in *The Economics of EMU*, and chapter three in *One Market, One Money* (1990), p. 81. The expected effects of a one percentage point reduction in nominal short interest rates in the UK economy are shown in K. B. Church et al., 'Comparative properties of models of the UK economy' in *National Institute Economic Review*, no. 145, August 1993, p. 106, table A5. In response to a one percentage point reduction in short-term nominal interest rates, after five years the LBS model shows GDP 3.8 per cent higher (0.75 per cent a year), the NIESR model

1.6 per cent (0.3 per cent a year), the Treasury model 1 per cent (0.2 per cent a year).

31 HM Treasury, *Financial Statement and Budget Report 1996–97* (London: HMSO, November 1995) pp. 50–1.

32 The net present value of GDP, now running at about £700 billion, can be calculated by multiplying it by the standard formula $1 + g/r−g$, where g is the real rate of growth and r is the real discount rate. The value of the formula, with $r = 0.045$, rises as g goes up from 0.025 to 0.0275, from 51.3 to 58.7. So the net present value of all future GDP rises by 7.4 times its annual amount, or just over £5,000 billion. If r, the rate of discount, falls by 1 per cent, the increase is far higher. All figures are in real terms.

33 Lawson (1992), p. 854.

34 See Richard E. Baldwin, 'On the microeconomics of the EMU', *The Economics of EMU*, pp. 30–1, section 5.

35 E. A. J. George, 'The economics of EMU', *Bank of England Quarterly Bulletin*, vol. 35 no. 2, May 1995, p. 196.

Chapter 4 The Virtues of Stable Prices

1 See Clive Briault, 'The costs of inflation', *Bank of England Quarterly Bulletin*, vol. 35, no. 1, February 1995.

2 Robert J. Barro, 'Inflation and economic growth', *Bank of England Quarterly Bulletin*, vol. 35, no. 2, May 1995.

3 See *One Market, One Money* (1990), graph 4.2, p. 91.

4 See also Christopher Johnson, *The Economy under Mrs Thatcher 1979–1990* (London: Penguin Books, 1991).

5 J. M. Keynes, *Essays in Persuasion* (London: Macmillan, 1931) p. 92.

6 Gavyn Davies, 'Express guide to the art of cutting inflation', the *Independent*, 16 January 1995.

7 *Taxation and Household Saving* (Paris: OECD, 1994) p. 38.

8 David Miles, 'Fixed and floating-rate finance in the UK and abroad', *Bank of England Quarterly Bulletin*, vol. 34, no. 1, February 1994, p. 36.

9 Andrew Wardlow, 'Investment appraisal criteria and the impact of low inflation', *Bank of England Quarterly Bulletin*, vol. 34, no. 3, August 1994, p. 260.

10 *One Market, One Money* (1990), graph 5.5, p. 121.

11 *One Market, One Money* (1990), graph 4.1, p. 90.

12 IMF, *International Financial Statistics* country tables.

13 Maastricht Treaty Protocol on the convergence criteria, article 1.

14 See Directorate-General for Economic and Financial Affairs, *Report on Convergence in the European Union in 1995* (Brussels: EU Commission, November 1995) box 1, p. 6.

15 See Christopher Johnson and Simon Briscoe, *Measuring the Economy* (London: Penguin Books, 1995), Chapter 5 'Inflation'.

16 Nicholas Oulton, 'Do UK price indexes overstate inflation?', *National Institute Economic Review*, May 1995, no. 152.

17 'The luxury-goods trade', *The Economist*, 26 December 1992, p. 91–4.

18 'Zero inflation', *The Economist*, 7 November 1992, pp. 21–3.

19 The ECB is described in the Maastricht Treaty, chapter 2 monetary policy, and in the protocol on the statutes of the ESCB and of the ECB.

20 See *OECD Economic Surveys: Germany*, 1994, diagram 10, p. 43.

21 *One Market, One Money* (1990), graph 4.6, p. 98.

22 James Meade, 'The EMU and the control of inflation', *Oxford Review of Economic Policy*, vol. 6, no. 4, winter 1990.

23 Andrew Blake and Peter Westaway, 'Should the Bank of England be independent?', *National Institute Economic Review*, no. 143, February 1993.

24 Treasury and Civil Service Committee, *The Role of the Bank of England* vol I, first report session 1993–94, HC 98-i. (London: HMSO, 8 December 1993) p. xxix.

25 Marjorie Deane and Robert Pringle, *The Central Banks* (London: Hamish Hamilton, 1994) p. 216.

26 Maastricht Treaty (1992), article 105 1.

27 Maastricht Treaty (1992), articles 108, 109e 5.

28 Maastricht Treaty (1992), article 107.

29 Lorenzo Bini Smaghi, 'Monetary institutions and monetary sovereignty in the EMU' in Driffill and Beber (1991), p. 269. See also Alberto Alesina and Vittorio Grilli, 'Reshaping monetary politics in Europe' in Canzoneri et al. (1992), tables 3A1 and 3A2, pp. 71–2.

30 See John Kay, 'Sharing responsibility is to pass the buck', *Financial Times*, 17 November 1995.

31 Philippe Moutot, *Preparing for Monetary Union; the View of the EMI* (London: International Conference Group, conference paper, 3 July, 1995).

32 Tommaso Padoa-Schioppa and Fabrizio Saccomanni, *Agenda for Stage Two: Preparing the Monetary Platform* (London: Centre for Economic Policy Research Occasional Paper no. 7, 1992) tables A–D.

33 M0 consists of notes and coin and commercial banks' deposits at the central bank. M3 consists of notes and coin and bank deposits held by nonbank residents.

34 See Michael Artis and others, 'A European money demand function' in Masson and Taylor (1993).

35 See H. M. Treasury, *Monetary Control* (London: HMSO Cmnd 7858, 1980).

36 Maastricht Treaty (1992), article 104.

37 Maastricht Treaty Protocol on statute of the ESCB article 12.
38 Maastricht Treaty (1992), article 105 5 and 6.
39 *Deutsche Bundesbank Annual Report 1993*, p. 92.
40 David Miles, *A Single European Currency: Options for the UK* (London: Merrill Lynch Global Fixed Income Research, 1 March 1995).
41 David Miles, 'Fixed and floating-rate finance in the UK and abroad', *Bank of England Quarterly Bulletin*, vol. 34 no. 1, February 1994.
42 *The Blue Book 1995* (London: HMSO, 1995) table 4.9.

Chapter 5 Costs and Benefits of Giving Up National Currencies

1 Maastricht Treaty (1992), article 109 1 4.
2 See Brigitte Granville, *Price and Currency Reform in Russia and the CIS* (London: Royal Institute of International Affairs, 1992).
3 Tommaso Padoa-Schioppa, 'The EMS: a long-term view' in Giavazzi et al. (1988), p. 373.
4 Barry Eichengreen and Charles Wyplosz, 'How to save the EMS' in Johnson and Collignon (1994), pp. 166–183.
5 Alan Walters, *Sterling in Danger* (London: Fontana, 1990) p. 78–80.
6 Treasury and Civil Service Committee, *The Autumn Statement* (London: HMSO HC 197 14 December 1987).
7 Scott Report (London: HMSO, HC 115–4, 1996), p. 1802.
8 See Steven Englander and Thomas Egebo, 'Adjustment under fixed exchange rates: application to the European Monetary Union', *OECD Economic Studies*, no. 20, spring 1993, p. 20.
9 E. A. J. George, *Bank of England Quarterly Bulletin*, 'The economics of EMU', vol. 35, no. 2, May 1995, p. 196.
10 *United Kingdom Economic Survey 1995* (Paris: OECD, 1995) p. 21. Also Christopher Johnson, *Competitiveness, Employment and the Labour Market* (London: Franco-British Council, 1995).
11 See Peter Bofinger, *Is Europe an Optimum Currency Area?* (London: Centre for Economic Policy Research, discussion paper no. 915, February 1994).
12 John Williamson, *Proto-EMU as an Alternative to Maastricht* (London: European Policy Forum, July 1995).
13 For a similar finding, see 'Buy hard: with a vengeance', *The Economist*, 26 August 1995, p. 76.
14 See Paul de Grauwe and Wim Vanhaverbeke, 'Is Europe an optimum currency area?: evidence from regional data' in Masson and Taylor (1993), chapter 5. For a clear textbook formulation see Paul Krugman and Maurice

Obstfeld, *International Economics* (New York: HarperCollins, 1994) chapter 21.

15 Robert Mundell, 'The theory of optimum currency areas', *American Economic Review*, no. 51, September 1961, pp. 717–25.

16 Joel Garreau, *The Nine Nations of North America* (Boston: Houghton Mifflin, 1983).

17 See Emerson and Huhne (1991), table 11, p. 110.

18 *United Kingdom Economic Survey 1995* (Paris: OECD, 1995), diagram 9, p. 19.

19 De Grauwe (1992), p. 32, table 2.1.

20 Tamim Bayoumi, *A Formal Model of Optimum Currency Areas* (London: Centre for Economic Policy Research, discussion paper no. 968, June 1994) pp. 22–3.

Chapter 6 How Governments Will Still Tax and Spend Under EMU

1 Maastricht Treaty (1992), article 3b.

2 A. Lamfalussy, 'Macro-coordination of fiscal policies in an economic and monetary union in Europe' in Delors Report (1989), tables 1–16, pp. 109–24.

3 *One Market, One Money* (1990), p. 100.

4 See *Kingsdown Enquiry* (1995), 'Fiscal autonomy', pp. 24–5. This describes a seminar in the House of Commons, which stated that 'Parliament would still have the power to tax and spend'.

5 Lawson (1992), p. 71.

6 Milton Friedman, 'The quantity theory of money' in *The New Palgrave Dictionary of Money and Finance*, edited by John Eatwell et al. (London: Macmillan, 1987) p. 31.

7 S. Howson (ed.) *Collected Papers of James Meade* (London: Unwin Hyman, 1988) Vol. I, p. 357.

8 James Meade, 'The EMU and the control of inflation', *Oxford Review of Economic Policy*, vol. 6, no. 4, winter 1990.

9 Maastricht Treaty (1992), article 109b and 109c.

10 A. Lamfalussy, 'Macro-coordination of fiscal policies in an economic and monetary union in Europe' in Delors Report (1989). Maastricht Treaty (1992), article 103. Lionel Barber, 'Delors calls for a "fiscal roof" over EMU', *Financial Times*, 13 October 1995.

11 See *One Market, One Money* (1990), tables 5.5 and 5.6, pp. 116–17.

12 For a discussion of the pros and cons of tax competition see Marc Vanheukelen, 'Taxation and EMU' in *Economie et Statistique*, pp. 77–80.

13 Ruding Committee, *Report of the Committee of Independent Experts on Company Taxation* (Brussels: European Commission, 1992).

14 Treasury and Civil Service Committee, *Cross Border Shopping*, first report session 1994–5 (London: HMSO HC 35–I, 23 November 1994). 'Tax on smoking', *Daily Telegraph*, 10 October 1995, p. 14. *Options for 1996: the Green Budget* (London: Institute for Fiscal Studies, 1995) pp. 69–80.

15 Margaret Thatcher, *The Downing Street Years* (London: HarperCollins, 1993) p. 553.

16 *OECD Economic Outlook*, no. 57, June 1995, tables A31–3.

17 Dick Taverne, *The Pension Time Bomb in Europe* (London: Federal Trust, 1995). Bill Jamieson, 'Pension timebomb', *Sunday Telegraph*, 10 December 1995.

18 The fiscal provisions of the Maastricht Treaty are in articles 104, 104a, 104b, 104c, and the Protocol on the excessive deficit procedure.

19 See Willem H. Buiter et al., *'Excessive Deficits': Sense and Nonsense in the Treaty of Maastricht* (London: Centre for Economic Policy Research, discussion paper no. 750, 1992). Also Neil Kinnock, *Design for Europe* (London: European League for Economic Cooperation, 1994).

20 Treasury and Civil Service Committee, *The 1994 Budget*, third report session 1994–5 (London: HMSO HC 79 11 January 1995) p. 90.

21 Maastricht Treaty Protocol on the excessive deficit procedure.

22 Maastricht Treaty (1992), articles 104c, 109e 4.

23 Maastricht Treaty (1992), articles 104, 104a, 104b.

24 See G. M. Caporale, 'Fiscal solvency in Europe: budget deficits and government debt under European Monetary Union', *National Institute Review*, no. 140, May 1992.

25 Gordon Brown, *Frost Programme*, BBC1, 1 October 1995.

26 In 1994, general government gross domestic fixed capital formation was £12.6 billion, or 1.9 per cent of GDP (*Blue Book*, 1995, table 9.1). There was another £7.7 billion in capital grants and transfers to other sectors, but this was excluded by the Maastricht definition.

27 H. M. Treasury, *Financial Statement and Budget Report 1996–97* (London: HMSO House of Commons paper, 30 November 1995) chapter 4.

28 See Ray Barrell and others, *The Employment Effects of the Maastricht Fiscal Criteria* (London: National Institute of Economic and Social Research, discussion paper no. 81, June 1995).

29 Maastricht Treaty (1992), article 104c.

30 Graham Bishop, *Fiscal Constraints in EMU* (London: Salomon Brothers Economic and Market Analysis, 27 September 1993).

31 Peter Norman and David Buchan, 'Bonn turns the screw to win Emu budget discipline', *Financial Times*, 11 November 1995. See also the refer-

ence to evidence by Dr Wolfgang Rieke, a former Bundesbank official, in *Kingsdown Enquiry* (1995), p. 19. 'He believed that more effective arrangements were needed to control fiscal policy at the European level.'

32 See 'Automatic stabilizers: their extent and role', *OECD Economic Outlook*, no. 53, June 1993, pp. 37–44.

33 Sir Donald MacDougall, 'Economic and Monetary Union and the European Community Budget', *National Institute Review*, no. 140, May 1992.

34 Charles Goodhart (ed.), *EMU and ESCB after Maastricht* (London: Financial Markets Group, London School of Economics and Political Science, 1992), part 2 'Fiscal policy and EMU'. Goodhart holds that EU fiscal stabilization requires a federal budget, while Bayoumi argues that automatic stabilizers built into national budgets should be sufficient.

35 *Public Finances and the Cycle*, Treasury Occasional Paper no. 4 (London: HM Treasury, September 1995).

36 Lord Healey, a former Chancellor of the Exchequer, used to talk about 'sado-monetarism'.

37 Delors Report (1989), p. 22.

38 Guillermo de la Dehesa and Paul Krugman, *EMU and the Regions* (Washington DC: Group of Thirty, occasional paper no. 39, 1992) table 3.

39 *General Report on the Activities of the European Union 1994* (Brussels: European Commission, 1995) tables 23 and 27.

40 Harvey W. Armstrong, *Regional Policy and Structural Aid* (Hull: Centre for European Union Studies, University of Hull with European Commission Representation in UK, 1995).

41 Lionel Barber, 'Brussels rules out big budget rise to fund EU expansion', *Financial Times*, 23 October 1995.

42 H. J. Brouwer et al., *Do we need a new EU Budget Deal?* (Brussels: Philip Morris Institute for Public Policy Research, June 1995) p. 18.

Chapter 7 The Transition to the Single Currency

1 Lord Tugendhat, Chairman, Royal Institute of International Affairs, 'Second thoughts on Europe', valedictory speech, 14 June 1995.

2 *One Market, One Money* (1990), p. 203.

3 'Monetarist' in this context does not mean the same as a monetarist in the sense of a follower of Milton Friedman.

4 Maastricht Treaty (1992), article 109j 3 and 4.

5 *Daily Telegraph*, 18 December 1995.

6 Maastricht Treaty Protocol on certain provisions relating to the United Kingdom of Great Britain and Northern Ireland. Protocol on certain provisions relating to Denmark.

7 Lorenzo Bini-Smaghi et al., 'The policy history of the Maastricht Treaty' in *The Monetary Future of Europe*, chapter 3, p. 26.

8 Cees Maas (chairman) and the group of experts, *Progress Report on the Preparation of the Changeover to the Single European Currency* (Amsterdam: ING Group, May 1995). EU Commission, *Green Paper on the Practical Arrangements for the Introduction of the Single Currency* (Brussels: EU Commission COM (95) 333 31, May 1995). European Monetary Institute, *The Changeover to the Single Currency* (Frankfurt: EMI, November 1995).

9 Maastricht Treaty (1992), article 103, articles 109e–m.

10 Collignon et al. (1994), tables 7, 10 and 13.

11 Maastricht Treaty (1992), article 109j.

12 European Monetary Institute, *Annual Report 1994* (Frankfurt: EMI, April 1995) p. 56, box 6.

13 Paul de Grauwe, 'An easier road to monetary union', *Financial Times*, 17 October 1995.

14 Confederation of British Industry, *A Europe that Works* (London: CBI, June 1995 p. 32).

15 Maastricht Treaty (1992), article 109j 1.

16 See Clifford Chance, *EMU: the Legal Road Ahead* (Paris: Association for the Monetary Union of Europe, November 1993).

17 See Malcolm Levitt and a working group, *Preparing the Transition to the Single Currency* (Paris: Association for the Monetary Union of Europe, 1994).

18 See Giovannini and Mayer (1991), chapters 9 and 10, for academic treatments of the currency substitution problem.

19 Noel Moore, *UK Currency Decimalization in 1971 and Possible Relevance to the Introduction of a European Currency Unit* (Paris: Association for the Monetary Union of Europe, August 1993).

20 Bertrand de Maigret, 'Lessons to be drawn from the experience of Brazil's 1994 successful currency change relative to Europe's move towards a single currency' (Paris: Association for the Monetary Union of Europe, *EMU for Business*, no. 3, 25 January 1995).

21 Speech to the annual conference of the Association for the Monetary Union of Europe, Frankfurt, May 1992.

22 Speech to the annual conference of the Association for the Monetary Union of Europe, Brussels, May 1995.

23 Lawson (1992), p. 275.

24 Lawson (1992), p. 310.

25 Maastricht Treaty (1992), article 109i 4.

26 See Lord Cobbold, 'The "Doppelmark" revisited, a simpler route to the single currency?' *The Treasurer*, October 1995.

27 *Survey on the Introduction of the Single Currency: a First Contribution on the Practical Aspects* (Brussels: Fédération Bancaire de l'Union Européenne, March 1995). *Implementation of a Single European Currency: Report on a Survey of UK Banks and Building Societies* (London: Association of Payment Clearing Services and British Bankers' Association, February 1995).

Chapter 8   The Single Currency and the Outside World

1 Maastricht Treaty (1992), article 109k.
2 Commission of the European Communities, *Exchange Rate Relations between Participating and Non-participating Countries in Stage Three of EMU* (Brussels: EU Commission interim report to the European Council CSE (95) 2108).
3 Charles Bremner, 'Commission urges Britain to join new pact for monetary stability', *The Times*, 8 December 1995.
4 John Major, 'Here are the questions that Europe still has to answer', *Daily Telegraph*, 18 December 1995.
5 Sarah Helm and Donald MacIntyre, 'Britain fears chaos and a divided Europe', the *Independent*, 16 December 1995.
6 Maastricht Treaty (1992), article 109g.
7 John Williamson, *Proto-EMU as an Alternative to Maastricht* (London: European Policy Forum, July 1995).
8 See John Arrowsmith, 'Economic and Monetary Union in a multi-tier Europe', *National Institute Economic Review*, no. 152, May 1995, and John Arrowsmith, 'Opting out of stage 3: life in the lower tier of EMU', seminar paper, London, June 1995.
9 For an account of the European Economic Area, see Bainbridge and Teasdale (1995), pp. 180–2.
10 'A mint with a hole in it' is a well-known advertising slogan. 'A hole with a mint in it' was coined to refer to Llantrisant in Wales, to which the British mint was decentralized.
11 Commissioner Hans van den Broek in reply to a question from the author, TSB Forum, London, 17 November 1995.
12 See Stefan Collignon, 'An Ecu zone for Central and Eastern Europe' in Barrell (1992) (ed.), pp. 191–211.
13 See David Vines, 'Crawling peg' in *New Palgrave Dictionary of Money and Finance*, vol. I, pp. 513–14.
14 Carlos Westendorp, *Progress Report from the Chairman of the Reflection Group on the 1996 Intergovernmental Conference* (Madrid: Ministry of Foreign Affairs, 1 September 1995) p. 11.

15 Richard Baldwin, *Towards an Integrated Europe* (London: Centre for Economic Policy Research, 1994).

16 Caroline Southey, 'No farm reform, no EU enlargement', *Financial Times*, 24 November 1995.

17 Richard D. Porter, *Estimates of Foreign Holdings of US Currency* (Washington DC: Federal Reserve Board, 1994).

18 Stanley W. Black. See 'Transaction costs and vehicle currencies', *Journal of International Money and Finance*, no. 10, December 1991, pp. 512–16.

19 *One Market, One Money* (1990), p. 182.

20 Speech to Bow Group/Association for Monetary Union of Europe conference on EMU, 23 February 1995 (London: International Conferences).

21 Lionel Barber, 'Banker supports single currency', *Financial Times*, 24 May 1995.

22 Speech to Bow Group/Association for Monetary Union of Europe conference on EMU, 23 February 1995 (London: International Conferences).

23 Final Report of the City Research Project, *The Competitive Position of London's Financial Services* (London: City Corporation, 1995). The report is notable for scarcely mentioning the single currency and its possible effect on the City.

24 Maastricht Treaty (1992), article 109.

25 See Y. Funabashi, *From the Plaza to the Louvre* (Washington DC: Institute of International Economics, 1989).

26 Maastricht Treaty (1992), article 109.

27 Maastricht Treaty (1992), article 105 2.

28 Paul Volcker et al., *Bretton Woods: Looking to the Future* (Washington DC: Bretton Woods Commission, 1994).

29 Jean Monnet, *Memoirs* (London: Collins, 1978) p. 428.

Chapter 9   The Economic and Political Case for UK Membership

1 Taylor, p. 140–1.

2 *Kingsdown Enquiry* (1995), p. 31.

3 *Frost Programme*, BBC1, 17 December 1995.

4 See Iain McLean, 'Economics and Politics' in *Companion to Contemporary Economic Thought*, edited by David Greenaway et al. (London: Routledge, 1991).

5 Maastricht Treaty Protocol on certain provisions relating to the UK, para. 7.

6 Speech at Chatham House, 21 September 1995.

7 Carlos Westendorp, *Progress Report from the Chairman of the Reflection Group on the 1996 Intergovernmental Conference* (Madrid: Ministry of Foreign Affairs, 1 September 1995) p. 18.

8 Speech to the European Movement by Rt Hon. Kenneth Clarke, Chancellor of the Exchequer, 9 February 1995 (HM Treasury: Press release 16/95 para 39).

9 *Kingsdown Enquiry* (1995), p. 34.

10 Green Paper, p. 4.

Bibliography

Bainbridge, Timothy with Teasdale, Anthony (1995) *The Penguin Companion to European Union*, London: Penguin Books.

Barrell, Ray (1992) *Economic Convergence and Monetary Union in Europe*, London: Sage Publications, for National Institute of Economic and Social Research and Association for the Monetary Union of Europe.

Barrell, Ray and Whitley, John (eds.) (1992) *Macroeconomic Policy Coordination in Europe*, London: Sage Publications, for National Institute of Economic and Social Research.

Britton, Andrew and Mayes, David (1992) *Achieving Monetary Union in Europe*, London: Sage Publications, for National Institute of Economic and Social Research and Association for the Monetary Union of Europe.

Canzoneri, Matthew et al. (eds.) (1992) *Establishing a Central Bank: Issues in Europe and Lessons from the US*, Cambridge: Cambridge University Press.

Centre for Economic Policy Research (1993) *The Monetary Future of Europe*, London: CEPR.

Chown, John F. (1994) *A History of Money from AD 800*, London: Routledge.

Collignon, Stefan et al. (1994) *Europe's Monetary Future*, London: Pinter.

Commission of the European Communities (1990) *One Market, One Money, European Economy*, no. 44, September 1990.

Commission of the European Communities (1991) *The Economics of EMU, European Economy* special edition, no. 1, 1991.

Commission of the European Communities (1995) *Green Paper on the Practical Arrangements for the Introduction of the Single Currency* (Brussels: EU Commission COM (95) 333, 31 May 1995).

Committee for the Study of Economic and Monetary Union (1989) *Report on Economic and Monetary Union and Collection of Papers submitted to the Committee for the Study of Economic and Monetary Union*, Luxembourg: Office for Official Publications of the European Communities. (Delors Report).

Connolly, Bernard (1995) *The Rotten Heart of Europe*, London: Faber & Faber.

Corry, Dan (1995) *Restating the Case for EMU*, London: Institute for Public Policy Research.

Council and Commission of the European Communities (1992) *Treaty on*

European Union, Luxembourg: Office for Official Publications of the European Communities. (Maastricht Treaty).

De Grauwe, Paul (1992) *The Economics of Monetary Integration*, Oxford: Oxford University Press.

Driffill, John and Beber, Massimo (1991) *A Currency for Europe*, London: Lothian Foundation Press.

Dyson, Kenneth (1994) *Elusive Union: The Process of Economic and Monetary Union in Europe*, London: Longman.

Emerson, Michael and Huhne, Christopher (1991) *The Ecu Report*, London: Pan Books.

Giavazzi, Francesco et al. (eds.) (1988) *The European Monetary System*, Cambridge: Cambridge University Press.

Giovannini, Alberto and Mayer, Colin (eds.) (1991) *European Financial Integration*, Cambridge: Cambridge University Press.

Goodhart, Charles (ed.) (1992) *EMU and the ESCB after Maastricht*, London: Financial Markets Group, London School of Economics and Political Science.

Gros, Daniel and Thygesen, Niels (1992) *European Monetary Integration*, London: Longman.

Insee (1994) 'Economic and Monetary Union', *Economie et Statistique*, special issue, 1994, Paris: Insee Info Service.

Johnson, Christopher and Collignon, Stefan (eds.) (1994) *The Monetary Economics of Europe*, London: Pinter.

Kenen, Peter (1992) *Emu after Maastricht*, Washington DC: Group of Thirty.

Kingsdown Enquiry (1995) *Report by the ACE Working Group on the Implications of Monetary Union for Britain*, London: Action Centre for Europe.

Lawson, Nigel (1992) *The View from No.11*, London: Bantam Press.

Masson, Paul and Taylor, Mark (eds.) (1993) *Policy Issues in the Operation of Currency Unions*, Cambridge: Cambridge University Press.

Panel of Independent Forecasters (1995) *May 1995 Report*, London: HM Treasury, May 1995, chapter and panel members' commentaries on EMU.

Panic, Mica (1992) *European Monetary Union: Lessons from the Classical Gold Standard*, New York: St Martin's Press.

Redwood, John (1995) *The Single European Currency*, London: Tecla.

Taylor, Christopher (1995) *EMU 2000? Prospects for European Monetary Union*, London: Royal Institute of International Affairs.

Temperton, Paul (ed.) (1993) *The European Currency Crisis*, Cambridge: Probus Publishing Company.

Uingerer, Horst et al. (1990) *The European Monetary System: Developments and Prospects*, Washington DC: International Monetary Fund (Occasional Paper no. 73).

Index